This volume brings together new essays from distinguished scholars in a variety of disciplines – philosophy, history, literary studies, art history – to explore various ways in which aesthetics, politics, and the arts interact with one another. Politics is an elastic concept, covering an oceanic breadth of mechanisms for conducting relations among variously empowered groups, and these essays offer a range of perspectives, including nations, classes, and gendered subjects, which examine the imbrication of politics with arts. Together they demonstrate the need to counteract the reductionist view of the relationship between politics and the arts which prevails in various ways in both philosophy and critical theory, and suggest that the irreducibility of the aesthetic must prompt us to reconceive the political as it relates to human cultural activity.

CAMBRIDGE STUDIES IN PHILOSOPHY AND THE ARTS

Series editors
SALIM KEMAL *and* IVAN GASKELL

Politics and aesthetics in the arts

CAMBRIDGE STUDIES IN PHILOSOPHY AND THE ARTS

Series editors

SALIM KEMAL *and* IVAN GASKELL

Advisory board

Stanley Cavell, R. K. Elliott, Stanley E. Fish, David Freedberg, Hans-Georg Gadamer, John Gage, Carl Hausman, Ronald Hepburn, Mary Hesse, Hans-Robert Jauss, Martin Kemp, Jean Michel Massing, Michael Podro, Edward S. Said, Michael Tanner.

"Cambridge Studies in Philosophy and the Arts" is a forum for examining issues common to philosophy and critical disciplines that deal with the history of art, literature, film, music and drama. In order to inform and advance both critical practice and philosophical approaches, the series analyses the aims, procedures, language and results of inquiry in the critical fields, and examines philosophical theories by reference to the needs of arts disciplines. This interaction of ideas and findings, and the ensuing discussion, brings into focus new perspectives and expands the terms in which the debate is conducted.

Politics and Aesthetics in the Arts

Edited by

SALIM KEMAL

University of Dundee

and

IVAN GASKELL

Harvard University Art Museums

CAMBRIDGE
UNIVERSITY PRESS

PUBLISHED BY THE PRESS SYNDICATE OF THE UNIVERSITY OF CAMBRIDGE
The Pitt Building, Trumpington Street, Cambridge, United Kingdom

CAMBRIDGE UNIVERSITY PRESS
The Edinburgh Building, Cambridge CB2 2RU, United Kingdom
http://www.cup.cam.ac.uk
40 West 20th Street, New York, NY 10011–4211, USA   http://www.cup.org
10 Stamford Road, Oakleigh, Melbourne 3166, Australia

First published 2000

Printed in the United Kingdom at the University Press, Cambridge

Typeset in 10/12.5pt Melior [CE]

A catalogue record for this book is available from the British Library

Library of Congress cataloguing in publication data

Politics and aesthetics in the arts / edited by Salim Kemal and Ivan Gaskell;
illustrations with Neil McWilliam and Michael Kelly.
p.   cm. (Cambridge studies in philosophy and the arts)
Includes index.
ISBN 0 521 45418 2 (hardback)
1. Aesthetics – Political aspects.   2. Arts – Political aspects.
I. Kemal, Salim.   II. Gaskell, Ivan.   III. Series.
BH301.P64P65 2000
111′.85–dc21   99–11073 CIP

ISBN 0 521 45418 2 hardback

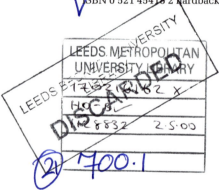

Contents

Contents

Illustrations

ix

Contributors

J. M. BERNSTEIN
Vanderbilt University

DAVID CARROLL
University of California, Irvine

DANIEL COTTOM
University of Oklahoma

PETER DE BOLLA
University of Cambridge

MICHAEL KELLY
Columbia University

NEIL MCWILLIAM
University of Warwick

LOUIS MONTROSE
University of California, San Diego

ANTHONY PAGDEN
The Johns Hopkins University

Editors' acknowledgments

There are many people we should like to thank, too many to list here. Jane Baston and Jane Whitehead, as always; Leo, Sara, and Rahim, as always; William and Kathryn Robinson. We would like to thank our Advisory Board members and the other readers and advisors on particular papers for the series, and those who have encouraged us through reviews, citations, and proposals for journals and further volumes. Perhaps it is fitting that a topic such as the relation of politics to aesthetics, so open to contention, so provocative of passion, and in some people's minds so entrenched in a system of received opinions and prejudices, should conclude the series. Throughout we have sought not only to bring together philosophers from both the analytical and continental schools, and theoretically minded practitioners of many other human science disciplines to consider common problems, but also to choose problems that in themselves challenge the theoretical status quo. The results have not fitted in with any existing orthodoxy, nor, we suspect, made many people feel more comfortable with their existing theoretical commitments. Our own choices have been informed by both politics and aesthetics: a politics and an aesthetics of surprise, quiet defiance, and disconcertion. With sincere thanks to all who have taken part in the series we now take our leave.

Contesting the arts: politics and aesthetics

SALIM KEMAL AND IVAN GASKELL

On June 30, 1939 the Fischer Gallery, Lucerne, Switzerland conducted an event that brought together art, aesthetics, and politics in a particularly acute manner. This was the principal auction of so-called "degenerate art": 126 paintings recently removed from German art museums under Nazi auspices. The actions of all involved resulted from political and aesthetic judgments on both politics and art. The politics of Nazism and Fascism – that is, of those who caused the works of art to be consigned – has often been described as having a constitutive aesthetic dimension; while those who made bids did so after having made political judgments about the probity of their actions, as well as aesthetic judgments about the works offered.

Nearly sixty years later, members of the US legislature fiercely attacked the National Endowment for the Arts in the wake of several controversial art exhibitions. In consequence, its funding was severely curtailed, and its terms of operation altered. Those attacking the NEA did so in part on ideological grounds (believing that the arts should not be publicly funded), and partly on ethical grounds (believing that the arts should not attack American values, iconically represented by the flag, nor condone gay or lesbian eroticism). All of these criteria led to political judgments expressed in the political forum centered on Congress. But they also involved aesthetic judgments which in turn affect the terms according to which the NEA itself is able to make aesthetic judgments.

This juxtaposition of the Nazi attacks on so-called "degenerate art" and Congressional attacks on the NEA and art it has funded is, of course, far from original, and is blunt rather than subtle. Yet, whether warranted or not, most importantly in this context this juxtaposition is itself political. As a political statement, it stems from

1

anger. Anger is so prevalent, whether explicitly or implicitly, whenever politics, aesthetics, and the arts are discussed together that it is almost always implicitly a fourth concept. It is a topic to which we will return.

The three concepts explicitly in play – politics, aesthetics, and the arts – interact with one another on many occasions, and not only, as in the instances cited above, when tensions run high. That those occasions are so many and varied is due to the elasticity of the concept of politics. Politics has long outgrown matters of government. Now it covers the mechanisms by which relations among variously – often differentially – empowered individuals and groups are conducted. Any relationship among humans, or between humans and other entities (such as "the environment") can be said to have a politics. In the cases of both the Nazi auction and the diminution of the NEA mentioned above, not only is there a politics of art, but also a politics of race, and of sex and sexual preference. We can speak of this development as a politicization of discourse. Its sustaining premise is that every relationship is a power relationship. Therefore any relationship among humans that purports to be principally mediated by, or sustained by, a shared interest in the arts, for instance, is *ipso facto* a power relationship. In this case, aesthetic and political judgments may become indistinguishable.

Politics comes in many shades, and not only of opinion. Its tonal range is immense, from the black-and-white of the politics of nations, classes, and parties, to the subtle grays of loosely defined interest groups. There is the passive politics discernible initially only to the analyst, and the active politics of the aggrieved. When we speak of the politics of art and the art of politics we speak of two quite distinct things. When we speak of the politics of aesthetics and the aesthetics of politics we also speak of two quite distinct things. This variety is hugely extended when we bear in mind the oceanic breadth of issues that politics can comprehend. How, then, are we to chart a course through such vast and often stormy seas? Our contributors offer a diversity of case studies as islands in this ocean, each with its own unique geography, where various currents meet. The same current may swirl past different islands, but no two occupy the same reach of ocean.

To discuss these issues, the chapters that follow are divided informally into three successive groups, though there are interconnections and overlaps between all of them. To set out the progress of these chapters briefly, before providing some more detail about each:

2

recent new historicist writings have argued for a particular relation between politics, understood as the state, and aesthetics, referring especially to drama.[1] At the same time, recently critical theory has maintained that some strains of contemporary philosophical writing have introduced a particular kind of politics by letting aesthetic issues inform philosophical discussion.[2] Working within the background of these writings, the first two chapters, by Louis Montrose and J. M. Bernstein, question a number of assumed connections between aesthetics and politics, suggesting that these are more complicated and nuanced than people have supposed. The following four chapters, by Anthony Pagden, Neil McWilliam, David Carroll, and Daniel Cottom, take up the understanding of politics by examining issues of identity and alterity, concerning strategies of dealing with the self and the Other, whether in terms of ethnicity, class, or subject. They implicitly operate in a context of a well-established understanding of politics that encompasses issues of nation, colonialization, class, and gender. Pagden discusses the ways in which colonialism dealt with the Other, in this case some influential French thinking about the New World. Carroll, McWilliam, and Cottom then look at the political formation of the aesthetic community itself in nation, class, and subject. The assumption of unity usual to the "nation" is disrupted by the classes and subjectivity that constitute that nation. To the considerations in the three preceding chapters, Cottom's discussion adds a recognition of the important element of an affective relation – anger – toward the questionable unities of state, nationhood, class, and culture. The final two chapters – by Peter de Bolla and Michael Kelly – offer accounts of confrontations with works of art, often of an irreducibly visual character. They explain the construction of the aesthetic community further by specifying the political nature of the objects that modernism reveres for perceived qualities such as unity and disinterestedness.

Let us look at some of the issues and arguments in more detail. The section on conceptual interactions begins with a chapter by Louis Montrose, "'From the stage to the state': politics, form, and performance in the Elizabethan theatre." Writing against the background of new historicist conceptions of the politics of state and stage, Montrose demonstrates how art and its institutions – here the newly emergent professional theatre – may or may not be implicated in the exercise of political authority in the narrow sense. He takes issue with arguments that would tie Elizabethan theatrical practices

3

to those of the Elizabethan state, and that in turn would tie Elizabethan theatricality to political absolutism. He notes that both the theatre's proponents and antagonists acknowledged the power of plays to effect moral changes in audiences for both good and evil. He pays particular attention to the equivocal role played by the Lord Chamberlain's Men (William Shakespeare's company) in the conspiracy of the Earl of Essex in 1601 by means of a performance of *Richard II* procured by the conspirators. He links this with a development of "personation" that gave importance to human agency in the shaping of affairs at the expense of divine providence. He discerns ambiguity, rather than straightforward ideology, in the relationship between theatre and state. The court and the theatre cannot be taken to have been symbolic or ideological equivalents: neither could the theatre fully sustain the mystique of the court, nor subvert it. So even in a relationship between political and art institutions that would seem to be theoretically simple in comparison with other relationships involving our three terms – politics, aesthetics, and the arts – matters turn out to be far more complex and equivocal than earlier commentators have suspected, or theoreticians might necessarily suspect.

In "Republican beauty, sublime democracy: civic humanism in Gadamer and Rawls", J. M. Bernstein examines terms of judgment in politics and the arts. He diagnoses that category confusions between the two result from an unsatisfactory resolution of ambiguities in Kant's conception of the aesthetic. He argues that Hans Georg Gadamer, relying on Kant, erroneously seeks to validate a grammatical connection so as to politicize, or "ethicize," the aesthetic; and he proposes that John Rawls does much the same in the other direction in constituting his notion of political liberalism, thus aestheticizing the political. Bernstein's motive, though, is not to chastise philosophical impropriety, but to draw attention to formal constraints and their breaching. These constraints matter, he contends, only insofar as they prohibit the realization of desires (here the desires signified by the miscegenation of the political and the aesthetic) which are themselves, in his account, powerful elements of cultural modernity.

These first two chapters define certain boundaries to interactions among our core concepts of politics, aesthetics, and the arts, in both historically pragmatic and contrastingly theoretical terms. The second group of chapters advances the discussion of politics into the realm of the constitution of alterities and selves, in part by turning to the formation of judgments. The exercise of judgment is both political and aesthetic. In his chapter, "Travelers, colonizers, and the aesthetics of self-conception: Denis Diderot on the perils of detach-ment," Anthony Pagden argues that even in the midst of imperial and colonial adventurism, some thinkers claimed that the commerce deriving from it blunted collective aesthetic sensibilities. For Diderot, the experience of travel, as well as settling, among people who were radically different from one's own had a decivilizing effect. In such cases – most spectacularly in that of the European penetration of the Americas – a diminution of moral sensibility followed from an inability to respond aesthetically to the conditions of alterity. Commerce ensured that this dulling effect should be returned from the deracinated colonists to their originating culture, leading to a decrease in its ability to foster an imaginative response to the new and the strange, and an inability properly to exercise a capacity for wonder. In Pagden's description of Diderot's critique of European expansion, politics and aesthetics are mutually dependent in the confrontation with alterity. Aesthetics is implicitly the barom-eter of politics, and the fraying of aesthetic judgment the conse-quence of imperial politics.

In the second of our chapters devoted to cultural alterity, "The aesthetics of nationalism and the limits of culture," David Carroll broaches the subject of nationalism. He contends that in recent analyses which examine the imaginary rather than the material constituents of nationalism, the aesthetic element – found mostly in the work of those poets and historians who define national identities – has been largely ignored. He holds that literary concepts of nationalism – though mutually or internally inconsistent – can none-theless be instrumental in constituting a national mythology. Further, he argues that an imaginary process of fabrication is integral to all forms of community. He analyzes the internal contradictions of nations: how accession by enculturation (such as acquiring linguistic proficiency) invariably exists in tension with exclusion by racism, for instance. Although criteria of accession and exclusion may be aesthetic, they are simultaneously political. Following Homi K. Bhabha and Jean-Luc Nancy, Carroll seeks to locate this tension internally, by identifying alterity as being within communities. Thus the image of a people is the repression of the alterity that actually constitutes it. Therefore that image is invariably fractured, incom-plete, or deferred. In these circumstances, Carroll points to the work of Edouard Glissant on the poetics of creolization, and the vital

5

instability of cultures constantly affecting each other as a pertinent aesthetics of culture.

David Carroll directs our attention towards internal contradictions in terms of national definition, demonstrating how a politics of nationhood can prompt a revision of aesthetic categorization, which then in turn could presumably modify perceptions of power relationships, insofar as they are conceived of aesthetically. While Carroll considers definitions of nationhood, Neil McWilliam, in his chapter, "Peripheral visions: class, cultural aspiration, and the artisan community in mid-nineteenth-century France," looks at internal divisions within a polity in terms of class. He examines the position of artisans who experimented with the possibilities of class permeability by aspiring to produce high-culture artifacts, and explores how art might provide the means of social redefinition. On the one hand, this was coupled with a tendency on the part of apologists to ascribe a moral vigor to the popular classes, uncorrupted by waste and privilege. On the other, conservatives insisted on cultural control as a means of maintaining deference for established hierarchies. This case study demonstrates how complex internal maneuverings for political advantage within a nation or polity can be articulated by means of competition for the definition and control of the arts. This is the case even when two major sets of protagonists share a fundamental conception of the responsibility of artists: in McWilliam's study both conservatives and artisan radicals believed that artists bore a responsibility for the moral well-being of the nation. Both shared a belief that art provided the moral instruction necessary for political responsibility, leaving the fundamental paradigm unchallenged.

If, in McWilliam's account, culturally ambitious artisans were in fundamental agreement with, even if at a disadvantage to, the bourgeoisie, true alterity lay in the emergence of the wage laborer whose artistic and social paradigms were quite distinct, and whose concerns were historically bound to eclipse those of the artisans. In this case the axes of alterity are almost exclusively between males, and seem to rescind any appeal to emotion. Yet, as we remarked earlier, wherever judgment is necessarily exercised – as in politics and aesthetics – it can be contested, giving rise, at times, to anger. Using examples from feminist scholarship, among others, Daniel Cottom recharges anger in relation to criticism with political urgency in his chapter, "The war of tradition: Virginia Woolf and the temper of criticism." He seeks a politics of anger beyond definitions that would confine anger to either a lack of self-mastery – reputedly female – or the irony of angry counsel against anger, or as a force of self-revelation "that breaks through regulating forms to reveal a hidden, inward, disruptive truth." Cottom observes that anger in texts (including, implicitly, his own) can go underground and therefore be difficult to locate, not necessarily declaring itself. He contends that emotions belong to our social beings, and therefore that our consideration of anger can be removed from a connection with neurosis to an association with cognition, rhetoric, and politics. Thus the slippery truth of anger invigorates a political perception of culture that cannot be confined to academic discourse, but must employ "fighting words" in contested domains of social action. These have involved the internal alterities in the US addressed by the civil rights and antiwar movements, feminism, and gay and lesbian rights and AIDS activism. Cottom's comments take on a particular urgency in the light of Paul Jay's effective exposure of the compromises of the academic regime in his discussion of the compromises of deconstruction.[3] Cottom's trenchant chapter offers an institutional critique of the academy, leaving the dispassionate reader wondering whether its forms and traditions can accommodate debate in terms adequate to the political task he adumbrates. Although Cottom's observations are predominantly about criticism and its temper, they might well be extended to art production in these and other areas where aesthetics interleaves a politics of anger. These four chapters have therefore addressed aspects of alterity under the broad headings of colonialism, national and class identity, and the politics of subjects, their emotions and gender. The final group of chapters echoes some of the themes already touched on, but concentrates on the issues of confrontation with the irreducible art object.

In "The discomfort of strangeness and beauty: art, politics, and aesthetics," Peter de Bolla deals with what he conceives as a basic evasion in our discussions of art: "that distinct area *of experience* that is called in the post-Kantian tradition affective response." Proposing that to regard art as no more than representations of ideologies allows its trivial politicization, he seeks to identify the peculiarly aesthetic aspects of the work in its relation to the affective response. He points out that Kantian aesthetic judgment is not purely subjective, but is also compelled by objects themselves. He explores the possibility that, as he puts it, "something is known to us in aesthetic experience which is not available to us as knowledge in

7

other forms of experience." He then approaches a work of art with this conception of the sublime as a form of knowing in mind, his chosen example being the paintings of Barnett Newman. He concludes from a description of a confrontation with such a painting that "the worldliness of the political must always remain adjacent to the timeliness of the aesthetic."

If Peter de Bolla approaches the encounter with the art object in a redefined Kantian manner, in "The political autonomy of contemporary art: the case of the 1993 Whitney Biennial," Michael Kelly calls attention to a philosopher who he sees as Kant's late modern counterpart, Theodor Adorno; for it was Adorno who famously asked how is art possible in the wake of an ethical and political outrage as extreme as Nazi genocide. Kelly offers observations on Adorno's exposition of the relationship between art and politics which suggests that each needs the other to define itself. He does so in the context of a detailed examination of the 1993 Whitney Biennial exhibition and the critical reactions it elicited, many of them politically based. That this particular contemporary art exhibition should have served as a focus for debate about the relationship between art and politics is well known, occurring as it did at a crucial time in the public debate (or so-called "culture wars") about politics and the arts in the US that saw the acknowledgment of symbols of culture as weapons on a battlefield. Kelly uses the occasion to render an account of confronting art itself, but also to describe various terms of encounter in that particular political and critical climate. He argues that theoretical accounts from Kant to Lyotard of the relationship between aesthetics and politics are not relevant to contemporary art, and that a recognition of the political autonomy of art, grounded in contemporary art practice, can allow us to redefine the issues, looking to contemporary art itself – rather than theory – for guidance.

The willingness of theorists to look attentively at the arts as untranslatable phenomena with their own dynamics that can contribute uniquely to human knowledge – whether through the exercise of judgment, or recognition that "the artwork is a knowing" (to cite de Bolla's epigraph) – marks an advance on an earlier state of affairs in which discursive reductionism obtained. Thinking along these lines, in which the aesthetic is revitalized to deal with the irreducibility of the artwork and our experience of it, in turn obliges us to reconceive the political in relation to art and human cultural activity as a whole, including politics more narrowly defined.

8

Analyses of the dynamic between our three core terms – politics, aesthetics, and the arts – have never been more at odds, but, as the chapters that follow demonstrate, existing suppositions about their relationship to one another have never been more contested, nor more fragile.

Perhaps one conclusion to be drawn from a voyage around this far-flung archipelago of politics and aesthetics is an acknowledgment of the politicization of discourse in the late twentieth century. The contributions to this book show that such a politicization, to be successful in sustaining intellectual attention, can never be reductive. Rather, it must incorporate modificatory terms and criteria – such as those of aesthetics – if it is to address complex questions raised by the arts and other forms of discourse in a suitably complex manner. Politics – however broadly defined – cannot alone offer adequate explanations of human creativity and communication. But then neither can aesthetics; and their necessary symbiosis is itself complex, calling for examination that most likely will undermine some of our most cherished assumptions – cherished because they are not disinterestedly academic, but affectively embroiled suppositions and convictions about self and Other. In this mental and social territory, anger will never be far beneath the surface, for, as the seventeenth-century historian and divine Thomas Fuller observed, "Anger is one of the sinews of the soul."[4] We must learn to harness it both effectively and justly.

Notes

1 See, for example, Stephen J. Greenblatt, *Shakespearean Negotiations: The Circulation of Social Energy in Renaissance England* (Oxford: Clarendon, 1988).
2 See especially Jürgen Habermas, *The Philosophical Discourses of Modernity* (Cambridge, MA: MIT Press, 1987), which identifies numerous aesthetic currents in contemporary philosophy, and a counterargument in N. Kompridis, *Crisis and Transformation: The Aesthetic Critique of Modernity from Hegel to Habermas* (Berkeley: University of California Press, 1999).
3 Paul Jay, "Bridging the Gap: The Position of Politics in Deconstruction," *Cultural Critique* (Fall 1992), 47–74. Jay tests various competing notions of deconstruction's relationship to politics by offering his own analysis of Jacques Derrida's essay, "The Principle of Reason: The University in the Eyes of its Pupils" (*Diacritics*, 13.3 (1983), 3–20). As Jay notes, "deconstruction has been largely responsible for helping us to see how the

assumptions, principles, and aims of academic institutions are structured and delimited by the languages and terms they employ and the philosophical assumptions that guarantee and legitimate them." Some would say that anyone acting on this awareness might be said to be acting politically, yet the action that would seem to be called for by deconstruction to undermine instrumentality would seem to be an endless deferral of action other than deconstructive analysis itself, which thereby constitutes a kind of political *mis en abîme*. In response, Jay describes Derrida's formulation of the "double gesture" to achieve a balance between critique on the one hand, and the grounds of its own validity on the other, to evade sterilization. This in itself, then, becomes the perceptible political position of deconstruction: that is, it is amenable to other political agendas for its use, in Jay's words, is "ultimately dictated by the politics of each critic who draws on it as well as by something inherent in deconstruction itself."

4 Thomas Fuller, *The Holy State and the Profane State* (London, 1642), book 2, ch. 8, "Of Anger."

"From the stage to the state": politics, form, and performance in the Elizabethan theatre

LOUIS MONTROSE

In her response to a parliamentary petition for the execution of Mary, Queen of Scots, Queen Elizabeth is reported to have told the joint delegation of lords and commons, "we princes . . . are set on stages, in the sight and view of all the world dulie observed; the eies of manie behold our actions; a spot is soone spied in our garments; a blemish quicklie noted in our dooings."[1] The first clause of this sentence has sometimes been invoked to epitomize what Stephen Greenblatt has called "the whole theatrical apparatus of royal power," and to make the point that "Elizabethan power . . . depends upon its privileged visibility."[2] Indeed, Greenblatt goes so far as to suggest that, because "a poetics of Elizabethan power" is synonymous with "a poetics of the theater," the drama produced in the Elizabethan public theatres is always already co-opted by the state: "It is precisely because of the English form of absolutist theatricality that Shakespeare's drama, written for a theater subject to state censorship, can be so relentlessly subversive: the form itself, as a primary expression of Renaissance power, helps to contain the radical doubts it continually provokes" (*Shakespearean Negotiations*, 64, 65). In this chapter, I shall be taking issue with arguments that bind the practices of the professional Elizabethan theatre to the practices of the Elizabethan state, and that bind Elizabethan theatricality to political absolutism.

For the moment, however, I wish to return to the initial quotation from Queen Elizabeth's reputed speech, which in its entirety seems to suggest that the "privileged visibility" of royal power also entails potential liabilities; that, if "kingship always involves fictions, theatricalism, and the mystification of power" (Greenblatt, *Renaissance Self-Fashioning*, 167), then fiction and theatricalism may also

Louis Montrose

be the very media through which royal power is demystified. Such is the possibility conveyed by Sir Henry Wotton, in the course of relating the accidental destruction of the Globe by fire during a performance of Shakespeare's *Henry VIII*:

> The Kings's players had a new play, called *All is true*, representing some principal pieces of the reign of Henry VIII, which was set forth with many extraordinary circumstances of pomp and majesty, even to the matting of the stage; the Knights of the order with their Georges and garters, the Guards with their embroidered coats, and the like: sufficient in truth within a while to make greatness very familiar, if not ridiculous.[3]

Wotton remarks upon a potential challenge to the authority of the great that is specifically stylistic and formal. What is at issue here is not the subversive political content of any particular play but rather the inherent capacity of dramatic representation in the public theatre to appropriate and to demystify the "absolutist theatricality" of the monarchy in the very process of staging it.

When the Lord Chamberlain's Men performed Shakespeare's *As You Like It* at the newly opened Globe at the end of the 1590s, Queen Elizabeth's subjects heard the compelling assertion that "All the world's a stage, / And all the men and women merely players" (2.7.138–9).[4] This declaration was both materially and symbolically affirmed in the very name, shape, and motto of the playhouse in which the play was being performed: the many-sided first Globe playhouse had as its sign the figure of Hercules carrying the globe; and as its motto, *Totus mundus agit histrionem*.[5] The metatheatricality of the Elizabethan drama does not necessarily obscure the privileged visibility of the royal actor. However, in the process of asserting that theatricality is a universal condition of social life, the common players assert their own privileged visibility within the circumscribed domain of the public and professional theatre; they manifest that the Globe is the locus of a theatrical power distinct from the "absolutist theatricality" of the queen. In what follows, my subject is the complicated dynamic existing between the Elizabethan theatre and the Elizabethan state, and the positioning of Shakespeare within that dynamic.

I

Throughout most of the sixteenth century, the Tudor regime had been engaged in a complex process of consolidating temporal and

12

spiritual power in the hereditary ruler of a sovereign nation-state. Consistent with this project, the Elizabethan government was actively engaged in efforts to suppress traditional, amateur forms of popular entertainment, including the civic religious drama. Such entertainments were perceived by the Elizabethan state to be tainted by the superstitions and idolatrous practices of the old faith. Because its loyalties tended to be local, regional, or papal, this traditional culture was regarded as a seedbed for dissent and sedition. Popular and liturgical practices, ceremonial and dramatic forms, were not wholly suppressed by the royal government but were instead selectively appropriated: In court, town, and countryside they were transformed by temporal authorities into elaborate and effusive celebrations of the monarchy; they became part of the ideological apparatus of the state.[6]

The suppression of religious and polemical drama and the curtailment of popular festivities were policy goals vigorously pursued by the Elizabethan regime from its very inception. The custom of celebrating the Queen's accession day began to flourish following the suppression of the northern rebellion and the York Corpus Christi play in 1569, and the promulgation of the papal bull excommunicating queen Elizabeth on Corpus Christi day 1570. The process of suppressing the mystery plays was virtually complete by 1580.[7] As Mervyn James puts it, "under Protestantism, the Corpus Christi becomes the Body of the Realm."[8] At the same time, the queen's privy council and the court nourished the professional theatre – if only to the limited extent that it could be construed as serving their own interests. By the 1570s resident professional acting companies, under the patronage of the monarch and her leading courtiers, were established in the vicinity of the City of London and the royal court at Westminster. Thus, the beginning of the fully professional, secular, and commercial theatre of Elizabethan London coincides with the effective end of the religious drama and the relative decline of local amateur acting traditions in the rest of England. Whether as a means of entertaining the court or diverting the people, the professional theatre seems to have been perceived by the crown as potentially if indirectly useful, both as an instrument for the aggrandizement of the dynastic nation-state and for the supervision and governance of its subjects.

With the building of the Red Lion in 1567 and the Theatre in 1576, the formerly itinerant professional players had their first designated playing structures. But it was not until the opening in

Louis Montrose

1599 of the first Globe, which was built from the timbers of the
dismantled Theatre, that a single company of professional players –
Shakespeare's company, the Lord Chamberlain's Men – had a
permanent home of which they themselves were part owners. At the
time the Globe was opened, the professional stage play was still an
emergent cultural form; the commercial theatre, an emergent socio-
cultural space; and the profession of actor, an emergent social
calling. These innovations could not be made to conform comfor-
tably to preexisting places in the traditional scheme of things. The
dominant Elizabethan view of that scheme, the orthodox Tudor
systematization of nature and society, is conveniently summarized
in the "Exhortacion concernyng Good Ordre and Obedience to
Rulers and Magistrates." This officially prepared and printed homily
was appointed to be read in Elizabethan churches, where (at least, in
principle) regular attendance was compulsory:

Almightie God hath created and appointed all thinges in heaven, yearth and
waters in a moste excellent and perfect ordre . . . Every degre of people, in
their vocacion, callyng and office, hath appoynted to them their duetie and
ordre. Some are in high degre, some in lowe, some kynges and princes, some
inferiors and subjectes, priestes and laimen, masters and servauntes, fathers
and chyldren, husbandes and wifes, riche and poorer and every one hath
nede of other . . . Where there is no right ordre, there reigneth all abuse,
carnall libertie, enormitie, syn and babilonicall confusion.[9]

This doctrine of a divinely appointed, unchanging, hierarchical, and
homological order was an ideological response to unprecedented
changes affecting English society in the sixteenth century: the
ramifications of the Tudor dynasty's efforts to concentrate authority
and power, both temporal and spiritual, in the person of the
monarch; religious controversy and persecution, and the sweeping
impact of Reformation policies upon economic, cultural, and spiritual life at all levels; the combination of population growth, price
inflation, unemployment and underemployment, and critical strains
upon what was even in good times little better than a subsistence
economy; transformations in agrarian modes of production, and
disruptions of traditional rural communities and values; widespread
geographic mobility and rapid social mobility; urban social problems
of unprecedented scope accompanying the spectacularly rapid
growth of London. Shakespeare's England was a traditional society
experiencing the dislocations of rapid change; and the ideology of
hierarchical and homological order that legitimated the Elizabethan

14

state could not effectively contain the ideologically anomalous realities of heterodoxy and social flux.

To some articulate Elizabethans, the popular theatre was an especially threatening innovation. Echoing the rhetoric of the homily on willful disobedience, Stephen Gosson declares the consequences of theatrical performance to be no less than the utter corruption of the social body and the destruction of the state:

> In Stage Playes for a boy to put on the attyre, the gesture, the passions of a woman; for a meane person to take upon him the title of a Prince with counterfeit porte, and traine, is by outwarde signes to shewe themselves otherwise then they are, and so within the compasse of a lye . . .
>
> We are commanded by God to abide in the same calling wherein we were called, which is our ordinary vocation in a commonweale . . . If privat men be suffered to forsake theire calling because they desire to walke gentlemen like in sattine & velvet, with a buckler at theire heeles, proportion is so broken, unitie dissolved, harmony confounded, that the whole body must be dismembred and the prince or the heade cannot chuse but sicken.[10]

Playing was without a place among traditional callings; and the players' assumptions of various roles – their protean shifts of social rank, age, and gender – seemed to some to be a willful confusion and subversion of the divinely ordained categories that had brought order out of chaos at the foundation of the world. The discrimination of statuses obsessed the guardians of the Elizabethan social order; those who did not know to keep their places might be punished. As antitheatrical tracts like Gosson's make explicit, the players were a stunning anomaly: they were men who made their living by pretending to be what they were not; their calling was to imitate the callings of others. The dramatic companies lavished money upon costumes, the readiest signs of social distinction in a stratified and deferential society. They bought the hand-me-downs of aristocrats and courtiers, in which to play at being aristocrats and courtiers. And when they were in costume, and in performance, they were exempt from the sumptuary laws that were so carefully designed to enforce a congruity between the appearance and the reality of status.[11] Thus, when these particular members of the commonwealth were laboring in their vocation, they were temporarily living a metasocial relationship to their fellow subjects and to their own society. In some significant respects, then, the protean Elizabethan common player was the very personification of the social facts denounced or suppressed in the homilies' scheme of things. He was – by profession – out of place.[12]

II

In 1574 the Earl of Leicester's Men were licensed by the queen to perform "as well for the recreacion of oure loving subjectes, as for oure solace and pleasure when we shall thincke good to see them."[13] In principle, only those companies of players who were the liveried retainers of great lords and could be employed occasionally for the solace of their masters and their masters' mistress were authorized to play in the public theatres. The queen thereby promoted the pleasures of her loving subjects, and also protected the players from the terms of the recent Acte for the punishement of Vacabondes and for the Releif of the Poore & Impotent (1572). This act was one of the key legal instruments employed by the Elizabethan state in its parallel attempts to enhance its disciplinary and its pastoral powers, to enlarge its capacity to control its subjects and to minister to their welfare. According to the terms of the act,

All and everye persone and persones beynge whole and mightye in Body and able to labour, havinge not Land or maister, nor using any lawfull Marchaundize Crafte or Mysterye whereby hee or shee night get his or her Lyvinge; & all Fencers Bearewardes Comon Players in Enterludes & Minstrels, not belonging to any Baron of this Realme or towardes any other honorable Personage of greater Degree [and who] shall wander abroade and have not Lycense of two Justices of the Peace at the leaste . . . shalbee taken adjudged and deemed Roges Vacaboundes and Sturdy Beggers.[14]

In the case of itinerant players, unstable locality was threateningly conjoined with unstable identity; vagabondage was conjoined with roguery. The distinction of liveried actors from rogues, vagabonds, and sturdy beggars was an attempt to accommodate the professional players to the status categories and social controls of a traditional, hierarchical, and deferential society. At the same time, however, it also implied an emergent recognition of the peculiar conditions of professional playing. The licensing of players depended upon a tacit recognition that their impersonations constituted a circumscribed and fictive mode of role-playing; and that professional playing was, in fact, not mere idleness but a paradoxical form of labor – a recognition that playing could actually be a "Crafte or Mysterye." Of course, at the same time that it afforded a means of protection to common players, the queen's restriction of license to those who "belonged" to trusted members of the aristocracy and were approved by the Justices of the Peace was also an assertion of royal authority, an authority both to allow and to limit the scope of her subjects' play.

Hostility to plays, players, and playhouses varied enormously in source, motive, and intensity. There were some who did not oppose occasional dramatic performances by amateurs, and/or private dramatic performances by professionals that were intended exclusively for elite audiences in the royal court, noble households, inns of court, colleges, or guildhalls. In such cases, the antitheatrical prejudice was aimed specifically at professional acting companies performing in open, public playhouses, whose audiences were largely though not exclusively composed of apprentices and servants, artisans and modest tradespeople.[15] In 1597, the lord mayor and aldermen of London petitioned the privy council to suppress stage plays, which were accused of causing numerous "inconveniences":

They are a speciall cause of corrupting . . . Youth, conteninge nothinge but unchaste matters . . . being so as that they impresse the very qualities & corruptions of manners which they represent . . . Wearby such as frequent them, beinge of the base & refuze sort of people or such younge gentlemen as have small regard of credit or conscience, drawe the same into imitacion.
They are the ordinary places for vagrant persons, Maisterles men, thieves . . . contrivers of treason, and other idele and daungerous persons to meet together . . . They maintaine idlenes in such persons as have no vocation & draw apprentices and other servauntes from theire ordinary workes and all sortes of people from the resort unto sermons and other Christian exercises to the great hinderance of traides & prophanation of religion established by her highnes within this Realm.[16]

The public playhouses were attacked as the breeding ground of plague and vice, traffic congestion and mob violence, inefficient workers and dangerous ideas. The common players were not only attacked because acting was thought to be intrinsically immoral, but also because it had suddenly become a means to relative affluence and upward social mobility for a group who had only recently been legally grouped with vagabonds, rogues, and sturdy beggars. Furthermore, the players were not only luring audiences away from the preachers, but were also stealing paying customers away from other commercial entertainments in which some of the great merchants and landlords of London had their own financial stakes.[17] London's city fathers saw the professional players not only as an affront to godliness and a threat to the social order but also as direct economic competitors.

An especially suggestive documentation of the city's attitude toward the players and toward their royal patronage is extant in a 1592 petition by the lord mayor to the Archbishop of Canterbury:

Louis Montrose

By the daily and disorderlie exercise of a number of players & playeng
houses erected within this Citie, the youth thearof is greatly corrupted &
their manners infected with many evill & ungodly qualities . . . In consideration whearof, wee most humbly beeseach your Grace . . . to voutchsafe us
your good favour & help for the refourming & banishing of so great evill out
of this Citie, which our selves of loong time though to small pourpose have
so earnestly desired and endeavoured by all means that possibly wee could.
And bycause wee understand that the Q. Majestie is & must be served at
certen times by this sort of people, for which pourpose shee hath graunted
hir lettres Patents to Mr Tilney Master of hir Revells, by virtue whearof hee
beeing authorized to refourm exercise or suppresse all manner of players,
playes, & playeng houses what-soever, did first licence the sayed playeng
houses within this Citie for hir majesties sayed service, which beefore that
time lay open to all the statutes for the punishing of these & such lyke
disorders. Wee . . . beeseach your Grace to call unto you the sayed Master of
hir Majesties-Revells . . . and to treat with him, if by any means it may bee
devised that hir Majestie may bee served with these recreations as hath ben
accoustomed (which in our opinions may easily bee don by the privat
exercise of hir Majesties own players in Convenient place) & the Citie freed
from these continuall disorders.[18]

The lord mayor's letter to Archbishop Whitgift suggests that the
crown was usurping and vitiating the moral and legal authority over
players that previously had been enjoyed and exercised by the city,
and that the instrument of this growing corruption and disorder was
the Revels Office itself. According to the lord mayor, the Master of
the Revels was charged to reform or suppress playing but instead he
actually countenanced it. (Mr Tilney, after all, gathered the fruits of
office by licensing plays, not by suppressing them.) Thus, from the
perspective of London's city fathers, the Master of the Revels – an
officer of the court – had now become the city's unappointed Lord of
Misrule; the licentiousness of the players was now licensed by
authority of the queen. The traditional task of the Office of the Revels
had been "to select, organize, and supervise all entertainment of the
sovereign, wherever the court might be."[19] The expansion of the role
of this court office to include the supervision of public as well as
courtly dramatic performances indicates that the Elizabethan regime
was attempting to subject the symbolic and interpretive activities of
its subjects to increasing scrutiny and regulation – at the same time
that it was inventing new sources of revenue for itself and its clients.
    The lord mayor made his appeal to the archbishop and his indirect
criticism of the court upon what he regarded as the common ground
of religious and civic responsibilities and spiritual and temporal
convictions. During the later sixteenth century, the religious opposi-

18

tion to players and to the newly established theatres included not only radical Puritan preachers but also orthodox Protestant ecclesiastics, who viewed the theatres as sharing the vanity and worldliness of the Holy Roman Church and as replicating its spectacular and heathenish rites. The two institutions were frequently identified with each other, and were made rhetorically interchangeable in Protestant polemics. Thus, for example, at the beginning of Elizabeth's reign, Bishop John Jewel ridiculed the papacy for bringing "the sacraments of Christ to be used now as a stage play . . . to the end that men's eyes should be fed with nothing else but with mad gazings and foolish gauds." Half a century later, the preacher William Crashaw understood theatricality as nothing less than the historically transmitted cultural heritage of Satan. In a sermon preached in London in 1607 he attacked "the ungodly Playes and Enterludes so rife in the nation: what are they but a bastard of Babylon, a daughter of error and confusion, a hellish device (the divels owne recreation to mock at holy things) by him delivered to the Heathen, from them to the Papists, and from them to us?"[20] In the context of such vehemently maintained convictions linking theatre and spectacle with papistical and satanic practices, the predilection of the queen, her court, and many in the Elizabethan nobility for dramatic and spectacular entertainments must have posed moral and political difficulties for some of the most righteous and articulate of Elizabethan subjects.

In a letter written from Venice in 1606, Sir Henry Wotton openly remarked upon the politics of spectacle as they were enacted in an alien state:

Yesterday was the Feast of Corpus Christi, celebrated by express commandment of the State (which goeth farther than devotion), with the most sumptuous procession that ever had been seen here . . . The reasons of this extraordinary solemnity were two, as I conceive it. First, to contain the people still in good order with superstition, the foolish band of obedience. Secondly, to let the Pope know (who wanteth not intelligencers) that notwithstanding his interdict, they had friars enough and other clergymen to furnish out the day.[21]

The English king's ambassador confidently deciphers the political purpose of this magnificent religious and civic ceremony: namely, to advance the interests of the ruling oligarchy of the Most Serene Republic against the unruliness of the Venetian populace, on the one hand, and against the authority of the Pope, on the other. Wotton, who had been a member of the Essex circle, was a well-schooled observer of the mysteries of state; doubtless, he found it both prudent and congenial to demystify the political appropriation of the feast of Corpus Christi in a context that was Italian, Catholic, and civic, rather than English, Protestant, and monarchical.

Among extant Elizabethan observations of the relationship between spectacle and power, one of the most cynical is to be found in the notorious "note Containing the opinion of on Christopher Marly" (1593), prepared for the privy council by Richard Baines shortly before Marlowe's death. Taking as his primary example the Machiavellian subtleties employed by Moses to maintain his power over the Hebrews, Baines's Marlowe asserts "That the first beginning of Religioun was only to keep men in awe." From the premise that the function of religion is, by mystification, to facilitate the power of the few over the many, it follows "That if there be any god or good Religion, then it is in the papistes because the service of god is performed with more ceremonies, as Elevation of the mass, organs, singing men, Shaven Crownes & cta. That all protestantes are Hypocriticall asses."[22] Baines's Marlowe gives his ironic approval to precisely those elements of Catholicism which the Protestant Bishop Jewel excoriates as "a stage play" that feeds men's eyes "with nothing else but with mad gazings and foolish gauds," precisely those elements that ambassador Wotton, with a politic detachment, observed in operation in Venice. As must have been evident to Marlowe and to some of his fellow subjects, including Wotton, the Elizabethan regime made a concerted effort to implement its own ceremonies of mystification; and it did so precisely by appropriating and elaborating, in a largely secular context, the ritual and iconic aspects of Catholic worship. However, by the very process of appropriating the spectacular theatre of medieval religion, the Elizabethan state contaminated its own strategies of legitimation. By the logic of radical Reformation thought, courtly culture was vulnerable to association with Catholic culture on the basis of their mutual association with theatricality and spectacle; and from this same perspective courtly culture could be perceived as tainted by worldliness, moral corruption, and deceptive illusion. Thus, at the same time that the iconic, verbal, and performative arts played a central role in entertaining the sovereign and aggrandizing the state, they were also a potential liability to the very reverence and assent which they were designed to procure. The criticism of the royal taste for theatrical entertainments that is obliquely implied in the lord mayor's 1592 petition to the Archbishop of Canterbury adumbrates an element of tension between court and city, between aristocratic and bourgeois cultures, between Anglican and Puritan modes of spirituality, that was to be articulated as an increasingly explicit ideological opposition during the Jacobean and Caroline reigns. The lord mayor's remarks also point towards a representational and ideological tension within Elizabethan royal policy: on the one hand, such policy sought to control and direct the iconoclastic energies of popular Protestantism through the institutions of a reformed Elizabethan church, of which the devout queen was the head; on the other hand, it sought to employ the representational resources of the arts to legitimate, to glorify, and to amuse a resplendent Renaissance court of which the magnificent prince was the center.

III

Throughout the course of Shakespeare's career in the theatre, the purpose of playing was much in dispute. The antic prince invented by the player/playwright avers that "The purpose of playing . . . is, to hold as it were the mirror up to nature, to show virtue her feature, scorn her own image, and the very age and body of the time his form and pressure" (*Hamlet*, 3.2.20–4). Plays imprint exemplary images of virtuous and vicious behavior upon the minds of their audiences, disposing them to emulate virtue and to repudiate vice. Hamlet implies that play can be serious and that jest can be earnest; that the seeming gratuitousness of play can mask its instrumentality. Through the persona of the prince, the Elizabethan playwright voices the notion that theatrical fictions are forms of ethically and politically purposeful play. Because the stage-play is both the product of a particular time and place and a circumscribed and reflexive space of representation, it may simultaneously exemplify and hold up to scrutiny the historically specific "nature" that it mirrors; it bears the pressure of the time's body but it may also clarify the form of the age. However, Hamlet's argument for drama's profound moral force is not presented unambiguously. The hero's subsequent behavior and the actual outcome of the dramatist's play are far more equivocal – both ethically and politically – than the high theatrical principles espoused by Hamlet might have led us to expect.

   Like some Elizabethan apologists for poetry, and like Shakespeare's Hamlet, those few who defend the theatre in print work within the rigorously behavioristic terms of the antitheatrical discourse but reverse its moral judgments. For example, Thomas Heywood defends his profession by claiming that those "that are chaste, are by us extolled, and encouraged in their vertues . . . The unchaste are by us shewed their errors."[23] If Heywood's defense is unambiguous, it is also conducted within too narrow and rigid a framework. For an Elizabethan perspective that emphasizes the affective power of theatrical performance – its pleasures and dangers – and does so in a rhetorically compelling fashion, we must look to Gosson, Stubbes, Rankins, and their successors, who attack the theatre for its immoral force. These unremittingly vituperative opponents represent plays, players, and playhouses as powerful agencies within Elizabethan society, and construe their power to be wholly malign. As early as 1577 – within a year of the opening of the Theatre – John Northbrooke writes that people habituated to playgoing are now unashamed to avow "that playes are as good as sermons, and that they learne as much or more at a playe, than they do at God's worde preached."[24] To the extent that the Elizabethan church was a state institution through which the regime sought to shape and channel the spiritual lives of its subjects, the perceived threat to reformed religion posed by the theatres could also be construed as a political threat to the authority of the state. Thus, in the 1597 petition quoted above, the city fathers appeal to the vital interests of the Queen's Privy Council with the charge that the theatres "draw . . . all sortes of people from the resort unto sermons and other Christian exercises, to the great hinderance of traides & prophanation of religion *established by her highnes within this Realm*" (Chambers, *Elizabethan Stage*, IV, 322; emphasis added). And in 1615, the author of *A Refutation of the Apology for Actors* gravely avers that "God onely gave authority of publique instruction and correction but to two sorts of men: to his Ecclesiasticall Ministers, and temporal Magistrates: hee never instituted a third authority of Players . . . Playes were ordained by, & dedicated to the Divell, which is enemy to God and al goodnes."[25] Those who attacked the theatre and those who defended it were agreed upon its compelling affective powers: Theatrical performance was thought to have the capacity to effect moral changes in its audience – whether for better or for worse. Plays might inspire, instruct, reform, delight, terrify, sadden, entrap, corrupt, or incite – in any case, they might do far more than pass the time.

The extensive antitheatrical discourse of Elizabethan and Jacobean pamphlets, sermons, and official documents provides a negative testimonial to the popularity and effectiveness of contemporaneous stage performances. To take this discourse seriously is at once to respect the intelligence and sincerity of contemporary opponents and to appreciate that the Elizabethan theatre may have exercised a considerable but unauthorized and therefore deeply suspect affective power upon those Elizabethan subjects who experienced it. The lord mayor's 1597 petition asserts, with palpable alarm, that the plays performed in the commercial theatres "impresse the very qualities & corruptions of manners which they represent . . . Whearby such as frequent them, beinge of the base & refuze sort of people or such young gentlemen as have small regard of credit or conscience, drawe the same into imitacion and not to the avoidinge the like vices which they represent." (Chambers, *Elizabethan Stage*, IV, 322). The actors have the power to impress images of corrupt human action upon the minds of the most vulnerable and dangerous groups in the general population, the lowly and the youthful. This power is here conceived of as material and absolute; and also as wholly malign, in that it always compels imitation, never aversion.

Despite the unremitting antitheatricalism of London's city fathers, the Elizabethan royal government was capable of viewing the public theatre in a moral light that was at least relatively positive. Such a position is evidenced by instructions from the privy council to the city in 1572, "in favor of certein persones to have in there howses, yardes, or back sydes, being overt & open places, such playes, enterludes, commedies & tragedies as maye tende to represse vyce & extoll vertwe, for the recreacion of the people, & therby to drawe them from sundrye worser exercyses."[26] Considerably later, at the turn of the century – a time of great socioeconomic uncertainty and political ferment, when London's professional and commercial theatres were enjoying unprecedented popularity and success – the privy council sought strictly to limit the number and location of playhouses, the frequency and times of performances, and the number of companies that would be allowed to play. In setting forth these orders, the privy council summarized the complex attitude of the state toward the theatre at the end of Elizabeth's reign:

Forasmuch as yt is manifestlie knowne and graunted that the multitude of the said houses and the misgovernment of them hath bin made and is dailie occasion of the idle riotous and dissolute livinge of great numbers of people, that leavinge all such honest and painefull Course of life, as they should followe, doe meete and assemble there, and of maine particular abuses and disorders that doe there uppon ensue. And yet nevertllelesse yt is Considered that the use and exercise of such plaies, not beinge evill in yt self, may with a good order and moderacion be suffered in a well governed estate, and that, hir Majestie beinge pleased at some times to take delighte and recreacion in the sight and hearinge of them, some order is fitt to bee taken for the allowance and mainteinance of suche persons, as are thoughte meetest in that kinde to yeald hir Majestie recreacion and delight, & consequentlie of the howses that must serve for publique playenge to keepe them in exercise. To the end therefore, that bothe the greatest abuses of the plaies and plaienge houses maye be redressed, and the use and moderacon of them retained, The Lordes and the rest of hir Majesties privie Councell, withe one and full Consent, have ordered in manner and forme as followeth.[27]

This order of the Queen's Privy Council reiterates the familiar claim that the professional players' public performances keep them in readiness to perform at court. However, the order's justification for the allowance of public playing goes well beyond consideration of the ruler's personal pleasures: it also justifies the allowance of a carefully limited and controlled public theatre on the grounds that such a theatre has its own legitimate place in a secure and flourishing commonwealth. The order fully acknowledges all of the massive social problems that were perennially blamed upon the theatres; nevertheless, it is unequivocal in its approach to correction in terms of greater control rather than complete suppression. The official understanding made explicit here is that, although the public theatre is *in practice* easily subject to abuse, it is by no means *in essence* corrupt or corrupting. The further implication is that, although public dramatic performance may indeed have considerable representational power, the actual ethical and political intent and consequences of such power can only be determined in local instances: the focus here is upon individual companies with specific repertoires, audiences, and playing venues; upon particular plays and the particular circumstances of their performance and reception.

IV

Such an understanding as that implied in the privy council orders of 1600 seems to me to be compatible with what we know of the part played by Shakespeare's company in the notorious Essex rebellion of 1601, and of the royal response to that performance. This singular conjunction of drama and sedition has been a basis for much generalizing about the political valence of the Elizabethan theatre; for this reason, it demands at least a brief consideration here.[28] On

24

the afternoon of Saturday, February 7, 1601, Shakespeare's company performed at the Globe a "play of the deposyng and kyllyng of Kyng Rychard the second" that was presumably – although not incontrovertibly – Shakespeare's *Tragedie of King Richard the second*.[29] This performance had been commissioned a day or two earlier by several of the conspirators; eleven of them – but not the earl himself – actually attended the performance. On the morning following, the Earl of Essex and his friends staged their own ill-conceived performance at Essex House and in the open streets of London. They failed to win over the populace; the conspiracy began to unravel almost immediately; and the attempted coup was crushed before the following day. Subsequently, in the course of investigating the conspiracy, the privy council questioned one of the Lord Chamberlain's players, Augustine Phillips, and took testimony from some of the conspirators regarding the Globe performance. As a consequence of the investigation, several of those who had arranged and attended that Globe performance as a prelude to their rebellion were tried and executed for treason; their procurement of the performance at the Globe was among the acts that were used in evidence against them.

The privy council's orders of 1600 had stipulated that "there shall bee about the Cittie two howses and noe more allowed to serve for the use of the Common Stage plaies," and that one of these should be the Globe as occupied by "the Servantes of the L. Chamberlen" (Chambers, *Elizabethan Stage*, IV, 330, 331). Given so recent and powerful a demonstration of the state's trust and favor, it may be thought that the implication of Shakespeare's company in the events of the Essex revolt would have proven disastrous. Nonetheless, the players' reputation and livelihood emerged from the crisis unscathed. Indeed, the Lord Chamberlain's Men performed at court before the queen just a few days later, on the night of Shrove Tuesday, February 24; on the morning following this latest commissioned performance, the Earl of Essex was executed for treason. This conjunction of dramatic and state performances may have been merely fortuitous, but it is tempting to see it as an intended royal response to the conjunction of tragic actions devised by the conspirators a little more than a fortnight earlier: from this perspective, the extension of an invitation to the common players of Shakespeare's company to perform again at court affirmed the continuity of royal favor toward the professional theatre, and simultaneously asserted the continuity of royal authority over the professional theatre; it made a symbolic statement that the state was secure and that its subjects were loyal.

What was the motive of the Essex party in requesting and subsidizing that particular performance of *Richard II*? Like the Elizabethan privy council, modern scholars and critics tend to assume that the performance was intended to incite the playgoing public of London to insurrection – or, at least, to predispose them to sympathize with the earl's claim that he had been victimized by the upstart caterpillars of the commonwealth who now controlled the sovereign, and that he was justified in rising to his own defense. There is a basis for this hypothesis in the events surrounding the publication and suppression of John Hayward's *Life and raigne of king Henrie the IIII* (1599), which clearly demonstrate that Essex had encouraged an identification of himself with Bolingbroke.[30] It seems to me that the hypothesis must also rely upon an assumption that the eleven conspirators who attended the performance in question did not have the capacious Globe to themselves, that they must have shared the dramatic experience with a reasonable number of ordinary playgoers upon whom the play could work the desired seditious effect.[31] The hypothesis that the conspirators expected the other spectators to identify Bolingbroke with Essex seems to assume that the Globe audience would have approved Bolingbroke unhesitatingly as the hero of the play. Such an assumption begs complex questions of intention, interpretation, and effect – issues about which the extant evidence allows us to do little more than speculate. There certainly existed at least an appearance of complicity by the Lord Chamberlain's Men in a seditious action that was of the gravest possible national significance; nevertheless, the perpetually suspicious and vigilant privy council quickly and unequivocally exonerated them. This benign official response to the players may have been due in part to the refusal of the inhabitants of London to give active support to the earl on the morning following the play. To the Elizabethan government, the spectacular failure of Essex in his attempt to arouse the queen's subjects in the streets of London may not have signified that the theatre was politically impotent but rather that there was no seditious intent in the players' performance of their playwright's play. In other words, the privy council may have judged dramatic intention by means of dramatic effect. Such an assumption implies, by negation, a fundamental conviction that the theatre was indeed powerful.

Unlike the players and the populace, however, the conspirators shaped the import of the play to their dangerous fantasies. Such is the implication of certain comments in the records of the revolt. There is, for example, the report of the trial of Sir Gilly Meyricke, at which the attorney-general cited Meyricke's insistence to the players, during arrangements for the performance, that "they must needs have the play of *Henry IV*," in which there was "set forth the killing of the King upon a stage." (By identifying the play in question with Henry IV rather than Richard II, the report strengthens its association with Hayward's notorious history.) Francis Bacon provides a vivid parallel description of Meyricke's theatrical enthusiasms: "so earnest hee was to satisfie his eyes with the sight of that tragedie which hee thought soone after his lord should bring from the stage to the state."[32] In conjunction, these comments strongly suggest that one of the conspirators' primary motives in commissioning the performance was to rouse *themselves* to action. They wished to witness a vividly dramatic reenactment of that historical event which they hoped to emulate in deed almost immediately following the performance. It seems, in other words, that they subscribed to the belief that drama has the capacity to imitate action and, by example, to impel its audience to action – an understanding shared by the theatre's most vocal defenders and detractors.

Richard II, as compellingly performed by the Lord Chamberlain's Men at the Globe, might well be thought to have stirred the conspirators to emulate Bolingbroke's successful precedent to have emboldened and resolved them to execute their dangerous and doubtful designs. Such an effect is clearly what at least one of the conspirators sought in the performance; and what, in principle, both critics and defenders of the theatre thought it to be capable of effecting. The subsequent exoneration of the players from any charge of complicity implies that neither in their play nor in their performance of it were they deemed by the authorities to be responsible for the constructions applied by the conspirators. There is evidence that the earl himself took a Hamlet-like interest in representations of aristocratic sedition and regicide, both written and acted. Consider the following charge, made during an earlier arraignment of the Earl of Essex, after he had defied the queen's command and returned to the court from Ireland:

His underhand permitting of that most treasonous booke of Henry the fourth to be printed and published, being plainly deciphered not onely by the matter, and by the Epistle itself, for what ende and for whose behoof it was

27

made, but also the Erle himself being so often present at the playing thereof, and with great applause giving countenance and lyking to the same.[33]

The official report appears to conflate Hayward's printed politic history with a dramatic entertainment on the same subject. This comment becomes particularly intriguing in conjunction with the famous and puzzling remark attributed to Queen Elizabeth, following the 1601 revolt, that "this tragedy was played 40tie times in open streets and houses" (Chambers, *William Shakespeare*, II, 327). There is no available evidence to confirm that the dramatic performances mentioned in either of these accounts were of Shakespeare's *Richard II*. Nevertheless, the two anecdotes constitute evidence suggesting that any public representation in late Elizabethan London of the dethronement and murder of King Richard II would have been politically volatile and have stirred strong topical interest.

Surely Shakespeare and his company were knowingly treading on dangerous ground in their original production of the play – let alone in their agreement to a special public performance for the Essex faction in 1601. What, then, may have motivated them to agree to such a performance? Let us consider the official record of the sworn statement taken from Augustine Phillips on February 18, 1601:

He sayeth that . . . Sr Charles Percy Sr Josclyne Percy and the L. Montegle with some thre more spak to some of the players in the presans of thys examinate to have the play of the deposyng and kyllyng of Kyng Richard the second to be played the Saterday next promysyng to gete them xls. more then their ordynary to play yt. Wher thys Examinate and hys fellowes were determyned to have played some other play, holding that play of Kyng Richard to be so old & so long out of use as that they should have small or no Company at yt. But at their request this Examinate and his fellowes were Content to play yt the Saterday and had their xls. more then their ordynary for yt and so played yt accordyngly.

(Chambers, *William Shakespeare*, II, 325)

The conspirators came to the players with the request for a specific performance of a play on a controversial and potentially dangerous subject. Understandably, the players resisted. Nevertheless, the lords and gentlemen were insistent, and the common players finally deferred to the wishes of their betters. Thus, one subtext of Phillips's deposition is the vulnerability of inferiors and clients to the pressures exerted by their superiors and patrons. But there is also another subtext that is ideologically at variance with the first, one based not upon codes of social deference or political allegiance but upon market calculations and professional judgments. The conspira-

tors presented their request to the players in purely commercial
terms "promysyng to gete them xls. more then their ordynary to play
yt"; the players resisted on a mixture of commercial and professional
grounds, "holding that play of Kyng Richard to be so old & so long
out of use as that they should have small or no Company at yt." The
players were finally persuaded by the conspirators, and their performance was rewarded according to the financially advantageous
terms agreed upon: they "had their xls. more then their ordynary for
yt and so played yt accordyngly." The players were to receive from
the conspirators substantially more than their usual take from a
public performance, and that profit would have been over and above
whatever they took in from the ordinary paying customers who may
also have attended. Although the topic was potentially inflammatory, it was also the case that *Richard II* had already been allowed for
public performance and for subsequent printing by the licensing
authorities – although not, perhaps, without prior censorship.[34] The
title page of the first quarto (1597), claims to present the play "As it
hath been publikely acted by the right Honourable the Lorde
Chamberlaine his Servants." The printing of a second and then a
third quarto in the next year, 1598, suggests that the play was in
demand – presumably by the same politic readership that, in the
following year, would be so eager to obtain copies of Hayward's *Life
and raigne of king Henrie the IIII*. Thus, we may have reason to
suspect that Phillips was being disingenuous when he claimed, in
1601, that the play was "so old & so long out of use as that they
should have small or no Company at yt." The motivations of the
players do not seem to have been political in any narrow sense of the
term, by which I mean actively seeking to promote the agenda of a
particular faction; they were, nevertheless, shaped by considerations
of a distinctly ideological character. More precisely, in agreeing to
perform the play in their public playhouse, the Lord Chamberlain's
Men seem to have been motivated by a combination of social
deference and commercial gain. This profitable but unstable mixture
points toward the conditions of emergence of the professional
theatre at an historically transitional moment. This theatre was
sustained by a frequently advantageous but inherently unstable
conjunction of two theoretically distinct modes of cultural production: one, hierarchical and deferential, based upon traditional relations of patronage and clientage; the other, fluid and competitive,
based upon market relations. The mix of patronage-based and
market-based modes of cultural production implied by the players'

acceptance of the conspirators' commission aptly manifested the ambiguous status of the professional players and their theatre within the shifting socioeconomic and cognitive frameworks of Elizabethan England.

V

It has sometimes been claimed that the salient point about the role of the theatre in the Essex conspiracy is that, in failing to catalyze a rebellion, it proved itself to be merely ineffectual and irrelevant. From this perspective, we are to conclude that the Elizabethan theatre was "powerless." For example, writing in reaction against the recently dominant critical tendency to politicize Renaissance drama, Paul Yachnin asserts that

> as a result of both the vigor of Elizabethan government censorship and the compliance of the players with that censorship, the theater of the late Elizabethan and early Stuart period came to be viewed as powerless, unable to influence its audience in any purposeful or determinate way. The dramatic companies won from the government precisely what the government was most willing to give: a privileged, profitable, and powerless marginality.[35]

Such a conclusion goes against the massive evidence that many guardians of Elizabethan religious and political orthodoxy thought that the theatre was very powerful indeed, and that it was powerful in the worst possible way. Furthermore, the persistent concern of the state to regulate the drama, even while tolerating or supporting it, does not argue for the perception that it was a trivial and impotent cultural practice. Yachnin argues that "the acquisition of their own theaters had the peculiar effect . . . of liberating the players from their dependence upon aristocratic sponsors and so freeing them to address a variety of topics in an objective spirit, and, at the same time, of diminishing the power of the theater to influence the political issues about which it was now free to speak" (60).

Yachnin seems to use the word *acquisition* to describe the move of the itinerant players into fixed houses circa 1576. This is to miss the distinction between the relationship of players to a playhouse that is merely a leased space and their relationship to a playhouse that is the collective property of the company – as was the case with the Lord Chamberlain's/King's Men after 1598. These changes profoundly affected the development of the players' socioeconomic

status and their collective professional consciousness.[36] Nevertheless, the characterization of the players as suddenly liberated from
dependence upon aristocratic patronage by their acquisition of playhouses is overstated. After all, there is considerable and familiar
evidence to affirm that the commercial theatre – and Shakespeare's
company, in particular – continued to maintain an important relationship to aristocratic and royal patronage, both financial and legal,
throughout the Elizabethan–Jacobean period. It is undoubtedly true
that the formal and thematic horizons of the drama were considerably enlarged by the increasing socioeconomic heterogeneity of its
audience. However, the consequence of such a change must have
been to complicate the ideological positioning of the professional
theatre, not to neutralize it. The commercial theatrical companies of
Elizabethan London were attempting to articulate and to satisfy the
collective desires of an increasingly large and diverse potential
market. This Elizabethan entertainment industry was hardly a disinterested venture; it had not left all ideology behind but was rather in
the vanguard of an emergent ideology of market capitalism.[37] Yachnin's association of the commodification of Elizabethan drama with
the achievement of objectivity and freedom is itself an observation
heavy with baggage from a later phase of that ideology.

    As an example of the players' paradoxical liberation into power-
lessness, Yachnin cites Shakespeare's *Richard II*, and its performance on the eve of the Essex revolt: "*Richard II* is able to
represent political issues openly by producing a political message
which is depoliticized (that is, incapable of exerting determinate
political influence) by virtue of being bifurcated, or two-faced"
("Powerless Theater," 66). Here Yachnin makes clear that what he
intends by the sweeping and provocative claim that the theatre was
powerless is the hardly controversial point that it could not intentionally produce and control specific political opinions and beha-
viors in its audience. By framing the issues in terms of drastic
antinomies – between "determinate political influence" and
"powerlessness," or between political "power" and the "freedom"
of artistic disinterestedness – Yachnin forecloses upon an analysis
of the more mediated, subtle, unintended, and/or unprogrammatic
ways in which the Elizabethan theatre appropriated, shaped, questioned, and publicly disseminated socially significant meanings,
values, and beliefs.

    Let me return again to the case of *Richard II*. "The overall meaning
or point of view" of Richard II, according to Yachnin, "is designed to

be indeterminate, open to a range of interpretations arrayed along an axis between orthodoxy, providentialism, and hierarchy at one pole and subversion, Realpolitik, and revolution at the other" ("Powerless Theater," 66). It is a critical commonplace that this play takes a multiple perspective upon the historical events it represents. But this critical commonplace must itself be historicized. The multiplicity of perspective characteristic of Shakespeare's plays has been construed, according to the canons of modern literary criticism, as a hallmark of Shakespeare's negative capability, aesthetic disinterestedness, intellectual inquisitiveness, and/or universal humanity. In an Elizabethan context, however, such characteristics may have had a specific and interested ideological valence. The providentialist ideology that provided the interpretive framework for some earlier Tudor historiography was also the basis for both the political discourse that legitimated the Elizabethan state and the personality cult that exalted the queen. As is made abundantly clear by so basic and widely disseminated a text as the official homily on willful disobedience, the principles of "orthodoxy, providentialism, and hierarchy" – which formed the core of this dominant discourse on Elizabethan state power – made no allowance whatsoever for alternatives or for indeterminacy. Those who advocated or appeared to advocate "subversion, Realpolitik, and revolution" – whether in print or in action – were guilty of sedition, and were frequently deemed to be satanic agents or to be merely depraved; they were subject to whatever control and punishment the regime could muster.

The tacitly antiprovidentialist *Realpolitik* of relevance to Shakespeare's *Richard II* and to the scholars and courtiers in the Essex circle was based upon the political reading and contemporary application of Tacitus's Roman history. Mervyn James characterizes Renaissance Tacitism as

the "politic" art by means of which the historical actor, his will powered by passion and interest, attained his objectives, which were understood in terms of the pursuit and preservation of dominance ... History simply became a field for the play of the heroic energy of the autonomous political will, seeking to dominate events by its command of the politic arts. It was an approach which, by comparison with that of the providentialist historian, could be thought of as "atheist"; for the historical actors it presented were seen as released from the sanctions and controls imposed by morality and law, and underwritten by religion.   (*Society, Politics and Culture*, p. 421)

One of the reasons why Hayward's history of Henry IV was of

interest to the Essex faction and of concern to the privy council was that it abandoned providentialist historiography and embraced a Tacitean/Machiavellian understanding of history and politics as processes shaped by the interaction of strumpet Fortune with the will and intellect of the individual human agent. In the formulation of F. J. Levy, "Hayward's book was the first realization in England of a history in which the causes of events were seen in terms of the interrelationship of politics and character rather than in terms of the working out of God's providence" ("Hayward, Daniel," p. 2).

Like Mervyn James's use of the term "historical actor," Levy's use of the term "character" is suggestive, particularly in light of his observation that Hayward's historical writing was both generally indebted to dramatic form and specifically influenced by the characterization of the royal actors in Shakespeare's history plays.[38] This suggests to me that the creation and motivation of characters in English history plays and tragedies of state – genres which were central to the late Elizabethan theatrical repertory – was a cultural development of considerable philosophical and political import. The sacred, dramatic ritual of the medieval church had a divine – that is, an instrumental – efficacy; the religious drama of the medieval Corpus Christi play imitated biblical history and divine revelation in "play"; the secular, professional, and commercial theatre of Shakespeare's London exemplified the reality that it played.[39] What is involved in these distinctions is a decisive shift in the coordination of playing dimensions: a reorientation of the dramaturgical axis from the vertical plane, which relates earthly events to a divinely ordained master narrative, to the horizontal plane, upon which human characters interact in an imagined social space. In conjunction with these changes – and, presumably, as a consequence of the professionalization of playing – the art of characterization seems to have undergone a dramatic change of its own, a change that may be apprehended in a significant terminological shift. Andrew Gurr has pointed out that "what the players were presenting on stage by the beginning of the [seventeenth] century was distinctive enough to require a whole new term to describe it. This term, the noun 'personation', suggests that a relatively new art of individual characterisation had developed" (*Shakespearean Stage*, pp. 73–4). A significant formal and stylistic component of this emergent mode of characterization was the development of the soliloquy into an effective theatrical convention for the expression of interior meditation, dialogue, or conflict. Raymond Williams has

33

observed that, in the later Elizabethan drama, the soliloquy instanti-
ates "new and subtle modes and relationships" in characterization
and in the dynamic between actors and audience; and that these
"were in themselves developments in social practice, and are
fundamentally connected with the discovery, in dramatic form, of
new and altered social relationships, perceptions of self and others,
complex alternatives of private and public thought."[40] Williams
resists the assumption that formal change merely reflects social
change, insisting instead upon a dialectical mode of ideological/
formal analysis: "The formal innovation is a true and integral
element of the [social] changes themselves: an articulation, by
technical discovery, of changes in consciousness which are themselves forms of consciousness of change" (*Culture*, p. 142).
Williams's conception of the connection between formal innovation
and social change is relevant not only to the device of the soliloquy
but to the whole phenomenon of personation as it emerged in the
drama of the late Elizabethan and Jacobean public and professional
theatres.

The conceptual and practical establishment of dramatic personation in English culture at the end of the sixteenth century is
consonant with the new importance being given to human agency
and to issues of individual conscience, interests, and will in the
most advanced historical, political, and economic speculations of
the day. In the long run, and from the widest perspective, the
development of the theatrical profession and the art of personation
were consonant with other material and ideological developments –
capital accumulation, market calculation, contractual relations, and
"possessive individualism" – that manifest the emergence of what
we now characterize as merchant capitalism and bourgeois subjectivity.[41] More immediately and particularly, these theatrical developments were consonant with the eagerness of the late Elizabethan
sociopolitical and intellectual elites to comprehend and justify
political and historical actions in terms of a Tacitean/Machiavellian
paradigm. Such an interest represented a conceptual challenge and a
perceived political threat to the absolutist pretensions of the sovereign. In the professional drama of the Elizabethan commercial
theatres, the shift of emphasis from a metaphysical to a social
dialectic implies that the locus of dramatic action had become the
temporal and mutable human realm of second causes; and the
increasing concern of the players and dramatists with individual
characterization – in the motivation of dramatic action – suggests

34

that this mode of drama is especially congenial to Tacitean/Machia-vellian views of historical process.

The celebrated remark attributed to Queen Elizabeth – "I am Richard II. Know ye not that?" – may suggest that she shared with the Taciteans of the Essex circle a habit of reading that found analogies and parallels between the shape of the past and the shape of the present. However, as the rest of her putative conversation with William Lambarde makes emphatically clear, the queen found the ideological implications of Tacitism to be not only seditious but sacrilegious:

> *W. L.* Such a wicked imagination was determined and attempted by a most unkind Gent. the most adorned creature that ever your Majestie made.
> *Her Majestie.* He that will forget God, will also forget his benefactors; this tragedy was played 40tie times in open streets and houses.
> (Chambers, *William Shakespeare*, II, 326–7)

As David Kastan has pointed out, Lambarde's use of the term *imagination* has a legal force, since the Tudor law of treason defined it in part as the "imagining and compassing of the death of a king."[42] Like the power of the imagination in Lambarde's usage, the power of the theatre in Queen Elizabeth's usage may take on an instrumental force. The queen's reference to "this tragedy . . . played 40tie times in open streets and houses" is usually taken by literary historians to refer to multiple performances of a tragic drama on the subject of Richard II, despite the puzzling implications of such a reading. The attributed royal remark seems to me more plausible when taken metaphorically, as an application of the *theatrum mundi* trope to the recurrent enactment of treason in a theatre-state in which "princes . . . are set on stages." In this sense, the remark attributed to the queen is cognate with Bacon's description of Sir Gelly Meyricke's "wicked imagination": "so earnest hee was to satisfie his eyes with the sight of that tragedie which hee thought soone after his lord should bring from the stage to the state." Whether or not Queen Elizabeth actually said that "we princes . . . are set on stages, in the sight and view of all the world dulie observed," the player-play-wright who was her subject probably read in Holinshed that she had. In any case, when he came to write his second tetralogy of English history plays, Shakespeare dramatized the theatricality of power as a recurrent contest among historical actors to control the personation of the king.

Shakespeare's *Richard II* does not explicitly advocate a Tacitean understanding of history and government, any more than it advocates the acts of "subversion, Realpolitik, and revolution" that it also represents. Instead, the play incorporates both providentialist and naturalist paradigms as opposing structures of meaning through which particular characters apprehend the shape of history; it mobilizes these paradigms as the conflicting terms in which characters enact and interpret the events in which they are taking part.[43] Elizabethan dramatic form has a rhetorical basis in the intellectual interplay of academic debating positions; it motivates ideas in terms of conflicts existing among, and within, human characters; and it incarnates these characters-in-conflict in professional players who interact upon a stage.[44] The performance of plays in the Elizabethan professional theatre operates a dialectic among characters within the play world; a dialectic between the fictional world of the characters and the experiential world of the audience; and a dialectic between the professional players and those who pay to see them play. Through this complex theatrical dialectic of illusion and estrangement, the Elizabethan drama produces that objectivity effect which has become its formal and ideological hallmark. To historicize this effect is to reveal the illusion of its objectivity, for the "objectivity" required to represent the dominant ideology as merely one among a range of possible positions is itself a perspective with profound political implications.

It is precisely by appropriating the official Elizabethan principles of "orthodoxy, providentialism, and hierarchy," and then (in Yachnin's terms) arraying them indeterminately along an axis of interpretive positions, that Shakespeare's history plays decenter those principles and demystify their claim to divine and immutable truth. Within the specific constraints of the dominant Elizabethan ideology, freedom of interpretation and indeterminacy of meaning were inherently dangerous and potentially subversive notions.[45] A local and practical – although not necessarily intended – consequence of theatrical illusion was that it could provide some measure of protection against the censorship, suppression, and punishment that otherwise threatened a cultural practice that was formally disposed to destabilize absolute and univocal claims. This is the historical and textual basis for the familiar modern celebrations of Shakespeare's ambivalence, complexity, universality, and/or transcendence of ideology. Through a complex of formal mediations, performed drama creates a multiplicity of perspectives; however, the very heterodoxy thereby created is itself – in principle – ideologically fraught. Thus, *pace* Greenblatt, "the English form of absolutist

36

theatricality" that characterizes the ideology of Elizabethan–Jacobean monarchy is radically destabilized when it is represented in Shakespearean theatre. And this is so precisely because "a poetics of Elizabethan power" is not synonymous with "a poetics of the theater" – because the form of theatricality in the public, professional theatre is itself predisposed to be antiabsolutist.

In its various manifestations – including the regulation of the drama – the concern taken by the queen and her council "for the recreation of oure loving subjectes" exemplifies the process of state formation through concerted efforts to expand and to systematize ideological state apparatuses.[46] The privy council attempted to restrict the number of professional acting companies and the number and location of playhouses; as early as the beginning of the 1580s, all plays for acting were made subject to censorship, licensing, and the payment of fees to the Master of the Revels. By such means as those I have already enumerated, the royal government at once enjoyed and protected but also sought to limit, control, and profit from the professional theatre. Regarding the attitudes of both the court and the city toward the theatre, one fact of central relevance is that the ideological as well as the physical and juridical locus of the theatre was at the intersection of royal and civic interests; in certain situations, the theatre could and did become a site where the differences between those interests might be articulated and engaged.[47] Perhaps the general point to be made here concerning the attitude of the Elizabethan state towards the Elizabethan theatre is that it was complex and equivocal; that it was not constant but was subject to numerous shifts, variations, and inconsistencies; and that some of these were the consequence of fundamental anomalies and contradictions, while others were the consequence of merely local or temporary exigencies. And what of the attitude of the Elizabethan theatre toward the Elizabethan state? The extant evidence concerning the ideological positioning of the professional playhouses and their plays – both from the plays themselves and from other sources – is, unsurprisingly, ambiguous, diverse, and contradictory. This suggests that, in practice, the Elizabethan theatre must have proved a rather unreliable ideological apparatus in the service of the Elizabethan state. On the other hand, as the circumstances of the Essex revolt suggest, it was at least equally difficult to enlist the professional Elizabethan theatre as a vehicle for concerted seditious action.

The Lord Chamberlain's Men gave a metatheatrical demonstration of the doubly mimetic capacity of drama – its status as a representation of, and provocation to, action – when they performed *Hamlet* at the Globe, as they almost certainly did not long before their infamous performance of *Richard II*. "The tragedians of the city" have come "to offer . . . service" to the prince. Although "their residence, both in reputation and profit, was better both ways," they are now compelled to leave their playhouse, temporarily reverting to itinerant status and seeking royal patronage because keen competition in the city's entertainment industry has hurt their profits (*Hamlet*, 2.2.316–62). The melancholy Hamlet is enthusiastic for the players' visit; and in this unwonted enthusiasm, the King seeks occasion to mollify his chiefest courtier, and to divert him from his malcontented brooding:

> It doth much content me
> To hear him so inclined.
> Good gentlemen, give him a further edge
> And drive his purpose into these delights. (3.1.24–7)

However, Claudius unwisely entrusts the office of Master of the Revels, and its licensing authority, to Hamlet himself:

> *King.* Have you heard the argument? is there no offense in't?
> *Ham.* No, no, they do but jest, poison in jest – no offense i'th'world.
> (3.2.230–2)

The antically disposed prince mocks the King's notion that the drama is an innocuous pastime; he has a rather different notion of what it would mean to "drive his purpose into these delights." Hamlet's sententious speech on "the purpose of playing" (3.2.1–45) is spoken in the context of his own particular purposes: "The play's the thing / Wherein I'll catch the conscience of the king" (2.2.604–5). A courtly command performance by the city's common players will be employed as an ethical instrument for the determination of political action; it will be placed at the center of the prince's design to delegitimate the monarch.

Immediately upon the arrival of the players, Hamlet requests that the company's leading player recite "a passionate speech" (2.2.431–2) describing the murder of Priam, and then, that these "tragedians of the city" (2.2.329) "play something like the murder of [his] father / Before [his] uncle" (2.2.596–7). It is for a double purpose that Shakespeare's Hamlet employs the theatre's powerful capacity to move its audience by a mixture of language and gesture: at once to confirm the King's guilt and to galvanize his own revenge, to rouse himself to regicide:

> I'll observe his looks;
> I'll tent him to the quick. if a do blench,
> I know my course. (2.2.597–9)

The strategies of Claudius and Hamlet enact opposed and complementary courtly attitudes towards the theatre: at the same time that
the monarch construes it as a means of diversion, his chiefest
courtier construes it as a means of subversion. In the very process of
catching the King in his metatheatrical mousetrap, however, Hamlet
himself becomes so affected by the power of theatrical mimesis that
he exposes his own suspicions and designs to the King. As repeatedly happens in *Hamlet*, the playwright's ironic designs defeat the
characters' purposes and puzzle their wills. Or, as the Player-King
puts it, in *The Murder of Gonzago*,

> Our wills and fates do so contrary run
> That our devices still are overthrown;
> Our thoughts are ours, their ends none of our own. (3.2.209–11)

Regardless of the divergent intentions and expectations of the
prince and the King, Hamlet's "mousetrap" has an ambiguous and
unpredictable effectivity within the world of Shakespeare's play. As
for the travelling company of professional players, their materially
self-interested motives are merely to maintain their livelihood and to
insure the continuance of royal patronage. They are hardly in a
position to refuse either Hamlet's choice of repertory – "Dost thou
hear me, old friend? can you play *The Murder of Gonzago*?" – or his
request for their inclusion in performance of "a speech of some
dozen or sixteen lines which [he] would set down and insert in't"
(2.2.537–8, 541–2). *Hamlet* is a tragedy of state that internalizes the
public and professional theatre's relationship to the court, thereby
foregrounding the cultural politics of that relationship. In its demonstration of a complex and contingent interaction of diverse interests,
the metaproduction of *The Murder of Gonzago* is emblematic of the
real but limited, diffuse, and unstable power of the professional
theatre within Shakespeare's society.

The inconclusive conclusions on offer here are not nearly as
exciting as the bold assertions that have become commonplace in
the critical literature on the Elizabethan theatre. However, from my
perspective, any general characterization of the relationship between
the Elizabethan theatre and the Elizabethan state in terms of an
either/or choice between subversion and containment, between
resistance and complicity, or between power and freedom, appears

39

to be hopelessly reductive.[48] A conceptual origin for the current critical notion of *contained subversion* may be located in the ambiguity of the Elizabethan term *license*, which implies that heterodoxy may be effectively controlled precisely by allowing it a conspicuously authorized expression. Although some recent discussions suggest that such a strategy was uniformly and unequivocally effective, the licensing of the Elizabethan drama by the Elizabethan state was merely an attempt at containment. Certainly, the Elizabethan state did attempt to contain the Elizabethan theatre. In practice, however, this attempt was inconsistent and haphazard, and was never uniformly and unequivocally effective. I suggest, furthermore, that it was wholly beyond the capacity of the Elizabethan state to achieve the uniform and absolute containment of alternative and oppositional discourses. Indeed, it could be argued that such total control is (as yet) beyond the power of any state. In particular instances and under particular circumstances, the Elizabethan drama-in-performance had the capacity to function as a sociopolitical instrument of domination and/or resistance. In the heat of this debate about the politics of the Elizabethan theatre, however, it should not be forgotten that this drama-in-performance was also, and simultaneously, a cultural practice and a cultural process that cannot be wholly reduced to a political function. Perhaps we need to remind ourselves that the Elizabethan drama-in-performance also had the capacity to function as a cognitive and therapeutic instrument – that is, to function ideologically, in the most general and most enabling senses of that term. In other words, the symbolic actions performed in the theatre had the immediate, if frequently transitory, capacity to stimulate the intellect and to promote the emotional well-being of its actual and vicarious participants. Plays-in-performance proffered aids to understanding and to endurance in the theatre of the world; they were, in Kenneth Burke's phrase, equipment for living.

In my view, the professional, public, and commercial theatre of Elizabethan London did have a subtle and diffuse power of its own, but the direction and effectivity of that power was uncertain and intermittent. It lay precisely in the combination of representational resources that enabled it to enact and to epitomize the *theatrum mundi* metaphor – resources that gave theatrical power its specificity as a cultural institution, form, and practice. My point is that the source of this power was in its very theatricality, and in the implications of theatricality for the construction and manipulation of social

rules and interpersonal relations – implications touching fundamental epistemological and sociopolitical issues of causality and
legitimacy, identity and agency. Even if, in the texts and scenarios of
particular plays, such implications were not foregrounded – indeed,
even if they were contained or suppressed – this power might
nevertheless make itself felt in the process of performance, in which
both the players and their audience participated actively in the
making of meaning.[49] The theatrical power I am trying to describe
did not lie in the explicit advocacy of specific political positions but
rather in the implicit but pervasive suggestion that all such positions
are situational, provisional, and motivated by the passions and
interests of their advocates. In this precise and limited sense,
Shakespearean drama as enacted in the Elizabethan theatre formally
contested the dominant ideological assertions of the Elizabethan
state.

Notes

This chapter was first published in Louis Montrose, *The Purpose of Playing:
Shakespeare and the Cultural Politics of the Elizabethan Theatre* (University of Chicago Press, 1996) and is reprinted by permission of the University
of Chicago Press.
1 "A Report of Hir Majesties most gratious answer, delivered by hir selfe
   verballie . . . in hir chamber of presence at Richmond, the twelfe daie of
   November 1586," in *Holinshed's Chronicles of England, Scotland, and
   Ireland*, 6 vols. (1808; rpt., New York: AMS Press, 1965), vol. IV, p. 934.
2 For the first quotation, see Stephen Greenblatt, *Renaissance Self-
   Fashioning* (University of Chicago Press, 1980), p. 167; for the second,
   Stephen Greenblatt, *Shakespearean Negotiations* (Berkeley: University
   of California Press, 1988), p. 64. The queen's speech is invoked in each
   instance.
3 Letter to Sir Edmund Bacon, July 2, 1613, in Logan Pearsall Smith, *The
   Life and Letters of Sir Henry Wotton*, 2 vols. (Oxford: Clarendon, 1907),
   vol. II, pp. 32–3. See also Stephen Orgel, "Making Greatness Familiar,"
   in Stephen Greenblatt, ed., *The Forms of Power and the Power of Forms
   in the Renaissance*, Genre Special Topics, 7 (University of Oklahoma,
   1982), pp. 41–8.
4 Shakespeare's plays are cited by act, scene, and line; I have used the text
   in *The Complete Works of Shakespeare*, ed. David Bevington, 4th edn.
   (New York: Harper Collins, 1992).
5 See Andrew Gurr, *The Shakespearean Stage, 1574–1642* (Cambridge
   University Press, 1970), p. 95. I first advanced an historicized account of
   the metatheatricality of the Elizabethan drama and the protean powers of

41

the Elizabethan players in "The Purpose of Playing: Reflections on a Shakespearean Anthropology," *Helios*, n.s., 7 (1980), 51–74.

6 On the process by which cultural practices were appropriated and invented in order to aggrandize the Tudor state, see Roy Strong, *The Cult of Elizabeth* (London: Thames and Hudson, 1977); Penry Williams, *The Tudor Regime* (Oxford: Clarendon, 1979), pp. 293–310, 351–405; Philip Corrigan and Derek Sayer, *The Great Arch: English State Formation as Cultural Revolution* (Oxford: Blackwell, 1985), pp. 43–71; David Cressy, *Bonfires and Bells: National Memory and the Protestant Calendar in Elizabethan and Stuart England* (Berkeley: University of California Press, 1989), pp. 1–129.

7 See Harold C. Gardiner, SJ, *Mysteries' End* (New Haven: Yale University Press, 1946); R. W. Ingram, "Fifteen Seventy-Nine and the Decline of Civic Religious Drama in Coventry," in *Elizabethan Theatre VIII*, ed. G. R. Hibbard (Waterloo, Ontario: University of Waterloo, 1982), pp. 114–28.

8 Mervyn James, "Ritual, Drama and Social Body in the Late Medieval English Town," *Society, Politics and Culture: Studies in Early Modern England* (Cambridge University Press, 1986), p. 41.

9 *Certain Sermons or Homilies (1547) and A Homily against Disobedience and Wilful Rebellion (1570): A Critical Edition*, ed. Ronald B. Bond (University of Toronto Press, 1987), p. 161. A second edition of the 1547 text appeared in 1559, almost immediately after the accession of Elizabeth, and this was reprinted frequently during the reign.

10 Stephen Gosson, *Plays confuted in five actions* (1582), facsimile edn. (New York: Johnson Reprint, 1972), sigs. C5r, G6v–G7v. Jonas Barish, *The Anti-Theatrical Prejudice* (Berkeley: University of California Press, 1981) is a magisterial intellectual history of antitheatricality in the West. Among the numerous recent studies of cross-dressing in Elizabethan theatre and society, see especially Laura Levine, "Men in Women's Clothing: Anti-Theatricality and Effeminization from 1579 to 1642," *Criticism* 28 (1986), 121–43; and Jean E. Howard, "Cross-Dressing, the Theatre, and Gender Struggle in Early Modern England," *Shakespeare Quarterly* 39 (1988), 418–40.

11 On sumptuary laws in early modern England, see N. B. Harte, "State Control of Dress and Social Change in Pre-Industrial England," in *Trade, Government and Economy in Pre-Industrial England. Essays Presented to P. J. Fisher*, ed. D. C. Coleman and A. H. John (London: Weidenfeld and Nicolson, 1976), pp. 132–65; Frank Whigham, *Ambition and Privilege: The Social Tropes of Elizabethan Courtesy Theory* (Berkeley: University of California Press, 1984).

12 On the profession of player in Elizabethan England, see Muriel Bradbrook, *The Rise of the Common Player: A Study of Actor and Society in Shakespeare's England* (Cambridge, MA: Harvard University Press, 1962); Gurr, *Shakespearean Stage*, pp. 19–81; Gerald Eades Bentley, *The Profession of Player in Shakespeare's Time, 1590–1642* (Princeton University Press, 1984).

13 Patent of May 10, 1574, reprinted in E. K. Chambers, *The Elizabethan Stage*, 4 vols. (Oxford: Clarendon, 1923), vol. II, pp. 87–8.

14 An Acte for the punishement of Vacabondes and for Releif of the Poore & Impotent (14 Eliz. I c. 5); rpt. in Chambers, *Elizabethan Stage*, vol. IV, pp. 269–71. The punishment prescribed was to be "grevouslye whipped, and burnte through the gristle of the right Eare with a hot Yron of the compasse of an Ynche about." The act was amended and continued in 1576 and 1584–5.

15 The classic work on the audiences of the Elizabethan theatres is Alfred Harbage, *Shakespeare's Audience* (New York: Columbia University Press, 1941). Harbage stresses the social heterogeneity and predominant commonality of the audiences in the public theatres. His conclusions are sharply challenged in Ann Jennalie Cook, *The Privileged Playgoers of Shakespeare's London, 1576–1642* (Princeton University Press, 1981), who argues that even the public theatres of the period were predominantly the playground of the privileged few. In reaction against Harbage's fundamentally democratic Shakespeare, Cook produces an emphatically elitist Shakespeare that flies in the face of much statistical and anecdotal evidence. For a critique of Cook, and a judicious and stimulating reconsideration of the whole question of the social composition of theatre audiences, see Andrew Gurr, *Playgoing in Shakespeare's London* (Cambridge University Press, 1987), esp. pp. 3–5, 49–79. Gurr's picture is more complex than those of Harbage and Cook, and takes into account variations among particular theatres and shifts over several decades. Gurr suggests "that despite the infrequent reference to their presence citizens were the staple, at least of amphitheatre audiences, throughout the period . . . Citizens . . . and their lesser neighbours the prosperous artisan class [were] a kind of silent majority in the playhouses" (64).

16 The Lord Mayor and Aldermen to the Privy Council, July 28, 1597; rpt. in Chambers, *Elizabethan Stage*, vol. IV, p. 322.

17 See the revealing comments of Thomas Nashe (1592) and Henry Chettle (1592), rpt. in Chambers, *Elizabethan Stage*, vol. IV, pp. 239, 243. The economic basis of hostility to the Elizabethan stage is stressed in Alfred Harbage, "Copper into Gold," in *English Renaissance Drama*, ed. Standish Henning, Robert Kimbrough, and Richard Knowles (Carbondale: Southern Illinois University Press, 1976), pp. 1–14.

18 The Lord Mayor to John Whitgift, Archbishop of Canterbury, 25 February 1591/2; rpt. in Chambers, *Elizabethan Stage*, vol. IV, pp. 307–8.

19 Gerald Eades Bentley, *The Profession of Dramatist in Shakespeare's Time, 1590–1642* (1971; rpt. Princeton University Press, 1986), p. 147. On the Revels Office, see also Chambers, *Elizabethan Stage*, vol. I, pp. 71–105; Janet Clare, *"Art made tongue-tied by authority": Elizabethan and Jacobean Dramatic Censorship* (Manchester University Press, 1990); Richard Dutton, *Mastering the Revels: The Regulation and Censorship of English Renaissance Drama* (University of Iowa Press, 1991).

Louis Montrose

20 See John Jewel, *An Apology of the Church of England* (1564), ed. J. E. Booty (Ithaca, NY: Cornell University Press, 1963), p. 36; William Crashaw, *The Sermons preached at the Crosse, Feb. xiiii, 1607* (1608), excerpts reprinted in Chambers, *Elizabethan Stage*, vol. IV, p. 249. On the hostility to the stage as a persistent feature of Western religious thought and polemic, see Barish, *Anti-Theatrical Prejudice.*
21 Letter to the Earl of Salisbury, Venice, May 26, 1606; rpt. in *Life and Letters of Sir Henry Wotton*, vol. I, p. 350.
22 Richard Baines, "A note Containing the opinion of on Christopher Marly Concerning his damnable [opini] Judgement of Religion, and scorn of God's word" (British Library Harleian MS 6848), printed in C. F. Tucker Brooke, *The Life of Marlowe* (London: Methuen, 1930), pp. 98–100. Machiavelli's commentary on Livy's account of Roman religion, *Discorsi*, 1.11–14, is a *locus classicus* for Renaissance perspectives on religion as political mystification.
23 Thomas Heywood, *An Apology for Actors* (1612), rpt. with I. G., *A Refutation of the Apology for Actors* (1615), facsimile edn. (New York: Garland, 1973), sig. Glv. Heywood goes on to recount some sensational case histories (sig. Glv–G2v), in which guilty creatures sitting at a play are so moved by the feigned action that they spontaneously confess their hidden crimes. All of "The Third Booke, Of Actors, and the true use of their quality" is relevant.
24 John Northbrooke, *A Treatise wherein Dicing, Dauncing, Vaine playes, or Enterluds, with other idle pastimes, &c., commonly used on the Sabboth day, are reproved by the Authoritie of the word of God and auntient writers* (1577); excerpts reprinted in Chambers, *Elizabethan Stage*, vol. IV, p. 198.
25 I. G., *A Refutation of the Apology for Actors* (1615), facsimile edn., pp. 57, 58.
26 Minute of City Court of Aldermen, May 20, 1572; rpt. in Chambers, *Elizabethan Stage*, vol. IV, p. 269. The Aldermen "agreed that Master Townclark shall devyse a letter for answer of thother, to be sent unto my Lord Burleighe, signifiing to his honour, that it is thought very perillous . . . to have such conventicles of people by such meanes called together, wherof the greatest number are of the meanest sorte."
27 "An order sett downe by the lordes and others of hir majesties privye Councell the 22 of June 1600 to restrain the excessive number of Plaie howses & the imoderate use of Stage plaies in & about the Cittye"; rpt. in Chambers, *Elizabethan Stage*, vol. IV, pp. 329–31; quotation from p. 330. See also the discussion in Glynne Wickham, *Early English Stages, 1300–1660*, 3 vols. in 4 parts (London: Routledge and Kegan Paul, 1959–81), vol. II, part 2, pp. 9–29. Wickham construes the document in the context of a crisis between 1597 and 1603 concerning the fate of the public theatres. The resolution by the crown in support of the theatres prepared the way for the more authoritarian control of the stage during the Jacobean reign; furthermore, by aligning itself unmistak-

ably with the theatre, "the monarchy . . . prompted all those who were [the theatres'] enemies to align themselves against the monarchy" (p. 26). It seems to me that this argument may also have moved in the other direction – that by aligning itself with the monarchy, the theatre prompted enemies of the crown to align themselves against the stage.

28 The topical connections were first fully set out in Evelyn May Albright, "Shakespeare's *Richard II* and the Essex Conspiracy," *PMLA* 42 (1927), 686–720; were contested in Ray Heffner, "Shakespeare, Hayward and Essex," *PMLA* 45 (1930), 754–80; and were reaffirmed and elaborated in Albright, "Shakespeare's *Richard II*, Hayward's History of Henry IV, and the Essex Conspiracy," *PMLA* 46 (1931), 694–719. A number of recent discussions have cited the special performance of *Richard II* to exemplify the involvement of the Elizabethan theatre in Elizabethan politics: see, for example, Stephen Greenblatt, "Introduction," in Greenblatt, ed., *Forms of Power*, pp. 3–5 and Stephen Orgel, "Making Greatness Familiar," in Greenblatt, ed., *Forms of Power*, p. 45; Jonathan Dollimore, "Shakespeare, Cultural Materialism and the New Historicism," in *Political Shakespeare*, ed. Jonathan Dollimore and Alan Sinfield (Ithaca, NY: Cornell University Press, 1985), pp. 8–9; and Leonard Tennenhouse, *Power on Display: The Politics of Shakespeare's Genres* (New York: Methuen, 1986), p. 88. For a valuable analysis of the relevant historical materials, and a critique of some recent anecdotal uses of the Essex episode in Shakespeare studies, see Leeds Barroll, "A New History for Shakespeare and his Time," *Shakespeare Quarterly* 39 (1988), 441–64. For an illuminating interpretation of the conspiracy in the context of the late-Elizabethan politics of honor, see "At the Crossroads of the Political Culture: The Essex Revolt, 1601," in James, *Society, Politics and Culture*, pp. 416–65.

29 The play is so identified in the deposition by Augustine Phillips (February 18, 1601), Shakespeare's colleague in the Lord Chamberlain's players. The text of the deposition is reprinted in E. K. Chambers, *William Shakespeare: A Study of Facts and Problems*, 2 vols. (Oxford: Clarendon, 1930), vol. II, p. 325. The first quarto of Shakespeare's play – "As it hath beene publikely acted by the right Honourable the Lorde Chamberlaine his servants" – had been printed in 1597; a second and a third quarto had been printed in 1598.

30 For a critical edition of the text and a detailed account of the controversy surrounding its printing and suppression, see *The First and Second Parts of John Hayward's "The Life and Raigne of King Henrie IIII"*, ed. John J. Manning, Camden Fourth Series, 42 (London: Royal Historical Society, 1992).

31 Filled to capacity, the Globe would likely have held about 3,000 customers (see Gurr, *Playgoing in Shakespeare's London*, pp. 18–22). Its audience for a successful play on a topical and controversial subject, performed on a Saturday afternoon, is likely to have numbered more than eleven. It is of course, possible, although highly unlikely, that the

Louis Montrose

conspirators really did have the Globe almost to themselves, and that they were content to have it so. In that case, however, we might then want to ask why they had not rather requested a private performance at Essex House.

32 The relevant excerpts from the report of the trial and from Francis Bacon's *Declaration of the Practises and Treasons . . . by Robert late Earle of Essex* (both 1601) are reprinted in Chambers, *William Shakespeare*, vol. II, pp. 325–6.

33 "An Abstract of the Erl of Essex his Treasons" (July 24, 1600), reprinted in Chambers, *William Shakespeare*, vol. II, p. 323. On the habits of reading in the Essex circle, which applied classical histories to current political conditions, see F. J. Levy, "Hayward, Daniel, and the Beginnings of Politic History in England," *Huntington Library Quarterly* 50 (1987), 1–34; Lisa Jardine and Anthony Grafton, "'Studied for Action': How Gabriel Harvey Read his Livy," *Past and Present* 129 (November 1990), 30–78; David Womersley, "Sir Henry Savile's Translation of Tacitus and the Political Interpretation of Elizabethan Texts," *Review of English Studies*, n.s., 42 (1991), 313–42; David Womersley, "Sir John Hayward's Tacitism," *Renaissance Studies* 6 (1992), 46–59.

34 Some 160 lines of the so-called "deposition scene" of *Richard II* (4.1) appear for the first time in print in the 1608 quarto, which advertises on the title page the additional material and the play's recent staging: "With new additions of the Parliament Sceane, and the deposing of King Richard. As it hath been lately acted by the Kinges Majesties Servantes, at the Globe." It is usually assumed that the additions in the 1608 text were part of the original version and were performed during the reign of Elizabeth but that the scene was censored in the Elizabethan printed editions. For a skeptical view of these assumptions, see Barroll, "New History for Shakespeare and his Time," pp. 448–9. For recent critical reviews of the issues, see Clare, *"Art made tongue-tied by authority,"* pp. 47–51 and Dutton, *Mastering the Revels*, pp. 117–27.

35 Paul Yachnin, "The Powerless Theater," *English Literary Renaissance* 21 (1991), 49–74; quotation from 50.

36 See Bentley, *Profession of Player in Shakespeare's Time*, pp. 14–15. Shakespeare's company was divided into a hierarchy of sharers, hired men, and apprentices; he was one of the sharers, with a direct financial interest in the company's properties, costumes, and scripts. Furthermore, he was the principal playwright for his company. Since scripts were bought outright from writers and were the exclusive property of the company, Shakespeare was in the very unusual position of holding "a reversionary interest in his own plays" (Wickham, *Early English Stages*, vol. II, part 2, p. 135). After 1598, he also became one of several "housekeepers" who owned shares in the Globe, and, subsequently, in the Blackfriars Theatre. Bentley points out that the Lord Chamberlain's/ King's Men were the only troupe of players with "a continuous existence throughout the period"; that they were "the only company operating two

46

theatres and maintaining over a long period of time the same system of ownership''; and that "none of the other score or more of London theatrical troupes in the period is known to have enjoyed the control of its own playhouse" *(Profession of Player in Shakespeare's Time*, pp. 12, 15). Shakespeare was, at one and the same time, a sharer and house-keeper in the Lord Chamberlain's/King's company and also its chief dramatist. He was uniquely positioned within a close-knit, stable, and extraordinarily successful joint enterprise. Thus he was able to enjoy both material and ideological conditions for artistic production that far surpassed those of most Elizabethan literary professionals and patronage poets, as well as those of his fellow dramatists.

37 For stimulating explorations of the relationship between the Elizabethan–Jacobean theatre and the emergence of market capitalism, see Don E. Wayne, "Drama and Society in the Age of Jonson: Shifting Grounds of Authority and Judgment in Three Major Comedies," in *Renaissance Drama as Cultural History: Essays from Renaissance Drama, 1977–1987*, ed. Mary Beth Rose (Evanston: Northwestern University Press and the Newberry Library Center for Renaissance Studies, 1990), pp. 3–29; Jean-Christophe Agnew, *Worlds Apart: The Market and the Theater in Anglo-American Thought, 1550–1750* (Cambridge University Press, 1986); Douglas Bruster, *Drama and the Market in the Age of Shakespeare* (Cambridge University Press, 1992).

38 On the probable debt of Hayward's printed history of Henry IV to Shakespeare's *Richard II*, see Levy, "Hayward, Daniel," pp. 16, 19; on the probable debt of his unfinished and unpublished continuation of the history to the later plays of Shakespeare's second tetralogy, see page 20 and note 57.

39 On the dramatic structure of medieval ecclesiastical rites, see O. B. Hardison, Jr., *Christian Rite and Christian Drama in the Middle Ages* (Baltimore: Johns Hopkins University Press, 1965); on the medieval conception of the civic religious drama as "game" and "play," see V. A. Kolve, *The Play Called Corpus Christi* (Stanford University Press, 1966), pp. 8–32.

40 Raymond Williams, *Culture* (London: Fontana, 1981), pp. 139–43; quotation from p. 142. See also "On Dramatic Dialogue and Monologue (Particularly in Shakespeare)," in Raymond Williams, *Writing in Society* (London: Verso, 1983), pp. 31–64.

41 On the ideological changes, focused upon the understanding of human nature, that heralded the emergence of capitalism and modernity in England, see C. B. Macpherson, *The Political Theory of Possessive Individualism, Hobbes to Locke* (Oxford University Press, 1964); and Albert O. Hirschman, *The Passions and the Interests: Political Arguments for Capitalism Before its Triumph* (Princeton University Press, 1978). On the complex relationship between these developments and the Renaissance theatre, see the important discussions in Wayne, "Drama and Society"; and Agnew, *Worlds Apart*, pp. 101–48.

42 See David Scott Kastan, "Proud Majesty Made a Subject: Shakespeare and the Spectacle of Rule," *Shakespeare Quarterly* 37 (1986), 459–75; quotation from 473. See also John Bellamy, *The Tudor Law of Treason* (London: Routledge and Kegan Paul, 1979), pp. 9–82, *passim*. As Kastan remarks, "Certainly both Essex and Elizabeth understood the playing of *Richard II* on the eve of the rebellion as part of the treasonous imagining, as an invitation to the populace to participate – either in the fiction or in fact – in the deposition of an anointed king" (p. 472).

43 A concise example of the juxtaposition of paradigms is offered by the Bishop of Carlisle's providentialist counsel to the beleaguered King Richard and its immediate translation into the terms of *Realpolitik* by the Duke of Aumerle:

> *Car.* Fear not, my lord. That Power that made you king Hath power to keep you king in spite of all. The means that heavens yield must be embraced, And not neglected; else heaven would,
> And we will not. Heaven's offer we refuse, The proffered means of succor and redress.
> *Aum.* He means, my lord, that we are too remiss, Whilst Bolingbroke, through our security
> Grows strong and great in substance and in power.
> (*Richard II*, 3.2.27–35)

Another example is provided in the juxtaposition of Richard's providentialist rhetoric in the speech immediately following (3.2.36–62) and the *Realpolitik* informing his "prophecy" to Northumberland after his fall (5.1.55–68).

44 On the homology between Elizabethan dramatic structure and rhetorical traditions of inquiry in humanist education, see Joel Altman, *The Tudor Play of Mind: Rhetorical Inquiry and the Development of Elizabethan Drama* (Berkeley: University of California Press, 1978).

45 For an overview of the legal and institutional aspects of Elizabethan censorship, see D. M. Loades, "The Theory and Practice of Censorship in Sixteenth-Century England," *Transactions of the Royal Historical Society* 5.24 (1974), 141–57; on the interacting practices of censorship and interpretation in Elizabethan literary culture, see Annabel Patterson, *Censorship and Interpretation: The Conditions of Writing and Reading in Early Modern England* (1984; rpt. with a new introduction, Madison: University of Wisconsin Press, 1990). On dramatic censorship, see Bentley, *Profession of Dramatist*, pp. 145–96; Clare, *"Art made tongue-tied by authority"*; and Dutton, *Mastering the Revels*.

46 For a general reading of Elizabethan policy in such terms, see Corrigan and Sayer, *Great Arch*, pp. 55–71. The concept of "ideological state apparatuses" is, of course, Althusserian: see "Ideology and Ideological State Apparatuses (Notes Towards an Investigation)," in Louis Althusser, *Lenin and Philosophy and Other Essays*, trans. Ben Brewster (New York: Monthly Review, 1971), pp. 127–86.

47 On "the struggle of Court and City," see Chambers, *Elizabethan Stage*, vol. I, pp. 269–307. The shifting history of the relationships among the Elizabethan state, the Corporation of London, and the Elizabethan commercial theatre is perhaps most readily traced in the collection of "Documents of Control," in Chambers, *Elizabethan Stage*, vol. IV, pp. 259–345. For a social historian's perspective on the relationship between the crown and the city in the 1590s, see Ian W. Archer, *The Pursuit of Stability: Social Relations in Elizabethan London* (Cambridge University Press, 1991), pp. 32–9. Archer's book barely mentions the theatres.

48 The view that an absolutist Elizabethan–Jacobean state allows or produces subversion so as to further its own hegemony is derived from a particular reading of Foucault and is most closely associated with the work of Stephen Greenblatt: see "Invisible Bullets" (1985), reprinted in Greenblatt, *Shakespearean Negotiations*, pp. 21–65; see, in particular, pp. 64–5, from which I quote at the beginning of this chapter. For a similar perspective, see Tennenhouse, *Power on Display*, esp. p. 15; Christopher Pye, *The Regal Phantasm: Shakespeare and the Politics of Spectacle* (London: Routledge, 1990), esp. pp. 43–4; Jonathan Dollimore, *Radical Tragedy: Religion, Ideology and Power in the Drama of Shakespeare and his Contemporaries* (University of Chicago Press, 1984), argues in stimulating if schematic fashion for the other side of the binary opposition, for a fundamentally contestatory relationship of English Renaissance drama to the dominant providentialist ideology. See also the provocative essay by Franco Moretti, " 'A Huge Eclipse.' Tragic Form and the Deconsecration of Sovereignty," in Greenblatt, ed., *Forms of Power*, pp. 7–40. For a more extended discussion and critique of the *subversion/containment* opposition, see my essay "New Historicisms," in *Redrawing the Boundaries: The Transformation of English and American Literary Studies*, ed. Stephen Greenblatt and Giles Gunn (New York: MLA, 1992), pp. 392–418.

49 For a brilliant and pioneering study of the importance of staging, performance, and actor–audience interaction to the collective creation of meaning in Elizabethan drama, see Robert Weimann, *Shakespeare and the Popular Tradition in the Theatre: Studies in the Social Dimension of Dramatic Form and Function*, ed. Robert Schwartz (Baltimore: Johns Hopkins University Press, 1978).

3

Republican beauty, sublime democracy: civic humanism in Gadamer and Rawls

J. M. BERNSTEIN

What, if anything, is the question about the relation between art and politics? Why should we so much as think that there is a question here that needs addressing? One plausible reason for thinking that there is no question that needs answering is because what might be called the language games of art *and* politics are now distinct and separate, and that it is in the nature of language games themselves that what is grammatically distinct is thereby self-sufficient, or that the history of modernity that has rendered these two language games distinct entails their grammatical self-sufficiency. Either way, to raise the question of art and politics is to commit a category mistake. To accuse one's opponents of a category mistake is a quick way of silencing debate; if different discourses have different grammars, and grammatical or categorical sets represent the minimum necessary conditions for intelligible utterance, then *a fortiori* questioning that seeks to relate distinct grammars offends against minimum conditions of intelligible utterance.

This gesture of silencing, whether originating from pragmatist complacency or a dogmatic postmodernism, must be question-begging; if discursive grammars are social products then only the vindication of the history whereby differentiated grammars have separated out can vindicate the second-order requirement that they be accorded (relative) a priori status. We do not lack such reflective histories, ones that seek to provide a priori credentials for these different domains of discourse. For example, Jürgen Habermas has sought to characterize cultural modernity in terms of the separation of the substantive reason expressed in religion and metaphysics into the three autonomous spheres of science, morality, and art, with each of these spheres possessing its own specific aspects of validity:

truth, normative rightness, authenticity, and beauty.[1] Since these spheres and aspects of validity replicate the divisions of Kant's critical system, we can perceive Habermas's analysis of progressive cultural rationalization as providing the historical grounds whereby Kant's transcendental method of legitimation is displaced by a form of rational reconstruction. Nonetheless, the goal is the same: providing (quasitranscendental) a priori status for particular historical grammars.

While there are internal or immanent ways in which the Kant/ Habermas story can be criticized,[2] I want here to proceed through an indirect interrogation of its account of categorical separation. After all, whatever formal constraints have been placed in the way of categorial miscegenation, those constraints matter only in virtue of the desires whose realization they prohibit. Those desires, expressing some sense in which the political and the aesthetic need or require supplementation from the other, are equally powerful elements of cultural modernity. Two slogans, the aestheticization of the political and the politicization of the aesthetic, are indices of those desires. While preliminary consideration of these slogans will not allay miscegenationist anxieties, it may adumbrate a potential field of inquiry worth pursuing.

AESTHETICIZING THE POLITICAL, POLITICIZING THE AESTHETIC

The belief that the political is in need of an aesthetic supplementation emerges at the intersection of two discrete if not unrelated phenomena: on the one hand, it can be seen as addressing the experience of atomization and fragmentation besetting modern, industrialized societies; on the other hand, it means to address the way in which the political order has been instrumentalized – political arrangements are now conceived of as means for securing cooperative social arrangements which are themselves means for attaining private ends. As the question of politics becomes one of just and fair cooperative arrangements for agents whose ends are extrinsic to political community, a corresponding shift away from considering political life the continuation of ethical life toward the idea of a science of politics occurs.[3] The connection among these alterations is direct: it is because of the dissolution of ethical life into a pluralized or fragmented society that the political sphere devolves from a mode of realizing the potentialities released by ethical

J. M. Bernstein

experience into a means for regulating forms of association no longer regarded as self-sufficient.

If it is the deprivation of political life as having the status of an end that problematizes it, the converse occurrence disquiets aesthetic experience. As artworks lose their cultic status or their power to represent the absolute (as in religious art), as art becomes autonomous, it becomes increasingly burdened by its own insubstantiality. The very idea of artworks or objects of aesthetic attention as purposeful (self-integrated and articulated) wholes without any external end or purpose – cognitive, ethical, or affective – secretes a dilemma: what is art (or aesthetic attending) for? This fundamental aporia in autonomous art and aesthetics is the mainspring of Kant's third *Critique*. Its dominant movement is determined by the goal of eliciting an autonomous grammar for aesthetic judgments, aconceptual but subjectively necessary judgments of the pleasure we take in various objects grounded in a disinterested perception of their formal finality. Yet, as Kant presses forward with his attempt to establish the grammatical autonomy of aesthetic judgments from cognitive and moral judgments, he simultaneously twists his analysis back into connection with what they are to be distinguished from. So, despite being aconceptual and only subjectively necessary, judgments of taste nonetheless token the fit (exemplified in the harmonious interplay of understanding and imagination) between our cognitive capacities in general and nature in general antecedent to all particular (conceptual and objective) judgment. And in claiming that "the beautiful is the symbol of the morally good," and that only in such light "does our liking for it include a claim to everyone else's assent," Kant provides aesthetic disinterestedness with a surprising moral quality.[4] This is aporetic because the more Kant emphasizes the connection between aesthetic judgments and cognitive and moral judgments the more ambiguous the claim to autonomy becomes, while the more he insists upon grammatical autonomy the more pointless aesthetic experience becomes.[5] If we uphold the first horn of the dilemma, we reduce art and aesthetic judgment to an anticipation of either scientific knowing or moral awareness, beauty becoming merely a sign of something else; while if we uphold the other horn of the dilemma, the voice of beauty says nothing either about our epistemic attachment to the natural world or about our relations to other human beings.

These tensions in Kant's theory would matter little if they did not so powerfully adumbrate and syncopate with repeated tensions in the practice of modern art. So the traditions of avant-garde and engaged art must be seen as responding to an unwanted and intolerable burden of autonomy through gestures that seek to either collapse the distinction between the institution of art and the world outside (the avant-garde) or to directly bring the political and moral concerns of social life into the center of the work of art itself (e.g., in Brecht and Sartre).[6] Conversely, each attempt to establish the social meaningfulness of art has been met with an equally pointed artistic critique that seeks to demonstrate that the value of aesthetic objects cannot be derived from their moral and political content, and that the distinction between the art world and the wider world of human endeavor cannot be summarily suppressed. And these tensions in the history of art are replicated by our aesthetic allegiances: we can sympathize with frustration at the vacuity of purely formalist art-for-art's-sake experimentation, wanting art to address our real moral and political concerns as fervently as we can find the desire for content a matter of philistine preaching and find ourselves incomprehensibly moved by the most abstract and dissonant works. However we inscribe these tensions – formalist modernism versus representationalism, dissonance versus harmony, absurdist antiart versus narrative realism – our particular judgments cannot be systematized, but continually traverse the distance between the extremes.

But why should this occur? Why should the most extreme reaction against autonomy, say the politicization of the aesthetic represented by socialist realism, so unequivocally fail? Why should the attempt to give aesthetic substance to an uncompromising humanism appear as both moralistic and aesthetically flat? How can the criteria in accordance with which works establish their aesthetic validity enjoin appreciation of works so apparently "inhuman"?[7]

Nor, in fact, are things simpler politically. Here too our allegiances are divided between incommensurable extremes. On the one hand, no one is surprised by evidence revealing both the deracinating effects of strong forms of individualism and anxiety about the dissolution of national communities. From the growth of resurgent communitarian political doctrines to their sociological counterpart demonstrating our desire for an escape back into the safety of a *Gemeinschaft* ruled by solidaristic "habits of the heart," instrumental, political culture is revealed as furthering the ends of a purely destructive modernity.[8] Yet, on the other hand, when we consider explicit programs for aestheticizing the political, when the ideals of organic communities and the state as a work of art are pursued as actual political ideals, then we are faced with not only the examples of Nazi Germany or the deployment of national identity as a repressive imaginary supplement that necessarily polarizes different social groups, making antagonism the source of unity, but equally with the socially repressive character of closed communities, their historical intolerance to outsiders of all sorts, and thus the point of the long history of struggle against communitarian ideals.[9] From this angle, the debate between liberalism and communitarianism, however factitious at the level of political theory, becomes the sign of extremes less easy to reconcile.

In pressing the case for the extremes as against the comfortable middle, my interest is in tapping an implicit grammatical self-consciousness, a self-consciousness that finds attempts to occupy a middle position both unavoidable and unsatisfactory. In both art and politics, in both our willingness to affirm and refuse calls for the politicization of the aesthetic and the aestheticization of the political, we are evincing an awareness of a grammatical aporia that seems deeper and more pervasive than any of its contingent exemplifications. Of course we believe that any rational polity will be premised on some fundamental communal attachments which must nonetheless acknowledge substantive differences in interests and value commitments. Although using extremely crude indicators, my claim here is that this commonsense belief cannot be answered in pragmatic terms that seek arrangements whereby both individualist and communalist goods are given adequate opportunity to be realized. Nor should this be news: from Schiller's *On the Aesthetic Education of Man*, the critique of rationalized modernity has employed the grammar of the aesthetic as its antidote. But the very tensions that make this critique appropriate, making the call for an aestheticization of the political have point, are equally at work within the aesthetic, hence giving point to, and undermining, the call for a politicization of the aesthetic.

One way of avoiding the detour through the aesthetic as essential to the diagnosis of modernity would be to focus on the logical question of means–ends rationality. From Descartes and Hobbes, it became plausible to argue that all cognition was fundamentally causal, and hence that whatever could be known to be either true or false was entangled in a nexus of causal relations. Cognition could determine what was good as a means but was unable to judge the goodness of ends. These, it was contended, were either objects of desire or posits of the will. The dominant strategy for combating the chaos of conflicting ends this restriction on the scope of cognition generated was to argue that some items were necessary or universal means to the pursuit of relative ends. As necessary and universal means, these items can be considered unconditional ends, ends each must have if they are to rationally pursue whatever other ends they might have. Something of this form is at work in Hobbes and in the two tests for the rationality of maxims which Kant proposes.[10]

Ignoring free-rider problems for Hobbes's analysis, and complaints about Kantian external reasons (a version of the free-rider problem), we cannot avoid noticing that these accounts do not restore ends to cognition. Hobbes is explicit about this, but so in a way is Kant. The irrationality of the maxim of giving lying promises depends upon its universalization (causally) engendering the collapse of the institution of promising, just as the irrationality of the maxim of refusing to give aid depends upon its universalization (causally) engendering conditions wherein one cannot receive the aid necessarily required for the pursuit of one's own ends. For Kant, irrationality does not lie in the causal consequences of what would occur if certain maxims were universalized, but in the contradiction between willing one's particular maxim and its universalized consequences. Nonetheless, the argument operates with nothing but causal and logical reasoning as its tools.[11]

The very idea of unconditional ends as delineated by Hobbes and Kant is reducible to the discovery of necessary and universal means. Hence, this whole form of argumentation construes the availability of ends to cognition as involving nothing more than standard means–ends rationality. Even the deployment of necessity and universality as criteria of rationality drags rationality into the domain of the logical and the causal. What would defeat the hegemonic claims of instrumental reason would be the demonstration that we could know certain ends to be *intrinsically* good, i.e., good in themselves and not good because they provide a means to anything else, without those judgments entailing that those ends are unconditionally good. So if playing the kazoo well is a good, it is an intrinsic good. This could be objected to on the grounds that masterful kazoo playing is good if at all only in virtue of the pleasure it might bring to player and listener. But this presupposes that the pleasurable is an independent criterion of goodness apart from the complex practices and activities through which human beings receive pleasure.[12]

If we now consider the grammar of intrinsic goods, then we cannot fail to notice how it overlaps with the grammar of the aesthetic:

things good in themselves, which yield pleasures that are objective but not unconditional, etc. Further, the preponderance of examples of goods internal to practices are derived from art and sport. Hence, even if it is conceded that there are intrinsic goods we are still left with the unsupported claim that it makes sense to want to import the grammar adhering to the cognition of such goods to political and ethical life. To say this is to suggest that the grammar of the aesthetic itself makes a claim which is extra-aesthetic, even if that claim can manifest itself only within the domain of art. Why should that be the case? And does the explanation of why it should provide reasons for believing that claim to be valid?

The opening pages of Gadamer's *Truth and Method* provide a genealogy of the aesthetic, understood in Kantian terms, which simultaneously explicates its grammatical relation to the ethicopolitical while validating that grammatical connection. This will lead Gadamer to attempt to politicize, or as we had better say in Gadamer's case, "ethicize" the aesthetic, an attempt I shall claim fails. I shall go on to argue that the grammatical connection between the aesthetic and the ethicopolitical uncovered by Gadamer in fact constitutes the distinctive claim of Rawls's *political* liberalism, thus making it an aestheticizing of the political. It too runs into difficulties that reveal both the necessary complementarity of the grammars constituting the political and the aesthetic, and their contingent but actual separation. Together, Gadamerian genealogy (the ethicization of the aesthetic) and Rawlsian political liberalism (the aestheticization of the political) reveal the aporetic identity and difference of aesthetics and politics.

A GENEALOGY OF THE AESTHETIC

According to Gadamer, modern aesthetic consciousness feels itself free to accept or reject artworks, and although we might challenge or dispute aesthetic judgments, their grammatical autonomy guarantees that neither reason (the citing of factual evidence) nor moral consciousness (the citing of agreed moral norms) can justifiably force us to alter such a judgment. However, aesthetic consciousness, our self-consciousness of ourselves as being *free* to accept or reject artworks on the basis of aesthetic judgments, belies a more basic experience whereby, once seized by the claim of an artwork, we no longer feel ourselves free to accept or reject the work on *our* own terms, that our experience of works is one of being somehow claimed by them, of demands being placed upon us. Gadamer's point here could be that disinterestedness, say, exposes us to a work the experience of which transcends mere liking. In fact, he regards the nature of the claim at issue as stronger. He contends that artworks from earlier times were not created for *aesthetic* acceptance or rejection. Our consciousness of art – aesthetic consciousness – is, Gadamer states, "always secondary to the immediate truth claim that proceeds from the work of art" (*PH*, 5). Aesthetic judgments alienate us from this funda- mental, cognitive engagement with artworks. The experience of aesthetic alienation is the experience of the gap between an original truth claim by a work and an aesthetic response to that claim.

Gadamer's concept of aesthetic alienation corresponds to the thesis that the grammar of the aesthetic makes a claim to generality transcending its placement within the art world. Perhaps this could be phrased as aesthetic experience always having the character of a defused cognition. The approach of the work of art, in truth, is a "shattering and a demolition of the familiar," which says to us both "'This art thou!'" and "'Thou must alter thy life'" (*PH*, 104). However, aesthetic consciousness is only able to respond to this address with the weakened, aesthetic, "This is beautiful (sublime, gripping, engrossing, etc.)." The cognition proper to a work of art hence becomes the protocognition of the judgment of taste. Yet, as I suggested above, the objectivity of the judgment of taste becomes peculiarly pointless unless it portends a more substantial cognitive claim, which is part of the reason why it seems to matter to us that judgments of taste themselves be objective. The premise of Gadamer's reflections is then a disequilibrium within aesthetic experience: aesthetic judgments' grammatical autonomy provides for an objectivity that while halting the decline of taste into preference simultaneously reduces or defuses the aboutness or object-directedness of aesthetic judgments to a heightened reflexive state.

Gadamer understands this defusing of the cognitive potential of art as an illegitimate consequence of the arrival of Enlightenment scientific rationality. He intends the genealogical analysis of aes- thetic alienation to be a first step in reestablishing art's cognitive status, which he regards as exemplary for his idea of hermeneutics. Art and the domain of the aesthetic thus become the places for a questioning of modernity. The terms governing this questioning are provided by Kant: reflective judgment, *sensus communis*, genius, sublimity, the transcendental imagination, etc. The configuration of these terms provides the grammar of the aesthetic whose full cognitive character Gadamer intends to reveal.

Gadamer's strategy in *Truth and Method* of siting the philosophical origins of aesthetic alienation in Kant's third *Critique* is less direct and negative than the section title, "The Subjectivization of Aesthetics in the Kantian Critique," would lead one to expect. Gadamer does want to urge that the Kantian doctrines of free beauty and pure judgments of taste entail a subjectification of aesthetics entailing an excising of truth claims from art, and an "untenable hermeneutic nihilism" in which "every encounter with [a] work has the rank and justification of a new production" (*TM*, 85). However, Gadamer also wants to credit Kant with securing the autonomy of aesthetic judgment from the dominion of conceptual judgment, and something more, namely, a salvaging and sequestering of the leading concepts of the humanist tradition: *Bildung* (culture), *sensus communis*, judgments and taste. Although aesthetic alienation is but one form of our alienation from the tradition, art and aesthetics nonetheless have a privileged position because they provide a refuge for the leading humanistic concepts, concepts whose suppressed truth claim, which just is the continuing claim that history and tradition makes upon us, continues to be heard *in* aesthetic claims. In providing a hermeneutic recovery of the human sciences in the opening pages of *Truth and Method* that is, by revealing the historical and ethical substantiality embedded in present aesthetic subjectivity, in the grammar of aesthetic judgment, Gadamer allows us to perceive the alienation of the humanist tradition in art. Our sense that art has a privileged position in combating scientistic culture is to be understood in terms of its inheriting, and subjectivizing, the concepts and grammar constitutive of humanistic discourse and cognition. What Gadamer identifies as the humanist tradition is, I shall suggest, best understood in terms of civic humanism.

Although not itself a concept belonging to aesthetics, *Bildung* in a sense anticipates and organizes the kind of grammar aesthetic discourse exemplifies. Implied by *Bildung* are disinterestedness, sublimity, beauty, aesthetic reflective judgment, and the type of generality and objectivity associated with judgments in the domain of art. According to Gadamer, *Bildung* involves more than a cultivation of given talents and capacities, more than a means of bringing about some end, for in *Bildung* what is acquired is preserved in itself. Gadamer follows Hegel in associating *Bildung* with progress away from immediacy and particularity toward universality. *Bildung* requires the sacrificing of immediacy – immediate desires, pleasures, opinions, emotions – for the sake of what is not immediate to the self. In Hegel's dialectic of master and slave this sacrifice is learned through the medium of work, where work is understood as desire restrained. In work the process of forming the thing, be it a physical or spiritual object, simultaneously forms the thing, shaping and transforming what is merely given, and leads the self toward sensitivity to and acknowledgment of the demands and claims of what is other than self. The goal of this general educative practice is to constitute the self as "a universal intellectual being" (*TM*, 13).

Gadamer begins with *Bildung* because he requires at the center of his account a conception of the interaction and cognition of what is outside the self that is more than representational; what is required is an account in which socialization, and by extension social interaction generally, is revealed as possessing a cognitive dimension, where cognition is shown to be self-transformative. In broad terms, we can say that the notion of *Bildung* anticipates and allows for the possibility of a political epistemology in which cognition, action, and solidarity are interconnected. Only if the process through which others and their claims are cognized can be shown to be objective, and that objectivity have a bearing on how one understands oneself and one's relation to others, can the very idea of a political or social epistemology be generated. Hence, only if socialization can be shown to be cognitive and normative at once can the present instrumentalist grammar of the political be overturned.

In analyzing *Bildung*, Gadamer's emphasis is less on the brute internalization of social norms and practices, and more on how what is internalized, our initial conceptual scheme, is revised and elaborated as new and unanticipated items and experiences are encountered. If having a conceptual scheme is possessing a system of coordination between self and world (including other persons), locating the self in a world in relations to others, then *Bildung* can be interpreted as the processual unfolding of that coordination, coming to have a self in relation to a world. Compressing a complex philosophical and psychoanalytic story, Gadamer interprets this process in starkly Hegelian terms, demonstrating how what is heteronomous, what is other than self (with respect to a given starting point), grounds, conditions and makes possible, autonomy and subjectivity. *Bildung* involves more than a suppression of immediacy and givenness; it involves as well a recognition, an

59

J. M. Bernstein

acknowledgment, a finding of conceptual space for other being, as a condition for self-possession. In this movement otherness, what appears as alien to the self, is recognized as no longer a limit to self-possession and self-consciousness, but a condition of it. And this means that *Bildung*, as a permanent mode of interaction with the environment, contains within it a moment of self-alienation and self-dispossession as a precondition for self-possession. In fact, this same process does occur in Kant, only there it is expressed in formal and individualistic terms. For Kant, self-alienation appears as the requirement of heeding the demands of the categories of understanding and the laws of reason, for it is through them that the givens of sense and desire are halted in their immediacy, and the objectivity and universality which ground the difference between self and world, thereby bringing them into coordination, is made possible. However, these categories are hardly "other" than subjectivity; categorial constituted understanding and categorical reason are not a given objectivity at the heart of subjectivity, as Kant thought, but a raising of modern subjectivity itself into a transcendental norm by reinscribing the historical process forming that universality and objectivity. Reflection transforms the *Bildung* of the modern subject into transcendental structures.

"Every single individual that raises himself out of his natural being to the spiritual finds in the language, customs and institutions of his people a pre-given body of material which, as in learning to speak, he has to make his own" (*TM*, 15). For Gadamer, the return to oneself out of alienation constitutes the "essence of *Bildung*" (*TM* 15). Gadamer models this confrontation, acknowledgment and recovery out of otherness, on our experience of the Other as "Thou." "The experience of the 'Thou' also manifests the paradoxical element that something standing over against me asserts its own rights and requires *absolute* recognition; and in that very process is 'understood' . . . One truth I refer to is the truth that becomes visible to me only through the 'Thou', and *only* by letting myself be told something by it. It is the same with the historical tradition" (*TM*, xxiii; emphasis mine). This modeling of hermeneutic experience on the confrontation with the "Thou" is taken up in Gadamer's claims that understanding only begins when something "addresses" us (*TM*, 266), and that this address occurs as an experience of a "strangeness" in the otherwise familiar Other (*TM*, 262).

Bildung is premised upon the experience of strangeness and address which is quite unlike, for example, the failure of a scientific hypothesis, since theories do not constitute the conceptual relations coordinating self and world generally. What is at issue here is the kind of strangeness that disrupts our understanding of the relation between self and world. In fact, neither our standard epistemological nor moral conceptual frameworks offer space to this type of experience. Such an address, however, is the categorially routine way in which works of art appear, and the grammar of the aesthetic a categorially routine way of cognitively dealing with such an address. But this is equally to say that the experience of strangeness, so to speak, has now migrated into the aesthetic notion of, above all, sublimity. Sublimity is the aestheticization of the experience of alterity (*RB*, 167–8), the removal of the grammatical experience of the address of the Other from what scientific cognition and morality must engage with into the safe quarantine of the art world. But if Gadamer is correct, only the experience of what is strange or sublime induces and reveals the kind of self-inhibition Kant relies on in his moral theory and analyses aesthetically in terms of disinterestedness. Kant's defusing and subjectivization of the entwinement of beauty and sublimity that is *Bildung* is accomplished in two steps. First, he reduces the sublimity of the object to an occasion whereby the sublimity of our own moral nature (the sublimity of the moral law) is brought to light: "sublimity is contained not in any thing of nature, but only in our mind, insofar as we can become conscious of our superiority to nature within us, and thereby also to nature outside us."[13] Secondly, having suppressed the sublimity of the object in favour of the sublimity of our moral nature, Kant consistently, if ambiguously, links both the possibility of judgments of taste and our interest in beauty to that moral nature (*TM*, 44–9).[14] For Gadamer, these acts of suppression and subjectification are the direct consequence of Kant's acceding to the thesis that only the causal judgments of the understanding are properly epistemic.

For Gadamer, the universality definitive of *Bildung* is an openness to what is Other, to other points of view and perspectives, where these latter are themselves viewpoints of possible others. "Our historical consciousness," Gadamer states, "is always filled with a multiplicity of voices that echo the past" (*TM*, 252); being able to hear and heed these voices is the achievement of *Bildung*, and the point of the human sciences; to hear and heed in this way is to have a sense for what transcends the self; it is to have a universal and common sense.

Following Vico, Gadamer regards common sense, the *sensus*

J. M. Bernstein

communis, as the sense that founds community: "what gives the human will its direction is not the abstract generality of reason, but the concrete generality that represents the community of a group, a people, a nation, or the whole human race" (*TM*, 21). Concrete generality is the routine equivalent of exemplarity.[15] In the humanist tradition the teaching of right action, the education for ethical life, proceeded by way of examples which revealed the appropriateness of what was done to the circumstances in question. Reliance on telling examples and an espousal of the idea that rhetoric involves fitting speech, saying the right thing for the occasion, both presuppose that practical knowledge is unlike theoretical knowledge in that in the former the subsumption of the particular under a universal rule is inadequate and inappropriate because what is essential in practical affairs is the demand of the concrete situation itself, not its fit with antecedent norms or theoretical expectations.

Practical knowledge, the capacity for making nonsubsumptive judgments of particular states of affairs, which becomes aesthetic reflective judgment in Kant, is termed *phronesis* by Aristotle. Later in *Truth and Method*, Gadamer develops the Aristotelian account of practical knowledge as a model for hermeneutical consciousness generally (*TM*, 278–89); the legitimacy of this move is underwritten by the idea that as historical beings we are practical beings. As practical and historical beings we become who we are through enculturation; and this enculturation, this continuous movement of the becoming-form-of-sense through the reflective comprehension of habitual activity and the becoming-sense-of-form in practical judgment, is a sense of community even if it is not recognized as such. When Vico defends common sense, then, he is defending the idea that "everyone has enough 'sense of the common' (*gemeinen Sinn*), i.e. judgment, that he can be expected to show a 'sense of community' (*Gemeinsinn*), genuine moral and civic solidarity, but that means judgment of right and wrong, and a concern for the 'common good'" (*TM*, 31). Against the background of such a sense of community the attempt to judge matters under universal rules of reason can be seen as a violation of the solidarity binding the community together, a disenfranchisement of the *sensus communis* to the point where it becomes senseless and uncommon. The concept of *sensus communis* in the *Critique of Judgment* is the ghost, the unacknowledged memory of the humanist sense of community, now severed from its determining role through the development of a universalistic morality written in the image of the new, universal, science.

The dislocation of *sensus communis* from the moral to the aesthetic domain is most clearly registered in the analogous dislocations
suffered by judgment and taste in Kant. Not only does the concept of
nonsubsumptive judgment lose its cognitive significance when transferred to the domain of aesthetics; but, even more noticeably, the
concept of taste loses its previous connection to the moral (*TM*, 33), a
connection which, according to Gadamer, goes back to the "ethics of
good taste" which is the comprehensive sense of the ethics of
measure of the Pythagoreans and Plato, and of the ethics of the mean
(*mesotes*) that Aristotle developed (*TM*, 38). In Europe, the ideal of
social *Bildung*, and with it the corollary notions of *sensus communis*,
judgment and taste, emerged in the "wake of absolutism and its
suppression of the hereditary aristocracy" (*TM*, 34).

Kant's reflective repetition of this tradition within his transcendental setting has three consequences. First, by resituating the
tradition in a transcendental setting he made it impossible to
acknowledge the claim to truth of the tradition (*TM*, 38) since
memory, having been reduced from its role as a constitutive form of
historical self-awareness to a psychological faculty (*TM*, 16), is no
longer operative as a constitutive element of *Bildung*. Secondly, in
grounding judgment in taste "he denies that taste has any significance as knowledge. It is a subjective principle to which he reduces
sensus communis" (*TM*, 40). Finally, in determining the universality
of taste and hence the *sensus communis* negatively – it is the free
play of not one but all our cognitive powers; and it abstracts from
subjective and private conditions of attractiveness and emotion –
Kant "is no longer considering the great moral and political tradition
of the concept of *sensus communis*" outlined above (*TM*, 41). Nonetheless, if Gadamer's genealogy holds, then the grammar of the
aesthetic is a subjectivized version of the grammar of classical
humanism. In unearthing the originary prehistory of Kantian aesthetics in the humanist tradition, Gadamer allows us to hear the
claims of that tradition as they reverberate in their alienated form of
"aesthetic" art and discourse. In so doing he means to return our
(alienated) aesthetic subjectivity to the historical substantiality from
which it arose.

As Gadamer is aware, the force of his retrieval of the humanist
tradition must remain muted until evidence can be provided that
there is a claim to *truth* in it; and to demonstrate this he must
demonstrate that the grammar of aesthetics "overflows" itself in the
direction of its origin, that is to say, he must demonstrate that art

transcends aesthetics by claiming us beyond aesthetic universality, by making truth claims. And further, these truth claims must themselves be such as to claim us for community; if this should fail to be the case, then it would not be the humanist tradition that would be claiming us through its originary overflow "in" aesthetics. Broadly, Gadamer must demonstrate that there is an internal connection between the phenomenon of aesthetic alienation with which we began and his genealogy of aesthetics.

Although inadequate in itself, Gadamer's conception of aesthetic differentiation goes some way toward fleshing out these claims. Gadamer explicates aesthetic consciousness, the aesthetic subjectivity inherited from Kant via Schiller (*TM*, 73–4), as founded in a process of abstraction which disregards a work's rootedness in a world. The act of abstraction, what Gadamer calls "aesthetic differentiation," makes the work available for aesthetic inspection; or, rather, aesthetic inspection itself, what is often interpreted as taking an "aesthetic attitude," as constituted by the Kantian grammar of the aesthetic, is the action of differentiation, separating the purpose, function, and meaningful content of a work from its formal and aesthetic character proper. What we designate in the idea of "aesthetic experience," and in the corresponding idea of works having "aesthetic form" or "aesthetic features," depends on a work of abstraction performed by consciousness. In performing this act of differentiation, aesthetic consciousness "distinguishes the aesthetic quality of a work from all elements of content which induce us to take up an attitude towards it, moral or religious, and presents it solely by itself in its aesthetic being" (*TM*, 77). Artworks become "worldless" precisely to the degree to which they become objects of aesthetic attention.

Aesthetic differentiation affects not only our mode of response to works of art, but equally the nature of artistic production. Artists create as individuals, worldlessly, even when the goal of their production is to create a public or community through their work, and hence to act as saviors in an unsaved world.

This claim has since determined the tragedy of the artist in the world, for any fulfillment of it is always a particular one, and that means in fact its refutation. The experimental search for new symbols or a new myth which will unite everyone may certainly create a public and create a community, but since every artist finds his own community, the particularity of this community-creating testifies to the disintegration that is taking place. It is only the universal form of aesthetic culture that unites everyone. (*TM*, 79).

Gadamer's contention here is that artistic production intends the full humanist process of *Bildung* aiming at the reformation of our *sensus communis*. However, since aesthetic production and reception are now structured by the worldless grammar of the aesthetic, what is created by works is not an ethicopolitical community, but an aesthetic community whose conditions of possibility, the grammar of the aesthetic, are simultaneously what prohibits those judgments from having extra-aesthetic status. To claim that it is only aesthetic culture that unites everyone is to affirm the grammar of the aesthetic as potentiating an objectivity beyond that available through particular works. But how can a grammar potentiate what its every employment refutes?

DEDIFFERENTIATION: GADAMER'S POLITICIZING OF THE AESTHETIC

Aesthetic differentiation reduces works to indeterminate nodal points mediating the exchange between their producers and receivers. Whether aesthetic consciousness comprehends itself in terms of the subjectivized concept of genius, be it in artistic production or reception, or in terms of aesthetic experience, the result is the same: the work itself is deprived of any intrinsic unity or integrity, it disintegrates into the multiplicity of experiences of which it is more the occasion than the object. "Basing aesthetics on experience leads to an absolute series of points, which annihilates both the unity of the work of art and the identity of the artist with himself, and the identity of the man understanding or enjoying the work of art" (*TM*, 85). As such, artworks lose their history; each becomes simultaneous with the present of its receiver and with each other in an empty time of recurring "nows."

For Gadamer, it is because aesthetics is aesthetic *consciousness* and aesthetic differentiation, an abstracting act of consciousness, that it is open to the countermovement of aesthetic dedifferentiation, which acknowledges the anterior ontological conditions of aesthetic consciousness. However much aesthetic differentiation leads to a disintegration and atomizing of culture, it must nonetheless be the case that the hermeneutic continuity that constitutes our very being, founding our identity through change and including our mediated unity and sameness with the Other, must operate here as elsewhere: "we encounter the work of art in the world and a world in the individual work of art" (*TM*, 86). Hence, we are capable of preserving the discontinuity of experience demanded by the provocation of the work of art within the continuity of our empirical existence. Artworks must come from and be drawn into the work of self-understanding, the continuous work of self-interpretation through the flux of experience that is the basis of human existence (see *TM*, xix, 147).

This contention clearly contradicts the careful distinction between the particularity of artistic production and reception on the one hand, and the generality of the grammar of the aesthetic on the other, acknowledged by Gadamer in his account of worldless artistic production. *Aesthetic dedifferentiation is Gadamer's attempt at a politicization of the aesthetic.* In criticizing it we can gain some insight into the grounds, worth, and limits of claims, like those of contemporary communitarians, that attempt to peremptorily figure modern political communities as if they were already substantial ethical communities, suppressing the aporetic character of our condition. Since the grammar of the aesthetic is the most unequivocal and purest bearer of an alternative grammar of the political, as I shall evidence in the next section, then in tracing the limits of the possibilities of aesthetic dedifferentiation, we simultaneously are tracing the obstacles to the political transformation of modernity.

The sources of Gadamer's illegitimate optimism are not difficult to locate. First, he underestimates or disallows "objective," categorial, and structural constraints on social practice. The inability of aesthetic culture to overcome the particularizing effects of modernity cannot be explained solely in terms of the *cultural* hegemony of the ideology of scientific knowing. Rather, that hegemony is itself a product of social and cultural rationalization that categorially and institutionally differentiates a previously (religiously) unified experience of the world into distinct practical forms. It is sphere differentiation which forces art into the cognitive/normative periphery of the modern social world, and thus silences the kinds of claims it makes.[16] The question of particularity is not solely one of a pattern of understanding, of aesthetic *consciousness*, but equally concerns what we can institute through one form of social practice; it concerns the more-than-doxic relations holding between different social practices and the institutions that embody them. This is what is illustrated by the failures of the avant-garde to remove the border separating the institution of art from everyday practice.

Secondly, the underestimation of what holds sway in modernity is necessitated by Gadamer's overestimation of the solidarity achieved through our shared possession of a common language. Gadamer appears to lack the theoretical resources to distinguish between community in some formal, minimal sense, the community of language users, say, and community in a more substantial sense, say of those who share a social identity capable of orienting their collective praxis. Possessing a language or a tradition in common is like a "convergent good," a good that many people each have an interest in promoting. In contrast, substantial community is like a "shared good," where part of what makes it a good is "precisely that it is shared, that is, sought after and cherished in common."[17]

Because Gadamer regards tradition as "the ever-active medium through which we sustain our social identities," he cannot but regard the linguistic community as a substantial community. But this gives to phenomena like aesthetic individualism only ideological force without anything objective corresponding to it. But, again, his own account shows how the system of artistic production and consumption has become individualized. Aesthetic differentiation and abstraction is not (only) a mental act but a real abstraction performed through social practice, just like abstract labor is a real social quality of labor under capital.

It might be argued that Gadamer never meant to claim that aesthetic differentiation could have the force here attributed to it. Yet in a passage in his 1975 essay, "The Relevance of the Beautiful," directly paralleling the one we have been discussing, he explicitly fowards his contradictory position.

At the very start I pointed out how the so-called modern age . . . had emancipated itself from the shared self-understanding of the humanist–Christian tradition. I also pointed out that the subjects that previously appeared self-evident and binding can now no longer be captured in an artistic form that would allow everyone to recognize them as the familiar language within which new statements are made . . . The artist no longer speaks for the community, but forms his own community insofar as he expresses himself. Nevertheless, he does create a community, and in principle, this truly universal community (*oikumene*) extends to the whole world.   (*RB*, 39)

In effect, Gadamer concedes the disappearance of the *sensus communis* while simultaneously keeping its force intact. This force derives from the fact that even modern works of art are still art, what artworks have been. Gadamer's strategy here, namely of showing how traditional characterizations of the artwork continue to apply to the works of the present, thereby establishing a continuity between past and present, begs the question at issue: does particularization and sphere differentiation affect the nature of art? Do the concepts that arguably still apply to works mean the same in the altered circumstances of modernity? Gadamer's own words suggest not, since the community formed around a modern work is only an aesthetic community, a community of the work; hence, modernity breaks, rather than merely suppressing or hiding, the original continuity between art and life. It is this event that Gadamer's carefully worked ontology of art, whose whole purpose is to generate a continuity between art and life, occludes. But with this continuity broken, the continuity between past and present art is also destroyed; aesthetic alienation bespeaks a kind of end of art. Insofar as a "truly universal community" now necessarily could be only an aesthetic community, aesthetic alienation would continue.

One might hypothesize that the aforementioned weaknesses in Gadamer's thought have a common origin, namely, the tendency in his thought to make unities and continuities dominate over ruptures and discontinuities. The event of a work addressing us is, indeed, for Gadamer an unanticipated, and in principle unpredictable, experience of strangeness and difference. Let us ignore the fact that Gadamer says too little in explanation of this sublime address. The work of understanding makes the strange familiar, thus incorporating the discontinuity of the address of the work into the continuity of a life praxis. But this is to say that, at the individual level, discontinuities are ingredients in the continuity of self-identity sustained through and by means of interpretive activity. An analogous unity and continuity obtains among the different horizons of understanding inscribing the worlds of socially and historically different peoples. Rather than make a weak claim about the accessibility of different horizons of thought and practice to our own, Gadamer contends that "in the process of understanding there takes place a real fusing of horizons, which means that as the historical horizon is projected, it is simultaneously removed" (*TM*, 273). Gadamer even goes so far as to claim that there is a "single horizon that embraces everything contained in historical consciousness" (*TM*, 271); with this claim the *sensus communis* is extended to a point where the difference between its reality and ideality collapse. And this argument blurs the historical force of the fate of art and the experience of aesthetic alienation, reducing the end of art to a contingent and temporary hibernation. In so doing, Gadamer flatly and bluntly cancels the question of modernity, reducing it to mere misunderstanding. Finally, this view contradicts Gadamer's own emphasis on and statement of the meaning of finitude: "Real experience is that in which man becomes aware of his finiteness . . . It proves to be an illusion that everything can be reversed, that there is always time for everything and that everything somehow returns" (*TM*, 320). This is the lesson of experience, the lesson of suffering, it does not appear to apply to Gadamer's account of art, nor, more generally, to the historical past.

SENSUS COMMUNIS AND OVERLAPPING CONSENSUS: RAWLS'S AESTHETICIZATION OF THE POLITICAL

While there is an evident ethical drive in Gadamer's attempt to restore the solidaristic claims of tradition, he quietly separates the recovery of the humanist tradition from the particular political claims of civic humanism. Indeed, one can read *Truth and Method* as substituting the human sciences, reconfigured as fully hermeneutical, for the politics of civic humanism, as if the texts and works of the tradition could replace and displace interaction with fellow citizens. If this is what has occurred, it would explain how Gadamer's radical critique of Enlightenment rationality should terminate in his quiescent appeals to "the tradition."

Classical republicanism is the view that only through the *active* participation of an informed citizenry can the goods of democratic regimes be prevented from being overrun by interest groups, power seekers, domination by bureaucracies, and the like. Civic humanism agrees with this ideal but adds the further thought that such participation is minimally a condition of the good life and maximally represents its realization.[18] My sense that civic humanism represents the political expression of Gadamer's position derives from the thesis that the requirement for participation in the classical republican tradition remains fundamentally prudential and pragmatic, whatever moral value is attributed to political participation, to the extent that citizens may legitimately have their primary ends elsewhere. Conversely, only within a regime conceived of in accordance with the ideals of civic humanism would it be the case that political activity had the character of *Bildung*.

Clearly, the overcoming of worldless particularity and the restoration of the idea of humanist *Bildung* is the fundamental ethical aim of Gadamer's project. In answer to the question "What is practice?" Gadamer replied: "Practice is conducting oneself and acting in solidarity. Solidarity, however, is the decisive condition and basis of all social reason. There is a saying of Heraclitus, the 'weeping' philosopher: The *logos* is common to all, but people behave as if each had a private reason. Does this have to remain this way?"[19] How could social reason, a significant *sensus communis* as the source of ethical *Bildung*, be realized, how could the collapse back into merely aesthetic communities be overcome unless the grammar of the aesthetic were desubjectivized and returned to its focal position in community formation and reformation? But what reason is there to believe that this transformation could be accomplished from within the aesthetic since as a separate domain it is constituted by what significant practice external to it refuses?

If the pluralization and particularization that Gadamer notes as the fate of the aesthetic is taken as a general symptom of the privatization of reason and hence of social goods, making those goods into mere individual preferences from the perspective of the neutral state, then the lowest level at which substantive *Bildung* could be systematically and effectively actualized under conditions of modernity is that of the political state. If so, then the conception of self as citizen becomes the necessary condition for the possibility of reintegrating ethical self-realization with personal self-realization. But this is just what civic humanism claims and requires. From this perspective it thus becomes plausible to interpret Gadamer's account of how the grammar of the aesthetic echoes with the claims of the humanist tradition as insinuating the grammar of the aesthetic as a subjectivized *political* grammar.

Gadamer's consistent revocation of the political in favor of tradition is premised upon the presumption that, ultimately, there is but one tradition, and that once access to it is made possible, its effectivity will generate the commonality suppressed by modern scientistic culture. This not only illegitimately presumes a unity to the classical tradition, but equally, and illegitimately as we have already seen, presumes its continuity with the conditions of modernity.

Now even if the extremely broadly sketched position to here is accepted as true, with the account of aesthetic alienation taken as explaining our adherence to the incommensurable extremes elaborated in the first section above, a deep problem remains. What if, along the lines of the model in which each successful work of art creates a community for itself, we construe modernity not in terms of atomism and fragmentation but merely in terms of radical pluralism? Would the sheer existence of such a pluralism, a body of reasonable comprehensive ethical and religious doctrines incompatible with one another, be sufficient to rule out the idea of a recovery of civic humanism? If pluralism is reasonable, would that be sufficient to rule out civic humanism as an option and reveal the aestheticization of the political as just that: the imposition of an aesthetic ideal on to a complex, plural social world? It is, in fact, just such a pluralism that leads Rawls to opt for an overlapping consensus as opposed to a thick *sensus communis* and hence to favor classical republicanism over civic humanism (*PL*, 205–6).

One may well wonder whether a classical republicanism strong enough to accomplish the securing of the requisite stability (freedom from the assorted evils that erode just institutions) is even intelligible apart from minimal civic humanism. While I doubt that such a separation is intelligible, it raises dark questions of political sociology to which no quick answers are available. But a response to such dark questions is unnecessary since the grammar of Rawls's political liberalism involves a politicization of the grammar of the aesthetic, so converging with Gadamerian hermeneutics; and Rawls's attempt to insulate reasonable pluralism from the perfectionist demands of a comprehensive civic humanism fails.

Political as opposed to moral (comprehensive) and prudential (Hobbesian) liberalism possesses solidaristic foundations, solidaristic content and has solidarity as its goal. The foundations of Rawls's theory is the public political culture of modern, constitutional democratic states in which citizens recognize one another as free and equal as is implied by their settled convictions (*PL*, 8). Rawls unflinchingly affirms these habits of the heart or "prejudices." Justice as fairness articulates these mutual recognitions into a doctrine; our purpose in embracing this doctrine is to "assure one another political justice" (*PL*, 42n). Such assurance is equivalent to the political recognition of self in the Other. Finally, it is by means of such public assurance that the goal of a well-ordered, which is to say, a continuing solidaristic, just political community is achieved.

Since Rawls perceives the plurality of competing and incompatible conceptions of the good as the major obstacle to the liberal state, it is unsurprising that he should restructure his theory to meet the ends of solidarity and stability, that is, that the aim of his theory of justice should itself be conceived of as practical (or as synthesizing the practical and the theoretical) rather than (purely) theoretical (*PL*, 9). The lack, or the persistent threat of a perceived lack of a political *sensus communis*, defines the explicit problem situation to which the idea of liberalism as a political rather than a metaphysical doctrine is meant as a response. While in part the notion of making liberalism political means simply restricting the scope of each claim or issue (the concepts of the person and autonomy, the morality of the theory, etc.) to the political sphere interpreted in terms of the basic structure of the institutions forming the background culture which grounds social cooperation, this scope restriction can have the pertinence Rawls intends only through a transformation of the grammar of political philosophy. The main elements of that transformed grammar are Rawls's notions of the reasonable as opposed to the rational and his idea of constructivism.

In terms that have sufficient currency for the purposes to hand, we can say that the grammar of the rational is monologic while the grammar of the reasonable is dialogic. The rational applies to how individual ends and interests are adopted, ordered, and affirmed together with the determination of the correct means for realizing them. In denominating the grammar of the rational monologic rather than, say, own-interested, we leave open the possibility that the content of rational reflection can be moral and even altruistic. What is excluded from rational reflection is the perspective of the Other in the processual order of reasons. What Rawls says about Scanlon's principle of moral motivation nicely encapsulates his main idea here: as reasonable agents we "have a basic desire to be able to justify our actions to others on grounds they could not reasonably reject – reasonably, that is, given, the desire to find principles that others similarly motivated could not reasonably reject" (*PL*, 49). We are not here attempting to discover what is true, say, what justice really is, but rather, acknowledging different starting points, different ideals, different weightings to aspects of experience, proposing both terms (standards and principles) and reasons for those terms that despite those differences others could accept and abide by. To proceed in this manner is to accept that some differences, like those between a utilitarian and a Kantian, are themselves reasonable.

The distinction between the reasonable and the rational sounds like a transformation of the distinction between hypothetical and categorical imperatives, or, more obliquely, that between *Verstand* (understanding) and *Vernunft* (reason). But this cannot be quite correct since neither second term directly makes the perspective of the other (morally represented by the duty of civility – *PL*, 217) constitutive, as is the case with what is reasonable. Rather, acting reasonably binds together categorical demands, the demands of justice, with reflective judgment: while fair terms of cooperation themselves might be monologically determined, the public proposing and justifying of such together with a willingness to consider grounds of reasonable disagreement, what Rawls calls "the burdens of judgment" (*PL*, 54–8), is a matter of judgment, taste, and tact. Political liberalism is a politically, i.e. dialogically, achieved construct wherein reason-giving is constrained to what can find a response in the other irrespective of private belief. Of course, this process of construction is not equivalent to forming an aesthetic reflective judgment in which no concept is announced as a consequence of reflective activity. But what ordinary reflective judgment and aesthetic reflective judgment share is the cognitive evaluation of some phenomenon without a concept in hand in order to guide it; rather, what concept(s) fit the phenomenon is a consequence of reflecting. So the very idea of the theory of justice being a construction entails that it is a product of reflection, with reasonableness (like Kantian disinterestedness in aesthetic judgments) marking the attitude or stand required of agents if they are to participate in such a constructive practice with the hope of coming to speak with a universal voice.

The reasonable encapsulates the ideal of mutual accountability with the goal of mutuality providing the scope restrictions on autonomous claims. That makes the notion of the reasonable coextensive with reason as constitutively social. The entwining of reflective judgment with categorical demands entails equating what is reasonable with an agent's public pattern of action. However, it is precisely this equation, according to Taylor, that is essential to the civic humanist tradition and is disallowed by Kant's moral philosophy, which always reverts instead to the matter of inner motive.[20]

Reasonableness provides for a political judgment of taste, like the discovery of reflective equilibrium, the harmonic accord of individual moral judgments and their principled articulation. It is because he deploys an aesthetic grammar of rationality, i.e. reasonableness, that Rawls can displace (Kantian) perfect procedural justice, which operates with "an independent and already given criterion of what is just" (*PL*, 72), issuing subsumptive judgments about cases, with pure procedural justice, where citizens themselves publically and practically specify the fair terms of their cooperation. Rawlsian citizens are not knowers but agents endeavoring to construct "the conception of a just constitutional regime" (*PL*, 93). The constructive activity of Rawlsian citizens is neither pure creation (these citizens, again, are bound by the tradition and culture of modern, constitutional democratic states) nor pure discovery, but rather the creative, and hence transformative exposition of the potentialities latent in our existing practices and culture. Because the procedure of constructing this conception of justice cannot be separated from what will bring the citizens operating it into accord, (re)creating an overlapping consensus (a *sensus communis*), then the historical truth of the conception and the *Bildung* of the citizens performing the procedure are identical. The original thin or indeterminate mutual recognition of one another provided by the political conception of persons as free and equal citizens with a sense of justice is dialectically transformed into an overlapping consensus through the construction of the conception of justice as fairness. In this account, construction and self-transformation are indissolubly linked.[21]

If these few remarks are in order, then it seems plausible to characterize the path from *A Theory of Justice* to *Political Liberalism* as movement from second to third *Critique* Kantianism. Implicitly, like Hannah Arendt before him, Rawls is finding in Kant's grammar of the aesthetic the outline of a (civic humanist) political theory.[22] That Rawls is operating with and requires an aesthetic grammar is entailed by his desire to come up with a judgment of the whole which is morally superior to and yet provides space for its constituent parts. In this sense, Rawls's persistent claim that his theory is not comprehensive while yet provisionally trumping all competing values is best understood in terms of the thesis that his theory is not subsumptive (and if not subsumptive, then, he believes, not comprehensive in a metaphysical sense). But if it is not subsumptive, then the rationality of the whole can only be reflective. This is what is at issue in the distinction between perfect and pure proceduralism. Because he fails to see that the grammatical commitments of reflective judgment themselves token pervasive ethical values, he falsely infers that his theory is not comprehensive. But there is no reason to believe that the subsumptive/reflective distinction has any direct consequences for the comprehensive/noncomprehensive distinction. Again, if Rawls's problem situation is one of unifying discrete elements without subsuming them, then the only available model to accomplish this end is that of aesthetic totalization, but if such totalization is more than a compromise, more than trading-off competing interests, then it must represent an ethical ideal of its own, namely, the classical ideal of unifying discrete items within a whole.

As has already been noted, Rawls demurs from the thought that his theory is civic humanist. Part of the reason for this is trivial: he defines even partially comprehensive doctrines as extending beyond the political to include nonpolitical values and virtues (*PL*, 175). This definitional restriction is followed through procedurally by his scope restrictions on the key terms informing his theory. These definitional restrictions take on substance when coupled with his affirmation that reasonable pluralism concerning the validity of comprehensive doctrines is a *permanent condition* of public culture under free institutions (*PL*, 129, 136). From this it follows that a unitary, and so comprehensive moral theory is necessarily unavailable for grounding a conception of justice; were one such insisted upon, it reasonably could lead to civil strife.

From this angle of vision, justice as fairness both is and is not our political *sensus communis.* It is, because it represents the conclusion of the construction that binds accord and theory. It is not our *sensus communis* because each individual's full reasons for finding it acceptable need not be the same: justice as fairness reasonably captures our fundamental moral ideals while respecting reasonable disagreement as to their ultimate ground and shape. Because justice as fairness furthers our moral powers, including our sense of justice, the resulting overlapping consensus cannot be regarded as skeptical or a mere *modus vivendi.*

Justice as fairness can appear as more than a *modus vivendi*, no matter what moral norms are invoked by it, only if, when its principles and ideals come into conflict with other values, it has sufficient weight to override them (*PL*, 138). Yet, if for actual citizens justice as fairness represents only an overlapping consensus, then why should they permit it to trump their strongest beliefs? To ask this question is to query why, both procedurally and actually, the reasonable must be taken as framing and subordinating the rational (*PL*, 339). An inadequate answer to this would derive from reasonable pluralism. Although Rawls seems to construe reasonable pluralism as a sociological fact about modernity, this would not be enough to sustain liberal justice as trumping other values since that fact could alter (say, by means of utilitarians taking control of the public media).[23] Let us, then, construe reasonable pluralism as a deep, metaphysical fact of modernity deriving from, firstly, the necessary conceptual indeterminacy of any full theory due to the complexity of relating evidence to theory, different weightings of evidence, the vagueness of central concepts, the differential experiences underlying our judgments, etc. (*PL*, 56–7); and secondly, the autonomy of modern citizens construed in terms of their power to form, revise, and rationally pursue a conception of the good. These two together are sufficient to make the *possibility* of reasonable pluralism permanent, but they are not enough to provide justice as fairness with trumping power. *The realization of this possibility would only make it rational to be reasonable.* But if this is correct, then the reasonable does not subordinate the rational, or rather, it subordinates it only so long as pluralism obtains. But that in itself would not make it irrational for utilitarians, for example, to seek a consensus nor illegitimate for utilitarian principles to become those of the state if such a consensus were achieved. If it remains rational to seek to achieve a consensus around a comprehensive doctrine, then the reasonable does not trump the rational, our grounds for being reasonable are reduced to rational calculation, and reason remains constitutively private.

This is enough to show how Rawls's theory could collapse into a *modus vivendi.* His reason for believing that no such collapse occurs can only derive from his belief that being reasonable is not merely a rational response to reasonable pluralism, but that reasonableness is a free-standing moral ideal that expresses an *affirmation* of reasonable pluralism, the plurality of human goods and the worth of autonomy. In brief, reasonable pluralism, the diversity of goods and autonomy if regarded as limitations or restrictions on the moral possibilities of justice, as generating a problem, only lead to reasonableness as a rational strategy; reasonableness becomes a free-standing ethical ideal only when these same items are explicitly affirmed as constitutive elements of the human condition contributing to its goodness. Paradigmatically, aesthetic practice has been the affirmation of the grammar of the reasonable, revealing it as free-standing rather then as a strategic response to conflict.

The equivocations of *Political Liberalism* are a consequence of Rawls adopting reasonableness as a free-standing ethical ideal while construing reasonable pluralism as a brute fact requiring accommodation. The central instance of equivocation is Rawls's construction of the original position as itself reasonable, thereby permitting its inhabitants to choose which conception of justice is best solely on the basis of what would be rationally best. As readers, our sense of justice and willingness to be reasonable is necessary if the device of the original position is to be acceptable. While the inhabitants of the original position know they are rational, they do not know they are being reasonable; they hence have no way of knowing that they are choosing more than a good *modus vivendi.* This keeps reasonable pluralism a problem, while for us watching the construction of the original position and selection of principles, the procedure is reasonable through and through; hence for us, the discovery/construction of political justice is only a matter of the public unfolding of standing solidarity with those with whom we are discoursing. The suppressed reasonableness of the representatives in the original position, however, continues to reverberate in the conclusion of the Rawlsian contract: justice as fairness neither unequivocally trumps nor fails to trump competing values, while the overlapping consensus is and is not our *sensus communis.*

Nor is this surprising. My claim here is that political liberalism is an aestheticization of the political: the Rawlsian grammar of the reasonable is the grammar of the aesthetic returned to its premodern public role. Hence, Rawls's fundamental strategy is equivalent to the dedifferentiation of the grammar of the aesthetic from the side of the political. In this respect, his general strategy is indistinguishable from Gadamer's. If so, then it is natural to expect it to run into analogous difficulties and ambiguities. Roughly, if there is a problem about political community, if real reasonable pluralism appears as what divides us decisively, this can only be because as citizens we are rational but not reasonable, our reasoning is private (monological) as is the reasoning called for in the bulk of our institutional practices. Conversely, if the reasonable is to reign as a free-standing ethical ideal, it would *a fortiori* trump the rational and pluralism would not be a problem. The reasonable is not a simple fact of public political culture, but an aesthetic ideal. It is the lack of the reasonable, and not, for example, the lack of an overlapping consensus, that keeps modern pluralism antagonistic and just arrangements instrumental. This becomes transparent if one considers the fact that from the perspective of reasonableness, irrespective of content, the very idea of free-riding is unintelligible. Rawls is hence operating with a deep metaphysical vision and a comprehensive ethical doctrine: the metaphysics is just Gadamer's hermeneutic ontology and the ethical doctrine is that of a civic humanism under conditions of reasonable pluralism for autonomous subjects. But this latter, under existing conditions, appears as an aesthetic ideal.

Evidence for the thesis that Rawls is operating with such an aesthetic ideal in which the reasonable is construed as free-standing only becomes explicit in his construal of a society with a democratic, constitutional state governed by justice as fairness as a social union of social unions. Elaborating von Humboldt's organic conception of social union as that which enables each "to participate in the rich collective resources of all the others," Rawls images such a union on analogy with the relation between good violin playing and that same playing as part of an orchestra, where violin playing represents the good of particular social practices and the orchestra a just society as a whole (*PL*, 321). In order for a society to conceive of its plural components not as warring factions but as elements within an organic whole, those elements, including, presumably for Rawls, diverse moralities, must be regarded both nonskeptically and as incomplete. Only in virtue of those two conditions does justice as fairness become an expression of our regard for the worth of others' goods and practices as well as of the necessity for them to be placed within a larger whole, and hence by extension an expression of our regard for the worth and goodness of the whole. Once these conditions are satisfied it becomes rational to regard society as purveying a more comprehensive good that enlarges the good of its parts (*PL*, 323).

The idea of a social union of social unions, which I would hazard comes closest to expressing the moral and aesthetic vision motivating Rawls's theory, is in fact stronger than what is given in the idea of an overlapping consensus. In order for comprehensive moral theories and free religious beliefs to fit the social union image, they can no longer be comprehensive in quite the sense they were prior to the arrival of modernity. A religious belief that ideally is encapsulated in all aspects of society, including its constitutional arrangements, and a doctrinally equivalent religion only now conceived as an object of "free" religious belief, are not the same. The good of free religious belief and unfree religious belief is not the same good since the movement from the latter to the former radically alters the relation between the believer and her or his god, as well as between her or his god and the gods of other believers. A free believer can hold both that her or his belief is true and that other beliefs while false have a point (they express something about the god relation), and hence are not a function of sheer ignorance or damnation. The difference is like the difference between a situation in which either violin playing or oboe playing are the good, but not both, and a situation in which both are good. The meaning of the good of playing the violin or the oboe must shift between the two situations, What holds for musical goods or religious goods holds equally for comprehensive moral theories.[24]

Here too, Rawls equivocates over the good of the reasonable, this time by suppressing the difference between the comprehensive good of unfree and free faith. It is, however, no accident that in delineating how an overlapping consensus is possible Rawls perforce uses three examples which underwrite the *autonomy* of the subject (*PL*, 145–6). If autonomy essentially involves the capacity to revise one's conception of the good, then an individual's comprehensive good must, as it were, intrinsically give expression to that fact. This is weaker than the claim that one's choice of a good life partially constitutes its goodness, since I think that thesis belies how our relation to the good feels from the inside: the good chooses us, not us it. But this can be true for goods conceived of as instrinsically good, good in themselves, without it following that such goods are in any sense comprehensive. On the contrary, the conditions of autonomy together with the thesis that there is more than one instrinsic good looks to be enough to entail the comprehensive good of political liberalism since to concede that there is more than one instrinsic good is to say that X plus one goods are choice-worthy – even if unchosen. And this is the minimum required to claim that there are a plurality of good lives not all of which any one person can realize, and that particular goods are enlarged by being placed into the comprehensive good of a union of unions. Value pluralism is only reasonable if nonskeptically affirmed; nonskeptical value pluralism requires incommensurable *goods*. Only with this affirmation do reasonableness and the idea of a social union of social unions entail one another.

Pace Rawls, political liberalism cannot be neutral in any significant sense. By the very fact that what counts as a possible good is always already restricted by its being good for autonomous persons and by being but one good amongst other goods, Rawls has already insinuated von Humboldtian perfectionism as constitutive. If the goodness of particular goods is partially constituted by their connection with other incommensurable goods, and that connection of goods is partially but necessarily established and expressed only through the principles and practices of a just state, then good lives are necessarily reasonable lives, and reasonable lives are the lives of virtuous citizens. Rawlsian civic humanism differs from standard accounts since in it political participation of the appropriate sort is not the privileged locus of the good life, but it is *a* privileged locus of such a life since without it one of our two moral powers and the constitutive good of liberal justice itself would lack expression. But that expression, the public reason of reasonable citizens, is the constitutive and constituting rationality of the liberal polity. Alas, the public reason of reasonable citizens is not the reason of our political and public culture.

SUBLIME DEMOCRACY

Apart from its ideality, one reason we might feel distinctly uneasy about Rawls's aestheticization of the political is because of the degree to which the reasonable pluralism of modernity is sublated within the organic totality of a social union of social unions. Could this liberal society be too well ordered, too solidaristic? And this cannot but matter since my central worry about Gadamer, and part of the point of my turning to Rawls, related to his (Gadamer's) suppression of modernity in making historical continuities predominate. Can the solidarity of modern, autonomous subjects be expressed through a *sensus communis*? What then happens to their autonomy? Has not the most persistent complaint against civic humanism, especially of the Rousseauian variety, been its apparent sacrifice of the individual to the organic collective? If Rawls's theory really is civic humanist, as I have been urging, then must not it be subject to the same criticism? And does not that failure demonstrate what is wrong with the aestheticizing strategy generally?

I think not. One reason for this judgment is encapsulated in the shift from political participation being the privileged locus of the good life to a privileged locus. That shift marks out both the space for plural good lives, or, more accurately, the plural ways of living out the good life of the citizen of a just liberal state. But if it is accurate to speak of the good life of a citizen of a just liberal state, then are we not again in a territory where, to use a well-known contemporary vocabulary, difference and otherness have ceded to the demand for unity and consensus?

The issues here are immensely complex since they relate, in part, to the precise range of options for living out the good life the state tolerates or makes available, its encouragement or tolerance for diverse experiments in living, and the like. Putting these issues aside as too complex to be answered here, we can nonetheless ask the broader question as to whether there is any possibility for citizens acting in excess of the liberal *sensus communis* and hence in excess of their identity as citizens? Or perhaps, is there some sense in which the constitution of the social identity of the self as citizen is made possible only by what does organically fit? These questions are driven not just by skeptical scruples but by aesthetic considerations. One distinctive component of the modern grammar of the aesthetic that does not have its locus in the discourse of humanism and as yet has not found expression in Rawls's aestheticization of the political is the idea of the sublime. For present purposes, let us simply identify the sublime as that which exceeds the demands of taste and the harmonic judgment of the beautiful, entangling, as the beautiful does not, both pain and pleasure. It is tempting to think, as Gadamer himself comes reluctantly to acknowledge, the experience of modernity, with its persistent transgression of closed structures and its emphatic refusal of closure in the name of freedom, first comes to grammatical awareness through the sublime, and only later in the experience of modern revolutions. The critical impetus of liberalism has always shared in this antiorganicist aspect of modernity, emblematically in the (illegitimate) slide from liberalism to libertarianism.

Although Rawls does not provide the citizens of the just liberal state with the oxymoronic right to revolution, he does approach this self-transcending ideal in elaborating the scope of the freedom of political speech in the following "fixed" points: "there is no such thing as the crime of seditious libel; there are no prior restraints on freedom of the press, except for special cases; and the advocacy of revolutionary and subversive doctrines is fully protected" (*PL*, 342). Rawls's account of the denial of seditious libel and of the development of the clear and present danger rule are exemplary: unless subversive advocacy is possible, and hence defaming the government impossible, allegiance to the state cannot itself be free; unless political speech can be dangerous and threatening we cannot discuss what matters most politically, for that "by its nature is often dangerous" (*PL*, 354).

While Rawls's defense of these constitutional theses draws heavily upon his earlier defense of pure proceduralism and public reason, the entire account serves to sustain the distinction between the authority of constitutional arrangements and citizens' judgments as to whether those arrangements (and their application to particular domains of social life) are indeed just. In Rawls's lexicon, the closure of that space would involve constitutional arrangements and the basic structure exhausting our two moral powers; but as powers, they are human capacities that are satisfied only through their exercise, and hence cannot be exhausted by any set of arrangements (*PL*, 335).

In pressing this aspect of Rawls's thought, two issues are at stake.

Firstly, below the surface here, but not far below, Rawls is considering the aporia of democratic authority: how to balance the sovereignty of a democratic citizenry with constitutional arrangements that legitimate and ground that sovereignty. To his credit, Rawls recognizes that this aporia cannot be solved or dissolved: it is constitutive of a democratic form of life. But the reason for this, the second issue, is because democratic authority is always divided between the autonomous activities of a citizenry and the constitutional arrangements that make those activities possible and efficacious. But this thought leads me to another, namely, that an essential feature of the solidarity of democratic peoples, something more evident in democratic movements than in the routine activities of deliberative democracies, is their opposition to any authority above themselves. To remind ourselves of this fact is equally to remind ourselves that solidarity has both positive and negative sources.

Arguably, it is the negative and critical sources of democratic solidarity that sustain its positive side. My guess is that this critical solidarity represents the sublime moment within just, liberal states; and that it is this critical, sublime source of solidarity that Rawls is gesturing toward but fails to theorize fully in his account of the freedom of political speech.

What makes the question of free speech a fundamental locus for the understanding of democracy is that it is where the pretheoretical, critical, and negative impetus to liberal culture meets with its institutional formation. How can liberalism avoid betraying its own antiorganicist celebration of autonomy while proceeding to provide a comprehensive morality that does not instrumentalize the political? Rawls's model of a deliberative democracy does, I think, aim to resolve this dilemma. But if free speech is going to be able to pick up antiorganicist sublimity, it must be pushed harder than Rawls allows; freedom of speech in the polity must be seen as echoing and replicating the constitution or construction of the polity as such. If constitutional arrangements only possess efficacy through an excessive acknowledgment of them, if those arrangements themselves are and are to be perceived as grounding an antiauthoritarian form of life, then the solidarity of a democratic people must have its source not only in reasonableness, the beauty of our construction and of the social union of social unions, but in the sublimity of our foundationless choice of such arrangements. If I were to begin this chapter again, I would open with these words of Georges Bataille:

Civic humanism in Gadamer and Rawls

CEASARIAN UNITY, ESTABLISHED BY A LEADER – A HEAD – IS OPPOSED BY THE HEADLESS COMMUNITY, BOUND TOGETHER BY THE OBSESSIVE IMAGE OF TRAGEDY. Life demands that men gather together, and men are only gathered together by a leader or by a tragedy. To look for a HEADLESS human community is to look for tragedy: putting the leader to death is itself tragedy, it remains a requirement of tragedy. A truth that will change the appearance of human things starts here: THE EMOTIONAL ELEMENT THAT GIVES AN OBSESSIVE VALUE TO COMMUNAL LIFE IS DEATH.[25]

Notes

1 Jürgen Habermas, "Philosophy as Stand-In and Interpreter," in K. Baynes, J. Bohman and T. McCarthy, eds., *After Philosophy: End or Transformation?* (Cambridge, MA: MIT Press, 1987), pp. 311–12. The following abbreviations will be used in the body of the text: Hans-Georg Gadamer, *Truth and Method*, trans. Garret Barden and John Cumming (London: Sheed and Ward, 1975), hereafter *TM*; Hans-Georg Gadamer, *Philosophical Hermeneutics*, trans. David E. Linge (Berkeley: University of California Press, 1976), hereafter *PH*; Hans-Georg Gadamer, *The Relevance of the Beautiful and Other Essays*, trans. Nicholas Walker (Cambridge University Press, 1986), hereafter *RB*; John Rawls, *Political Liberalism* (New York: Columbia University Press, 1993), hereafter *PL*.

2 See, for example, Thomas McCarthy, "Reflections on Rationalization in the Theory of Communicative Action," *Praxis International* 4.2 (1984), 77–91.

3 See Jürgen Habermas, "The Classical Doctrine of Politics in Relation to Social Philosophy," in *Theory and Practice*, trans. John Viertel (Boston: Beacon Press, 1973), pp. 41–81.

4 Immanuel Kant, *Critique of Judgment*, trans. Werner S. Pluhar (Indianapolis: Hackett, 1987), §59, p. 353.

5 See my *The Fate of Art: Aesthetic Alienation from Kant to Derrida and Adorno* (Cambridge, Mass.: Polity Press, 1992), pp. 29–44.

6 Peter Bürger, *Theory of the Avant-Garde*, trans. Michael Shaw (Minneapolis: University of Minnesota Press, 1984).

7 Jean-François Lyotard, *The Inhuman: Reflections on Time*, trans. Geoffrey Gennington and Rachel Bowlby (Cambridge, Mass.: Polity Press, 1988). In saying this I do not mean to deny that some works manage to occupy a middle position, only that the extremes continue to be compelling.

8 Robert Bellah, Richard Madsen, William M. Sullivan, Ann Swidler, and Steven M. Tipton, *Habits of the Heart* (London: Hutchinson, 1988).

9 Philippe Lacoue-Labarthe, *Heidegger, Art and Politics*, trans. Chris Turner (Oxford: Blackwell, 1990), pp. 61–76.

10 For a defense of Kant's two strategies, see, for example, Onora O'Neill, *Constructions of Reason: Explorations of Kant's Practical Philosophy* (Cambridge University Press, 1990).

11 I elaborate this argument in detail in my *Adorno: Disenchantment and Ethics*, forthcoming.

12 This is a version of a standard anti-utilitarian argument that overlaps with Alasdair C. MacIntyre's treatment of goods that are external and internal to practices. See his *After Virtue* (London: Duckworth, 1981), pp. 173–7.

13 Kant, *Critique of Judgment*, §28, p. 264.

14 Ibid.

15 On the logic of exemplarity, see ibid., §§46–7, pp. 307–10; for a discussion of this, see Bernstein, *Fate of Art*, pp. 89–108.

16 My own preference here is for a Weberian account of rationalization as entailing sphere differentiation; see ibid., pp. 225–32.

17 Charles Taylor, "Philosophy and the Human Sciences," in *Philosophical Papers*, vol. II (Cambridge University Press, 1985), p. 96.

18 This distinction is not common; it is usual to consider both these under the heading of "civic republicanism." However, the distinction is important for Rawls. He borrows his notion of civic humanism from Taylor (see ibid., pp. 334–5).

19 Hans-Georg Gadamer, *Reason in the Age of Science* (Cambridge, MA: MIT Press, 1982), p. 87.

20 Taylor, "Philosophy and the Human Sciences."

21 Although I lack the space here to elaborate this claim, a further element revealing the convergence of Rawls and Gadamer is their joint employment of constitutional or legal reasoning as a model of public reason or, what is the same, hermeneutical rationality; see *PL*, pp. 231–40 and *TM*, pp. 289–305.

22 Hannah Arendt, *Lectures on Kant's Political Philosophy*, ed. Ronald Biner (University of Chicago Press, 1982).

23 For a weaker version of the line of argument I am pursuing in this paragraph, see Stephen Mulhall and Adam Swift, *Liberals and Communitarians* (Oxford: Blackwell, 1992), pp. 224–5. In general, my critique of Rawls overlaps with that of Mulhall and Swift. I should here like to thank Stephen Mulhall for both his patience in listening to my fumblings and his sage advice over things Rawlsian.

24 Ibid., pp. 220ff.

25 Georges Bataille, *Visions of Excess: Selected Writings, 1927–1939*, trans. and ed. Allan Stoekl (Minneapolis: University of Minnesota Press, 1985), p. 210.

4

Travelers, colonizers, and the aesthetics of self-conception: Denis Diderot on the perils of detachment

ANTHONY PAGDEN

I

In this chapter I wish to examine one powerful critique of the European overseas empires of the eighteenth century, and the impact that they had had upon societies which had created them. This is the claim that imperial expansion, colonization and even tourism, has, together with the abundance of goods modern commerce has inflicted upon our senses, blunted our collective aesthetic sensibilities. Arguments of this kind can be found in a number of eighteenth-century writers, in Hutcheson, in Shaftesbury, in Rousseau, in Herder, even in Kant. But one of its least studied, yet most widely diffused, proponents was Diderot.

Like so much of Diderot's more compelling ideas, his indictment of empire is to be found in a number of commentaries, contributions, and (fictional) continuations of texts by other authors. Much, indeed, of Diderot's writings on both aesthetics and politics – and for Diderot the two were inextricable – takes this form. The *Lettre sur les sourds et les muets* (a critique of Charles Batteux's *Les Beaux-Arts reduits au même principe*), the *Eloge de Richardson*, the translation of (and also commentary on) Shaftesbury's *Inquiry Concerning Merit and Truth*, the *Refutation* of Helvetius's *De l'Homme*, and the *Supplément au voyage de Bougainville* (a series of fictional missing passages from, and reflections on, Bougainville's *Voyage autour du monde*) are all texts which supplement, challenge, evoke, and finally remodel other works.[1] The only major exception is his most sustained, and most influential work on aesthetics, the *Recherches philosophiques sur l'origine et la nature du beau*. But even that was given its title by his pupil and first biographer Jacques-André Naigeon in 1798 and first appeared anonymously as the article on "Beau" in the *Encyclopédie*.

85

By far the most enigmatic of these self-effacing supplementary texts, however, is the contributions Diderot made to the 1780 edition of the abbé Thomas Guillaume Raynal's *Histoire philosophique et politique des établissements et du commerce des Européens dans les Deux Indes*. The *Histoire*, the work of a renegade Jesuit and former editor of the *Mercure de France*, first appeared in 1770 and became an immediate best-seller. More than thirty editions were printed between 1770 and 1787.[2] Napoleon later declared himself to be a "zealous disciple of Raynal" and, significantly in view of what he did there, took a copy of the book with him to Egypt.[3] The title of the work alone was sufficiently striking to guarantee it a readership. The first part, the claim to be both a *philosophical* and a *political* history, made it, as Raynal went to some lengths to explain in the preface to Book I, unique. "I have questioned the living and the dead," he assured his readers, "I have assessed their authority; I have compared their testimonies; I have clarified the facts."[4]

From text to text Raynal had traveled the world with "the august image of the truth" always before him as a guide. And he hoped that if his history "still finds some readers in the centuries to come, I wish it to be apparent how much I was free of passions and prejudices."[5] The second part of his title was equally striking. Here, it claimed, was a history which brought together the two halves of the planet, the East and the West, and the two hitherto unrelated spheres of European colonial activity into one work. It was as if the gaze of the European, "elevated above all human considerations," could "glide above the atmosphere" and thus indeed unite "the globe beneath himself."[6]

The first edition of the work, though extensive in its range, was neither very original nor, in any sense, the radical document it was to become. In subsequent editions, however, it was reworked probably by a number of the lesser and greater *philosophes*, to the extent that the original text was reduced to little more than a narrative structure for a series of striking juxtapositions by other hands. By the time the final edition appeared in 1780, these had transformed the work into a kind of mini *Encyclopédie* on the political, intellectual, and social implications for Europe of colonization. The most original and sustained of these contributions were by Diderot. They were also far more uncompromising in their anticolonialism than the more moderate and reconciliatory tones of Raynal's original text.[7] If in the words of Diderot's own riposte to his friend Frédéric Grimm, Raynal's work finally became "the book that I love and that kings and their courtiers detest, the book that gives birth to Brutuses,"[8] this is almost entirely because of his own presence in the text.

Like many of his contemporaries, Diderot detested empires. He detested them because they were necessarily based upon conquest, because they violated the political rights and disrupted the lives and customs of others, and because they generated political relationships dependent upon slavery and fear, rather than amity and trust. He hated them, too, because they were overextensions of the natural human social unit, the society which is never so large that the ruler has no idea who his subjects are, how they live, or by what laws they ought to be governed.[9] "Can one conceive of the means of subjecting to the same rule," he said of the Russia of Catherine the Great (one of the few places outside France he ever visited), "peoples who cannot understand each other, who speak seventeen or eighteen different languages and who retain customs and superstitions from time immemorial to which they are more attached than to life itself?"[10]

Furthermore, it was not only the imperial powers themselves that stood to lose from the process of cultural, and finally moral, disintegration that such overreaching necessarily involved. It was the race itself, for all "Enormous monarchies," as Hume had phrased it, were "probably, destructive to human nature; in their progress, in their continuance, and even in their downfall."[11]

For Diderot, the disruption posed to the natural evolution of society by such extended empires could be seen at every level of human experience. Diderot's ambition was always, in Naigeon's words, to create a natural and experimental history of man,[12] which would constitute a refutation of the materialism of Helvetius and Buffon, a history which would explore the conflict between the apparent homogeneity of the physical makeup of the species and the huge diversity of behavior of which its individual members were capable. It was to provide the "preliminary concept of man" which, rather than theological abstractions, had to precede all moral and aesthetic judgment.[13] Diderot had also begun his literary career as the translator of Shaftesbury's *Essay Concerning Merit and Virtue*. Although in later life he was to reject much of Shaftesbury's Neoplatonism and what he took to be the Englishman's utilitarian approach to aesthetics, he remained convinced throughout his life of the truth of Shaftesbury's claim that "All things in the world are united," that the human sphere, in common with the physical, was ordered according to a single "union and coherence."[14] As he said again and again, in a number of different contexts, everything, if it

were to carry meaning, had to be linked (*enchaîné*) to everything
else. The unrelated, detached phenomenon would be entirely unintelligible. As he phrased it in his only attempt at a sustained
philosophical work, *De l'Interprétation de la nature* (1753),

> If phenomena are not linked to one another there can be no philosophy.
> Phenomena are all linked so that the condition of each might be imperma-
> nent. But if the condition of beings is one of perpetual vicissitude; if nature
> is still at work in spite of the chain that links phenomena, there can be no
> philosophy. All our natural science becomes as ephemeral as words.[15]

And what applied to the world of nature, applied equally to the
world of human experience. "In the universe all is one," he wrote of
Shaftesbury's own Neoplatonism, "This truth was one of the first
steps of philosophy and it was a giant's step . . . All the discoveries
of modern philosophers unite to establish the same proposition."[16] It
followed, therefore, that if the European empires had been responsible for the creation of social and political evils, they must have had
deleterious consequences for our aesthetic sensibilities also.

II

For Diderot, as later for Kant, aesthetic judgment was communicative.[17] It was, in the term which Kant had taken from Shaftesbury
and the Scots, a *sensus communis*, which had meaning only insofar
as it was communicable to all the members of any *possible* community.[18] Diderot went to some length in the *Recherches philosophiques sur l'origine et la nature du beau* (1752) to refute Francis
Hutcheson's claim that there might exist an "Internal Sense."[19]
Hutcheson's attempt to harness Lockean sensationalism to a generalized conviction that there must exist some universal register of
what was beautiful, had, he believed, produced something very
close to a reformulation of the older, discredited conception of
innate ideas which Locke had done so much to destroy.[20] Like
Shaftesbury – to whom he was intellectually far closer than he was
prepared to admit in the *Recherches philosophiques* – Diderot was
uneasy with the moral, as well as the aesthetic, implications of a
purely sensationalist theory of knowledge. But he was not prepared
to accept anything so clearly detached from the realm of experience,
and thus independent of our moral faculties, as an "internal
sense."[21] Hutcheson also supposed that even if we were able, as
individuals, to unlearn all that we had experienced as civilized

beings, our aesthetic appreciation of the world would be unimpaired. As Diderot summarized the argument, were "an austere philosophy, inimical to luxury" to drive us to "break statues, overturn obelisks, turn our palaces into huts and our gardens into forests," the *individual* would be no less sensitive by these actions to "the real *beauty* of these objects; internal sense would rebel against it; and it would be reduced to making a merit of its courage."[22] For Diderot this was absurd since no one could exercise judgment, or any faculty, in the absence of the world of persons or things to which it belongs. All aesthetic, and crucially all *moral*, understanding must, therefore, be the product of a specific and artificial environment, of a "civilization." It cannot, for instance, be the case that our capacity for aesthetic judgment, for "taste" (*goût*), exists equally in "savages" and in infants as it does in civilized adults. *Le Goût* is a faculty, but like all faculties it has to be exercised in society with other beings. "What, therefore, is taste?" Diderot asked. "A facility acquired through repeated experiences to apprehend the true or the good, together with the circumstance that makes it beautiful, and to be promptly and vividly struck by them."[23] In Diderot's view, all that Hutcheson and his followers had demonstrated was that "there is something obscure and impenetrable in the pleasure that the *beautiful* induces in us."[24] Neither was he prepared to accept the utilitarian claim that what we take to be beautiful is simply that which, in some sense, gives us pleasure.[25] (In the *Recherches philosophiques* he rather perversely attributes this view to Shaftesbury, although Shaftesbury's theory of "disinterestedness," the claim that aesthetic judgment is independent of our ordinary theoretical and practical concerns, certainly cannot be construed as a form of utilitarianism.) All aesthetic judgment, he argued, had relied upon association, what, in the *Recherches philosophiques*, he calls *rapports*.

But amongst the qualities common to all the things that we call *beautiful*, which should we select to be the thing for which the term *beautiful* is the sign? Which one? It is evident, it seems to me, that it can only be the one whose presence causes all to be *beautiful*; of which the prevalence or rarity, if it is susceptible to prevalence or rarity, causes all to be *beautiful* to a greater or lesser extent; of which the absence causes them to cease to be *beautiful*; which cannot change its nature without causing a change to the *beautiful* in kind, and of which the opposite quality would turn the most *beautiful* into the disagreeable and ugly; that by which, in a word, *beauty* is instituted, grows, varies infinitely, deteriorates and disappears. Now, only the concept of *association* [*rapports*] is capable of producing these effects.[26]

At one level these *rapports* are, it is clear, the internal relationships which impart harmony to a work of art. But they also constitute the relationships which exist between the world and the viewer, the reader or – although Diderot rarely discusses music – the listener. An image, a line of poetry, or a musical phrase only acquires "beauty" when seen in harmonious relationship to other parts of the whole to which both they, and the viewing, reading, listening agent, simultaneously belong.[27] Beauty is dependent upon its meaning, and meaning cannot, as we have seen, be detached from the natural world itself.[28] It would seem to follow not merely, to use Diderot's own example, that a single line of poetry acquires its beauty (and its meaning) from its literary context – the reader's knowledge of what follows and precedes it – but that it relies, too, upon the specific culture of the "civilization" to which the reader belongs. (This is why Diderot believed that certain kinds of painting and poetry were appropriate to certain kinds of government.) The line from Corneille's *Horaces*, "Qu'il mourût" (That he should die), would not only fail to move – it might even, as Diderot suggests, seem comic or absurd, in some other context – without the previous, and equally famous phrase "seul contre trois, que voulais-tu qu'il fît?" (alone against three, what do you wish him to do?); it would also fail without the dramatic setting, and the essentially republican sentiments, on which the entire story of Roman parental sacrifice is based.[29] In other societies – our own for instance – such sentiments, unless they were assumed to be purely theatrical, might seem merely self-destructive. Underpinning these claims is not only Shaftesbury's "union and coherence of the whole"; there is also a conviction that connectedness of this kind translates into the world of sensation (and crucially into the moral world) as a sense of order. And on this account "taste" – the faculty with which we register the appropriateness of the *rapports* which constitute our aesthetic experience – can be expressed as a sense for order. "The taste for a general order," he wrote in *Entretiens sur le fils naturel* of 1757, his imaginary conversation with the playwright Dorval,

dominates us from tenderest infancy; it is older in our soul . . . [older] than any considered sentiment; and it is thus that my soul turns me against myself; it acts in us without our perceiving it; it is the germ of courtesy [*honnêteté*] and good taste; it carries us to the good as long as it is not vitiated by passion; it follows us even in our errors; then it sets out the means of the most advantageous manner for ill.[30]

A similar insistence determined the inflexibility of Diderot's taste in painting. "A well composed picture," he wrote in the article on *Composition en peinture* in the *Encyclopédie*, "is a whole contained within a single point of view in which the [various] parts pursue the same end and, by their mutual correspondence, form an ensemble as real as that of the parts of a living body."[31] Such order, furthermore, constituted not only a harmony among the various parts of a single whole, it also determined what he called "the conformity of our judgments with things." Beauty, that is, is in art precisely what truth is in philosophy: the exact (although not literal) representation of the world.[32] Because of this it cannot be separated from the other domains of experience to which all humans are subject, namely all that goes under the name of custom (*mœurs*). For Diderot, as for Shaftesbury, there could be no obvious disassociation between the aesthetic and, in the broadest cultural sense of the term, the moral, anymore than there could be a disassociation between the various parts of which the natural world itself is composed. What was perceived by our "taste" to be beautiful had also to be what was grasped by our "moral sense," in Shaftesbury's formulation, as good.[33] For the man of "taste," the fact of the beauty of a thought and action, a belief, a work of art, or a mathematic theorem was proof of its goodness. "Either one considers associations [*rapports*] within customs," he wrote, "and one has *moral beauty*; or one considers them in works of literature and one has *literary beauty*; or one considers them in works of music and one has *musical beauty*," even, and crucially for one so concerned as Diderot was with the arts and crafts, "men's mechanical works" (les ouvrages mécaniques des hommes) conformed to the same general rule, to produce "*artificial beauty*" (le beau artificiel).[34] It followed from this that a "good" play or poem would have a moving, morally improving subject matter, as well as displaying technical excellence. "In order to judge here where good taste is to be found," he wrote to Sophie Volland in 1762, "one has to decide where good manners are to be found." Art could be no more a matter for individual choice than morality (or, indeed, the correct equation). The young libertine who found "a little turned-up nose, laughing lips, a bright eye, a resolute bearing," to be charming was expressing a preference for the moral worthlessness that sustained such images. "His taste is reduced to this," Diderot concluded, "I love vice; and mine to this: I love virtue. It is thus for almost all judgments; they resolve themselves finally into one or other of these words."[35] "If the moral system is corrupt," he wrote of the theatre, "taste must needs be false."[36] It was this single belief, consistently, ruthlessly, applied which makes his art criticism of the 1760s, for all its frequent brilliance, ultimately so restricted. It was "the moral painting" of Greuze, "the first who took it into his head, amongst us, to give manners to art," that won his admiration.[37] He could appreciate Boucher's skills, his handling of color, even the breadth of his imagination. But for Diderot his *art* was always degraded and degrading because of what it depicted. "The degradation of taste," he wrote, "of color, of composition, of characters, of expression, of design, followed step by step the depravation of moral manners." And inevitably, in time, the subject matter had come to contaminate the technique. If everything in the universe constituted a single whole, nothing within a culture or even within a single work of art could remain isolated or sanitized for long. As a painter, Boucher had everything "but for the truth," but because he did not have *that*, he was in no real sense an artist.[38]

III

Taste for "the beautiful," and a taste for the morally good, is a faculty which has to be exercised in the company of others. Ultimately it is what all true civilization must be based upon. The kind of morality which sustains the Tahitian society Diderot describes in the *Supplément au voyage de Bougainville*, while it may have created a society which is free from crime and – in the sense that everyone in it pursues the interests of the community – free also from corruption, is also a fairly bleak, undifferentiated place. Like most eighteenth-century social theorists, Diderot could recognize, and applaud, the value of the simple natural lives supposedly lived in Canadian woods, Pacific islands, in republican Rome, or even closer to home among the villagers of the Vaud. Diderot may not have had much confidence in the ultimate progress of Western civilization, but one part of him at least valued highly the plurality which only that civilization seemed able to bring. From his writing desk he could see that even within Europe, beset as it was by a miserable populus concerned exclusively with survival and the restrictive power of established religion, "the progress of enlightenment is limited."[39] Beyond the limits of the civilized world, however, no "Enlightenment" was possible at all. If he admired the stoicism which the savage, Canadian Indian, Tahitian or "Brames" seemed to possess, he seems also to have shuddered at the conditions which made it necessary. He was appalled by what Rousseau had applauded, by the absence of the arts and sciences among such peoples, and by what his Neapolitan contemporary Francesco Antonio Grimaldi described as "the mask which makes him like his fellow" which all "savages" seemed to wear.[40] He knew, as Jean Starobinski has characterized it, that "The expansion of civilized activity is constantly overtaken by the risks of failure: and what constitutes an obstacle is not solely what remains ungovernable in nature, but the power of destruction that civilization brings within itself."[41] Civilization had its obvious moral and cognitive dangers. But it also had its rewards. And one of these was moral and aesthetic *understanding*. For the "savage," irreproachable though he may be, is "good" because his faculties are still inert. In the, perhaps fortunate, circumstances in which he finds himself, he has never had to exercise either moral or aesthetic judgment. He does only what nature dictates to him. Such a condition was, Diderot wrote in refutation of Helvetius's *De l'Homme*, clearly a state of true innocence and, equally surely, civilization was "a state of war and crime." But that "the savage state is preferable to the organized state. I deny it." The mere absence of violence did not prove that such states were, in any meaningful sense, "happy" ones.[42] Happiness (*bonheur*), like taste (*goût*), is the outcome of an exercise of judgment. "Yes, Mr. Rousseau," he declared at his most extreme, "I prefer refined vice clothed in silk to ferocious stupidity dressed in animal skins."[43] Savages were not exactly stupid; but their wisdom certainly did not lead to true *bonheur* and was, in any case, useless to any civilized being, except as a point of reference. True *bonheur*, for Diderot, unlike Rousseau, was not innocence, but the product of the exercise of virtue. A vicious person, or one who does not, as neither the child or the savage properly can, know the distinction between good and evil, cannot be truly "happy," however content or satisfied he or she may be.[44] The Tahitians of the *Supplément au voyage de Bougainville* (who are, in any case, knowing observers of the European world) offer a powerful critique of the civilized man's social, and above all sexual, mores, because they speak with the voice of nature. But they can do that only because, as they have never experienced what civilized man has experienced, they are able to stand outside the whole process of cognition. (Although as the *vieillard* who curses Bougainville for having brought "civilization" – "We follow the pure instinct of nature: and you have tried to efface its character from our souls" – to his island knows, they cannot remain so for long.[45]) In this respect the savage would seem

93

to be little different from an animal, for animals who also possess something akin to "our first apprehensions and to our most coarse and mechanical sensations," are, as savages seem to be, "incapable of forming that association of ideas that alone can produce reflection in which the essence of thought yet consists."[46]

Because they are the products of reflective action, civilizations are also inescapably plural and dynamic. However we may be guided by their image, true ideal types can only *exist* in a simple, and hence "savage," world. "The ideal model of beauty," Diderot told his friend Frédéric Grimm, "the true line that corrupts itself, that disappears and that will only perhaps be rediscovered perfectly in a people by a return to the state of barbarism; for that is the only state in which men convinced of their ignorance are able to reconcile themselves to the slowness of groping uncertainty; the others remain mediocre precisely because they are born, so to speak, knowledge-able."[47] Such a return, however, was not an option for civilized man. "The destiny that rules the world wishes that all should pass. The happiest condition of a man, of a state, has its term."[48] It was this which made the contemplation of ruins – an eighteenth-century pastime of which Diderot was particularly fond – so instructive. For in ruins "he associates with the objects a procession of incidental and moral ideas about the energy of human nature and the power of peoples."[49] The evasion of this process was not an option, not even, in the end, for "savages," and while cultural pluralism was clearly part of the human condition, some degree of what all the peoples of the world could recognize as civility was the lot of all mankind. Civilization is a learning process, and Diderot's whole project – insofar as it possesses any coherence – was concerned with the origins and the development of things.[50]

It was this which gave the ancients their particular cultural value. Diderot's involvement in the dispute between the ancients and the moderns was firmly on the side of the moderns. He knew that modern man had achieved things which the ancients could never even have dreamt of. He knew, too, that for the moderns to copy the ancients was to misunderstand their peculiar heuristic value.[51] For unlike the Tahitians, whose world offers a point of view upon our own, but remains, nonetheless, firmly beyond our own, the Greeks and the Romans are our immediate ancestors.[52] They stand this side of the threshold of civility but still so close to the state of nature that their contact with it is direct and unmediated.[53]

For Diderot, however, as for many other eighteenth-century social theorists, the model for the development of civilization, of knowledge itself, was provided by the history of language. Speech is not only the earliest, and the most crucial human social act, it was also widely believed that there was a close correlation between language and structure of the human mind. The human mind possesses the capacity for grasping the interconnectedness, the wholeness of the universe, of which it is the only fully reflective part. But it does so in the form of a sign – what Diderot termed an *"hiéroglyphe"*.[54] "The word must paint the thought and be its image," he wrote in his article on *Inversion* in the *Encyclopédie*. "But thought is indivisible and consequently cannot itself be the immediate object of any image: one must of necessity resort to abstraction."[55] In order to make this accessible to rational understanding, it has, to use a term which Diderot borrowed from Condillac, to be "decomposed."[56] We can, that is, *perceive* things as single immediate wholes, but we can only *understand* them temporally and serially. Linearity is a necessary condition of true thought as opposed to unstructured reflection. "So we can observe what we do when thinking," wrote Condillac, "we are able to realize it; consequently we can learn to guide our reflection. Thus to think becomes an art and that art is the art of speaking."[57] Language – *la parole* – and representation – *l'image* – operate in precisely the same way. The picture the painter creates on his canvas, is, like the completed speech-act, the outcome of a process of de- and re-composition. "Our soul," wrote Diderot in the *Lettre sur les sourds et les muets* of 1751,

is a picture in motion which we paint after ceaselessly: we use plenty of time to render it faithfully: but it exists as a whole and all at once: spirit is not reckoned step by step like expression. The brush executes only in duration what the eye of the painter enfolds in an instant. The formation of languages requires decomposition; but to *see* an object, to *judge* it beautiful, to *feel* an agreeable sensation, to *desire* possession, is the state of the soul in a single instant.[58]

Decomposition is the defining feature of civilization, and as such is a process which, while we all perform it unreflectively, has, nevertheless, to be learned. It is a cognitive operation to which neither the child nor the "savage" can have complete access. This is one reason why "Savage" societies have no arts (although they do have crafts) and no sciences, since both of these demand decomposition. "Savage" languages – as numerous travelers claimed to have observed – lack the abstractions and universals with which civilized men do their thinking. They are, however, rich in metaphors – for of all the forms of speech, metaphor most closely approximates to the original undecomposed image – and in complex compound nouns. Since nonlinearity shared something with the original harmony between man and the natural world, "primitive" languages were believed to be able to capture in this way entire images with a single word. "A savage whose language is not yet formed," explained Pierre Louis Moreau de Maupertuis in 1756, "can conflate and express all at once the pronoun, the verb, the number, the object and the adjective and say in a single word: *I killed a large bear.*"[59] The languages of the ancient world, because they too were closer to the creation of the original speech-act, also preserved some of this immediacy. Latin and Greek – or so Diderot claimed to believe – "gives in a single word . . . the state of the soul," of the original aesthetic impulse, and "this word once uttered, all is said, all is heard."[60] He, omitted, however, to provide any examples.

IV

Decomposition is also the process by which we develop both our sense of taste and our understanding of what is morally good. As we have seen, the action of painting precisely mirrors the action of language acquisition. Our customs, too – although Diderot was never very clear on this point – are the products of similar internalized, and now unreflective cognitive processes. Because they originate in this way, within particular cultures, they are also precisely characterized by what Diderot described as a "national character" (*esprit national*). Each such *esprit*, he believed, is composed of two elements, one, "the moral," is variable and allows for variations over time, the other, the physical, is fixed and dependent upon climate.

Insofar as these [two] causes act contradictorily, the nation is insensate. It does not begin to adopt the spirit that befits it until the moment when its speculative principles coincide with its physical position. It is thus that it advances with great strides towards the splendor, opulence and happiness that it could promise itself by the free use of its local resources.[61]

Tear the two apart again, and what will inevitably follow, as from any disassociation of the parts of a natural whole, is a collapse back into a state of disorder. In the human world this meant a return to the condition of barbarism. Like Herder after him, however, Diderot was prepared to believe that no matter how a people's social world might change, they remained in some sense what their environment had willed them to be.[62] Look, he said in the *Histoire*, at the Indians of "Indostan," a people who have suffered for centuries at the hands of a tyranny by comparison with which even the Spaniards might seem benign, yet they still remain "mild, humane, timid," incapable of revolt, their only vice being their timidity. "Morality does not alter physique," he wrote in his Refutation of Helvetius's *De l'Homme*, "but it constrains it and this constraint ends by removing all its primitive natural energy."[63] The Indians owed their gentle nature to their "climate," not to their present social and cultural state. The complete collapse of a culture which had once rivaled that of the Egyptians and to which the Greeks had gone to learn their science "even before Pythagoras," is entirely to be attributed to the barbarism of India's Mughal rulers.[64]

Given a wider, more general definition, however, "climate" could be made to include the land, and a love of the land, "the first instinct, the first bond of society, without which all the other artificial ties have neither resilience nor duration," became the principal force behind love of *patrie*.[65] Yet for Diderot, climate, even in this extended sense, operated only at the level of the needs and desires we all share. It may make men gentle, as it did with the Indians, or, as it has done with the Tartars, make them fierce or, again like the Native Americans, disinclined to hard labor. But the full force of the *"esprit national"* is "moral" – it belongs, that is, to *mores*, to the civil and religious law, the habits and customs, the *habitudines* which constituted, in Pascal's celebrated phrase, "a second nature which destroys the first."[66] It is the product of sustained moral and intellectual judgment, of the exercise of "taste," and cannot be detached from any other aspect of the culture by which it is sustained. It is, of course, what Diderot, like Shaftesbury, understood by "patriotism." It was a feeling close to friendship, heroic as was friendship, and explicitly non-Christian – and thus to be found in all cultures everywhere. Because it, in common with both "taste" and "moral sense," was in this way communicative, it had, "if it be allow'd anything at all" to imply, in Shaftesbury's words, "something *moral* and *social*. The Notion itself presupposes a naturally *civil* and *political* state of Mankind."[67] It should not be confused, as it so often was by those whom Shaftesbury described contemptuously as "patriots of the soil," with the kind of blindness to the qualities of others which had prevented his own countrymen from recognizing that they were "the *latest Barbarous*, the last *Civiliz'd* or *Polish'd* People of Europe."[68] True love of one's country was an essential part of the new benevolence towards all peoples, the truly cosmopolitan (or *mondaine* as Diderot called it) recognition of the relative worth of *all* the cultures of the globe. A national character of this kind must also, of course, have a precise geographical location, what Diderot calls a "metropolis." "The metropolises of empires," he wrote in the *Histoire*, "are the hearths of the national spirit, that is to say, the places where it shows itself with the greatest energy in speech."[69] To wish to abandon this metropolis was a form of cultural, cognitive, aesthetic, and hence moral, suicide. What, asks A in the *Supplément au voyage de Bougainville*, could have driven Bougainville himself to abandon his "meditative state" and embrace the "active, hard, wandering and dissipated profession of the traveler"?[70] Paradoxically – but Diderot was fond of paradoxes – it is the savage who, because he has yet to form such attachments and is therefore at home everywhere, has yet to be, in the words of B, "carried on the ocean without the restrictions of the fantasies from which one can no longer extricate oneself."[71] But, of course, like everything else the savage "knows," he is in this only following his instinct. Civilized man, in losing that instinct, has had to learn the virtues of the home life.

Diderot's disapproval of travel belongs to an ancient European tradition, one which locates the source of all civility – which is, after all, a life lived in cities (*civitates*) – in settled communities, and which looks upon all modes of nomadism as irredeemably savage. All men other than pilgrims who leave their native homes are suspect. Crossing the ocean was an act contrary to nature, for the gods – or God – had filled half the world with water precisely in order to keep humans apart.[72] Because of this, said Diderot, there was "no state more immoral than that of the traveler." He who travels constantly, he wrote in the *Histoire*, "resembles the proprietor of an immense dwelling who, instead of sitting beside his wife amongst his children, would spend his whole life visiting his apartments." What he carries with him from room to room is a catalog of human vices: "Tyranny, crime, ambition, misery, curiosity, I know not what spiritual disquiet, the desire to know and to see, boredom, the disgust of an expended happiness, these have expatriated and will expatriate men in all times."[73]

Such men are generally to be found among those who seek to fulfill ambitions for which their native land offers no scope. They are, that is, the products (or the victims) of what no civilization can avoid: the inescapable gap between ever-increasing human needs

and the society's capacity to meet them. Happiness for the children
of Prometheus, as Helvetius had pointed out, was "a device which
had always to be remade."[74] But no matter what the original motive
for departure might have been, everyone who abandons his metropolis, and with it his *esprit national*, is compelled to become
another kind of being. Our identities are like masks. They are
carefully built up for us by the cultures to which we belong. But like
masks – like the identities which the actor assumes on a stage – they
remain inherently unstable. Detach anyone from his *patrie* for too
long, and inexorably his identity will begin to fall away. "I only
make exceptions in rare circumstances," wrote Diderot of such
beings.

To the extent that the distance from the capital grows, this mask drops away.
It falls at the frontier. From one hemisphere to the other what becomes of it?
Nothing. Beyond the equator a man is neither English, Dutch, French,
Spanish, nor Portuguese. Of his country he retains only the principles and
prejudices which authorize or excuse his conduct.[75]

"Expeditions over time" have thus

given birth to a new species of nomadic savage. I speak of these men who
traverse so many lands that they end up belonging to none; . . . of these
amphibians who live on the surface of the waters . . . who truly have neither
fathers, mothers, children, brothers, relations, friends, nor fellow citizens;
for whom the sweetest and most sacred associations are extinguished.[76]

This identity-less European traveler has, in a sense, reversed the
journey which his ancestors once made from the state of nature to
civil society. By traveling through space, he has gone backwards in
time, by going from Europe to America or India or the Pacific, he has
also gone from civility to savagery. But the person he has thus
become, the person who now lies beneath the mask, is not the *bon
sauvage*, the natural man, whom, on Diderot's account, Bougainville
had met on Tahiti. For all great revolutions, as Diderot said in
another context, change irradicably the human and social land-
scapes over which they move.[77] The principles and prejudices
which the mask of civility inevitably leaves behind clutters the mind
of the new savage quite as much as it did that of the old civil man.
This decomposed civil being is what Diderot nicely calls "a domestic
tiger who reenters the forest."[78] He has loosened, if still not entirely
lost, the hold which civilization once held over him. He has shed his
identity, the mask of his being, and with it the capacity for the kind
of imaginative "decomposition" which is the source of all rational

thought, of all art and all science. Since he cannot, however, fully unlearn what he once knew, he has become not a true "savage," but what Diderot characterized as a "barbarian," one whose contact with civilization, however insubstantial, has rendered him incapable of innocence, yet also insensitive to the joys of nature, of art, and even to the delights of human society.[79] Even Bougainville himself, enlightened mathematician though he was, after years of traveling had almost reached this condition. "I am now so far from the sanctuary of the sciences and the arts," he warned his readers, "that my ideas and my style can only have taken too great an imprint of the wandering and wild life that I have led for twelve years."[80] Such deracinated beings must, on Diderot's account of how we form our moral and aesthetic judgments, be no longer capable of either good taste or of good customs. Like the savages whom they had come to resemble, like the Native Americans who produced wonderful copies of Flemish Madonnas out of quetzal feathers, the European traveler and colonist could imitate the cultural products of the civilized world, but generate none of his own. His very act of colonization is, itself, a denial of the civilizing instinct, the instinct to create and metamorphose. In America and India, all the Europeans had ever attempted to do was to replicate, their sole objective being to resist, and deny, the temporal process which makes them human. "Nothing is more bizarre," Diderot wrote, "than to see Europe transported and reproduced, so to say, in America, in the name and form of our cities; in the laws, the manners and the religion of our continent."[81] The imagination, as Diderot had said elsewhere, borrowing a metaphor from d'Alembert (or d'Alembert from him), is,

The art of lifting a corner of the veil and to show to men a corner of the world they inhabit that is ignored or rather forgotten. The instigator is himself sometimes unsure if the thing he reveals is a reality or a chimera, if it ever existed beyond himself; so he is at the final limit of human energy and at the extremity of the resources of art.[82]

Like the artist with whom he is here compared, the traveler and the discoverer have revealed to the general gaze an increasing number of unknown and neglected corners of the world. But for them the act of travel and discovery, the raising of the veil, does not have the power, as it would have for the true artist, to move them over into an act of creation.[83] Because traveling is itself a mode of dislocation both in space and time, it can only return in upon itself.

It is precisely for this reason that America "did not give birth to any prodigy in the heads of the Spaniards," when they first arrived in a world which was, in almost every significant respect, wholly unlike anything with which they were familiar. The ancients had invested all natural phenomena with a sense of wonder, transforming every stone, mountain, tree, and wood into a personalized, magical force. But when the moderns arrived in America, "an entirely new nature remained mute beneath the gaze of the Spaniard."[84] All these men had done was to transport to the New World the wonders of the ancient, the Amazons, the Fountains of Eternal Youth, the eternally ageless Hyperboreans.[85] In Europe these things – fantastic though they might have been – belonged, nevertheless, to an understanding of nature. They had originated in the Greeks' direct encounter with this world. In America, they were mere imitations, as detached and meaningless as the stone castles the Portuguese had built in Benin. These travelers and colonists, incapable of any true aesthetic response, were similarly detached from any moral sense. Once out beyond the limits of their *patrie*, they bore "at the bottom of their hearts the fatal germ of a depredation which grew swiftly to a inconceivable fury, when, beneath another sky, far from all public prosecution and the imposing scrutiny of their fellow citizens, neither decency nor fear could, by their effects, stop them."[86]

The social and political consequences of this mode of decivilization were, of course, well known. Diderot was also aware that commerce, *le doux commerce*, which in Montesquieu's celebrated phrase had "made men gentle," had created inescapable lines of communication between Europeans at home and the new breed of deracinated beings overseas, lines which carried back as easily as they carried out. The European empires and the world economy which the new commercial societies now sustained meant that nothing which occurred in one part of the globe could be fully insulated from anything which happened anywhere else. The disassociation which had overtaken the European colonists overseas had seeped back home to infect, in turn, the mother country. "Approximately two centuries after the depopulation of Europe to Asia," said Diderot summarizing the entire history of European overseas expansion, came the migration into America, and "this revolution substituted chaos for nothingness and mixed amongst us the vices and products of all climates."[87]

Commerce may have had the effect of familiarizing people who once believed that their cultures were the only possible measure of all things with a diversity of human types of which they had no previous experience. But the outcome of this had not been tolerance or the erosion of superstition, but rather a decrease in the capacity for imaginative response to the new and the strange similar to that which the first deracinated travelers had experienced when confronted with the wonders of the natural world in America. "The variety of religions and nations has familiarized the coarsest spirits with a species of indifference towards the object that had most struck their imagination."[88] It is not only that Europeans themselves should have become anesthetized to sensation, in the way that doctors cannot be moved to pity by the sight of blood and suffering,[89] it is that the entire culture in the centuries following the voyages of Columbus and Vasco da Gama had grown weary, unable properly to exercise their capacity for wonder. "The variety, the multiplicity of objects that industry has presented to the spirit and to the senses, has divided human affections and enfeebled the energy of all the senses."[90] In a world in which every action must have consequences that affect us all, the travel of a few has thus left us all ultimately the poorer.

Notes

All the quotations from eighteenth-century French texts have been translated by Ivan Gaskell.

1 See Georges Daniel, *Le style de Diderot: légende et structure* (Geneva: Droz, 1986), p. 138: "Un discours s'enchaîne a un autre discours, qu'il continue, qu'il complète, qu'il développe, qu'il peut même développer indéfiniment, au risque, à chaque instant, de l'infléchir en le faisant déborder vers on ne sait quelles questions et régions étrangères au sujet." See also Daniel Brewer, *The Discourse of Enlightenment in Eighteenth-Century France. Diderot and the Art of Philosophizing* (Cambridge University Press, 1993), pp. 62–3.

2 For the printing history, see Anatole Feugère, *Bibliographie critique de l'abbé Raynal* (Angoulême: Imprimérie ouvrière, 1922), pp. 15–48.

3 Quoted in Hans Wolpe, *Raynal et sa machine de guerre. L'Histoire de Deux Indes et ses perfectionnements* (Paris: Editions Genin, 1956), p. 8.

4 "J'ai interrogé les vivans et les morts," he assured his readers, "J'ai pesé leur autorité; j'ai opposé leurs témoignages; j'ai éclairci les faits."

5 "[T]rouve encore quelques lecteurs dans les siècles à venir, je veux qu'en voyant combien j'ai été dégagé de passions et de préjugés." I have used the edition of 1781. *Histoire philosophique et politique des établisse-*

mens et du commerce des Européens dans les deux Indes, 10 vols. (Geneva), vol. I, p. 3. Hereafter cited as *Histoire*.

6 Ibid. "élevé au dessus de tous les considérations humaines" could "plâne au-dessus de l'atmosphère" and thus indeed unite "le globe au-dessous de soi." This section, however, was in fact written by Diderot.

7 I have followed the now definitive reconstruction of Diderot's contributions in Gianluigi Goggi, *Denis Diderot. Pensées detachées. Contributions à L'Histoire de Deux Indes*, 2 vols. (Siena, 1976–7), and Michèle Duchet, *Diderot et "L'Histoire de Deux Indes" ou l'écriture fragmentaire* (Paris: Editions A.-G. Nizet, 1978).

8 "Le livre que j'aime et que les rois et leurs courtisans détestent, c'est le livre qui fait naître des Brutus": "Lettre apologétique de l'abbé Raynal à M. Grimm," in Diderot, *Œuvres philosophiques*, ed. Paul Vernière (Paris: Garnier, 1956), p. 640.

9 For a more detailed account of Diderot's critique of European imperialism, see Anthony Pagden, *European Encounters with the New World* (London and New Haven: Yale University Press, 1993), pp. 141–80.

10 "Conçoit-on le moyen d'assujettir a une même règle des peuples qui ne s'entendent pas qui parlent dix-sept à dix-huit langues différentes, et qui gardent de temps immémorial des coutûmes et des superstitions auxquelles ils sont plus attachés qu'à leur vie même?" (*Histoire*, vol. X, p. 28).

11 "Of the Balance of Power," in *Essays Moral, Political, and Literary*, ed. Eugene F. Miller (Indianapolis: Liberty Classics, 1985), pp. 340–1.

12 *Mémoires historiques et philosophiques sur la vie et les œuvres de Denis Diderot* (Paris, 1821), p. 291. The most perceptive studies of this aspect of Diderot's thought, and of the place of the *Histoire des Deux Indes* within it, are those of Girolamo Imbruglia. See in particular, "Dopo L'Encyclopédie. Diderot e la sagezza dell'immaginazione," *Studi settecenteschi* 11–12 (1988/9), 305–58, and "Diderot e le immagini della pirateria nel '700,'" *Belfagor* 45 (1990), 493–511.

13 *Salon de 1767*, in *Salons*, ed. Jean Seznec and Jean Adhémar, 3 vols. (Oxford University Press, 1957–67), vol. III, p. 148: "notion préliminaire de l'homme."

14 Anthony Ashley Cooper, Third Earl of Shaftesbury, *The Moralists: A Philosophical Rhapsody*, Treatise V of *Characteristicks of Men, Manners, Opinions, Times*, 2nd corrected edition, 3 vols. (London, 1714), vol. II, p. 287.

15 "Si les phénomènes ne sont pas enchaînés les uns aux autres, il n'y a point de philosophie. Les phénomènes seraient tous enchaînés, que l'état de chacun d'eux pourrait être sans permanence. Mais si l'état des êtres est dans une vicissitude perpétuelle; si la nature est encore à l'ouvrage malgré la chaîne qui lie les phénomènes, il n'y a point de philosophie. Toute notre science naturelle devient aussi transitoire que les mots": *Œuvres philosophiques*, pp. 240–1. Jacques Chouillet has written that from this date on Diderot's entire project can be seen as an

attempt to "réunir toutes les existences possibles en une seule 'nature'"
and thereby to "mettre fin à la trop fameuse distinction de deux
substances dont la persistance a si longtemps retardé le développement
de la pensée occidentale": *La Formation des idées esthétiques de
Diderot, 1745–1763* (Paris: Armand Colin, 1973), pp. 325–6.

16 "Dans l'univers tout est uni. Cette vérité fut un des premiers pas de la
philosophie, et ce fut un pas de géant . . . Toutes les découvertes des
philosophes modernes se réunissent pour constater la même proposition": footnote to the translation of the *Essay Concerning Merit and
Virtue* (as *Essai sur le mérite et la vertu*, 1745), in *Œuvres complètes*, ed.
Jules Assevat and Maurice Tourneaux, 20 vols. (Paris, 1875–7), vol. I,
p. 26.

17 "I say that taste can with more justice be called a *sensus communis* than
can sound understanding; and that the aesthetic, rather than the intellectual, judgement can bear the name of public sense, i.e. taking it that we
are prepared to use the word "sense" of an effect that mere reflection has
upon the mind; for then by sense we mean the feeling of pleasure. We
might even define taste as the faculty of estimating what makes our
feeling in a given representation universally communicable without the
mediation of a concept." Immanuel Kant, *The Critique of Judgement*, ed.
and trans. James Creed Meredith (Oxford University Press, 1991), p. 153.
See also Hans-Georg Gadamer, *The Relevance of the Beautiful and Other
Essays*, ed. Robert Bernasconi (Cambridge University Press, 1986),
pp. 19–20. Kant had read Diderot's article "Beau" in the *Encyclopédie*
with admiration and recommended it to his pupil Johann Georg
Hamann. See Roland Mortier, *Diderot en Allemagne* (Paris: Presses
universitaires de France, 1954), p. 151.

18 In this, of course, it differs from "common sense," which is the understanding shared by a particular community, and may, therefore, be
entirely false for other communities. For a discussion of the definition of
this term, see Onora O'Neill, *Constructions of Reason. Explorations of
Kant's Practical Philosophy* (Cambridge University Press, 1990),
pp. 24–7.

19 In *Œuvres esthétiques de Diderot*, ed. Paul Vernière (Paris: Garnier,
1988), pp. 399, 402–5; Francis Hutcheson, *An Inquiry into the Original
of our Ideas of Beauty and Virtue* (London, 1725), pp. 7–8. Hutcheson,
however, insisted that "All beauty is relative to the sense of some mind
perceiving it" (p. 35). The "Internal Sense" is a faculty and consists in
the ability to perceive the connections between the separate information
received from our individual external senses. In this respect it would
seem to be little different from Diderot's "rapports."

20 "The only pleasure of sense that our philosophers seem to consider,"
wrote Hutcheson in implicit rejection of Lockean sensationalism, "is that
which accompanies the simple idea of Sensation." *An Inquiry*, p. 6.

21 "Twas Mr. Locke," wrote Shaftesbury to Michael Ainsworth in 1709,
"that struck at all fundamentals, threw all order out of the world, and

made the very idea of these . . . unnatural, and without foundation in our minds." Quoted in Charles Taylor, *Sources of the Self. The Making of the Modern Identity* (Cambridge University Press, 1989), p. 253, n29.

22 "Une philosophie austère, ennemie du luxe [to drive us to] brisera les statues, renversera les obélisques, transformera nos palais en cabanes, et nos jardins en forêts, [the *individual* would be no less sensitive by these actions to] la beauté réelle de ces objets; le sens interne se révoltera contre elle; et elle sera réduite à se faire un mérite de son courage" (*Recherches philosophiques sur l'origine et la nature du beau*, in *Œuvres esthétiques*, p. 400).

23 "Qu'est-ce donc que le goût? [Diderot asked.] Une facilité acquise par des expériences réitérées, à saisir le vrai ou le bon, avec la circonstance qui le rend beau, et d'en être promptement et vivement touché" (*Essais sur la peinture*, in *Œuvres esthétiques*, p. 738).

24 "[I]l y a quelque chose d'obscur et d'impénétrable dans le plaisir que le *beau* nous cause" (*Recherches philosophiques*, in *Œuvres esthétiques*, pp. 400–1).

25 Ibid., p. 411. Shaftesbury was always hostile to the notion (developed by Hutcheson) that aesthetic appreciation could be detached from an idea of the good, and in this respect, beauty could be associated with the useful. See, for instance, *Miscellaneous Reflections*, Miscellany III, Cap. II, in *Characteristicks*, vol. III, pp. 180–1. "Thus beauty and truth are plainly joined with the notion of utility and convenience." As Vernier has observed, Diderot's critique is in fact directed against one of his own notes to his translation of Shaftesbury's *Essay*. For Shaftesbury's notion of "disinterestedness" and its influence on aesthetic theory until Kant, see Paul Guyer, *Kant and the Experience of Freedom. Essays on Aesthetics and Morality* (Cambridge University Press, 1993), pp. 50–60.

26 "Mais entre les qualités communes à tous les êtres que nous appelons, *beaux*, laquelle choisirons-nous pour la chose dont le terme *beau* est le signe? Laquelle? Il est évident, ce me semble, que ce ne peut être que celle dont la présence les rend tous *beaux*; dont la fréquence ou la rareté, si elle est susceptible de fréquence et de rareté, les rend plus ou moins *beaux*; dont l'absence les fait cesser d'être *beaux*; qui ne peut changer de nature, sans faire changer le *beau* d'espèce, et dont la qualité contraire rendrait les plus *beaux* désagréables et laids; celle en un mot par qui la *beauté* commence, augmente, varie à l'infini, décline et disparait. Or, il n'y a que la notion de *rapports* capable de ces effets" (*Recherches philosophiques*, in *Œuvres esthétiques*, p. 418).

27 Ibid., pp. 420–2. Unsurprisingly perhaps Diderot makes very little use of painting in his attempt to explain the use of *rapports*, although most of his examples of the operation of "Taste" in his other writings are pictorial.

28 Cf. Diderot's observations on mathematics in this respect, *Mémoires de mathématiques*, in *Œuvres complètes*, vol. IX, pp. 104–5.

29 *Recherches philosophiques*, in *Œuvres esthétiques*, pp. 422–4.

30 "Le goût de l'ordre en général nous domine dès la plus tendre enfance; il est plus ancien dans notre âme . . . qu'aucun sentiment réfléchi; et c'est ainsi qu'elle m'opposait à moi-même; il agit en nous, sans que nous nous en apercevions; c'est le germe de l'honnêteté et du bon goût; il nous porte au bien tant qu'il n'est point gêné par la passion; il nous suit jusque dans nos écarts; alors il dispose les moyens de la manière la plus avantageuse pour le mal" (*Entretiens sur le fils naturel*, in *Œuvres esthétiques*, p. 128). The speaker is Dorval, but it is clear that "Moi" agrees with this sentiment.

31 "Un tableu bien composé est un tout refermé sous un seul point de vûe, où les parties concourent à un même but, et forment par leur correspondence mutuelle, un ensemble aussi réel, que celui des membres dans un corps animal" (*Encyclopédie ou dictionnaire raisonée des sciences, arts et métiers* [Neufchatel, 1765], vol. III, p. 772a, and see in Jacques Chouillet, *La Formation des idées esthétiques de Diderot, 1745–1763* [Paris: Armand Colin, 1973], p. 376).

32 *Entretiens sur le fils naturel*, in *Œuvres esthétiques*, p. 160

33 *An Inquiry Concerning Virtue, or Merit*, Book I, Part III, Section I, Treatise IV of *Characteristicks*, vol. II, p. 42.

34 "Ou l'on considere les rapports dans les moeurs," he wrote, "et l'on a le *beau moral*; ou on les considère dans les ouvrages de littérature, et l'on a le *beau littéraire*; ou on les considère dans les pièces de musique, et l'on a le *beau musical*" *Recherches philosophiques*, in *Œuvres esthétiques*, p. 420).

35 "Pour juger ici de quel côté est le bon goût il faut bien déterminer de quel côté sont les bonnes mœurs . . . [The young libertine who found] un petit nez retroussé, des lèvres riantes, un œil éveillé, une démarche déliberée [to be charming was expressing a preference for the moral worthlessness] . . . Son goût, se reduit à ceci: j'aime le vice; et le mien à ceci: j'aime la vertu. Il en est ainsi de presque tous les jugements; ils se résolvent en dernier à l'un ou à l'autre de ces mots" (Letter of September 2, 1762, in *Œuvres complètes*, vol. XIX, p. 20).

36 "Si le système moral est corrompu il faut que le goût soit faux" (*De la poésie dramatique*, in *Œuvres esthétiques*, p. 281). Cf. Roland Mortier, *Diderot and the "Grand Gout." The Prestige of History Painting in the Eighteenth Century* (Oxford: Clarendon, 1982), pp. 4–5. "Truth, poetry and morality: these three concepts cannot be separated without producing an incomplete work of art."

37 "[L]e premier qui se soit avisé, parmi nous, de donner des mœurs à l'art" (*Salon de 1765*, in *Salons*, vol. II, p. 144).

38 "Le dégredation du goût, de la couleur, de la composition, des caractères, de l'expression, du dessin, a suivi pas à pas la deprévation des mœurs" (Ibid., p. 75).

39 "[L]es progrès de la lumiere sont limités" (Diderot to Sophie Volland, October 30, 1759, *Correspondence de Denis Diderot*, ed. Georges Roth, 16 vols. [Paris: Editions de Minuit, 1955–70], vol. II, p. 299).

40 Francesco Antonio Grimaldi, *Riflessioni sopra l'inegualianza tra gli uomini* (1779–80), in *Illuministi Italiane*, ed Franco Venturi (Milan and Naples: Riccardo Riccardi), vol. V, p. 562, and see Anthony Pagden, "The 'Defence of Civilization' in Eighteenth-Century Social Theory," *History of the Human Sciences* 1 (1988), pp. 33–45.

41 "L'expansion de l'activité civilisée est constamment doublée par ses risques d'échec: et ce qui lui fait obstacle n'est pas seulement ce qui demeure indomptable dans la nature, mais la puissance de destruction que la civilization porte en elle même" (Jean Starobinski, *Diderot dans l'espace des peintres suivi de Le Sacrifice en rêve* [Paris: Réunion des musées nationaux, 1991], pp. 58–9).

42 *Réfutation suivie de l'ouvrage d'Helvétius intitulé L'Homme*, in *Œuvres complètes*, vol. II, p. 287.

43 "Oui Mr. Rousseau, j'aime mieux le vice raffiné sous un habit de soie, que la stupidité féroce sous une peau de bête" (Ibid., p. 411).

44 Ibid., p. 432.

45 "Nous suivons le pur instinct de la nature: et tu as tenté d'effacer de nos âmes son caractère" (*Œuvres philosophiques*, p. 466).

46 "[N]os premières appréhensions et à nos sensations grossières et les plus machinales . . . incapables de former cette association des idées qui seule peut produire la réflexion, dans laquelle cependent consiste l'essence de la pensée" (*Encyclopédie*, vol. I, p. 469a). And see the observations of Girolamo Imbruglia, "From Utopia to Republicanism: The Case of Diderot," in *The Invention of the Modern Republic*, ed. Biancamaria Fontana (Cambridge University Press, 1994), pp. 78–9.

47 "Le modèle ideal de la beauté, ligne vrai qui se corrompt, qui se perd et qui ne se retrouveroit peut-être parfaitment chez un peuple qui par le retour à l'état de Barbarie; car c'est le seul condition où les hommes convaincus de leur ignorance puissent se résoudre à la lenteur du tâtonnement; les autres restent médiocres précisement parce qu'ils naissent pour ainsi dire, sçavants" ("Addresse à mon ami Mr. Grimm," *Salon de 1767*, in *Salons*, vol. III, p. 61). For Diderot, "*médiocre*" implied rational and informed judgment, the opposite of child- or savage-like innocence on the one hand, and religious enthusiasm on the other.

48 "Le destin qui règle le monde veut que tout passe. La condition la plus hereuse d'un homme, d'un état a son terme" (Ibid., p. 125).

49 "[I]l se jouit encore aux objets un cortège d'idées accessoires et morales de l'énergie de la nature humaine, et de la puissance des peuples" (Ibid., vol. II, p. 118).

50 Cf. Starobinski, *Diderot dans l'espace des peintres*, p. 56. "La contemplation philosphique par excellence . . . est celle de la genèse, de la destruction, de la métamorphose des mondes."

51 "Réformer la nature sur l'antique, c'est suivre la route inverse des Anciens qui n'en avoient point; c'est toujours travailler d'après une copie" (*Salon de 1767*, in *Salons*, vol. III, pp. 61–2).

52 As the character B says to A at the end of the *Supplément au voyage de Bougainville*, "Imitons le bon aumônier, moine en France, sauvage dans Taiti." To which A replies, "Prendre le froc du pays où on l'on va, et garder celui du pays où l'on est" (*Œuvres philosophiques*, p. 515).

53 On this point see Yvon Bélaval, *L'Esthetique sans paradoxe de Diderot* (Paris: Gallimard, 1950), p. 148.

54 See Renata Mecchia, *Le Teorie linguistiche e l'estetica di Diderot* (Rome: Caracci editore, 1980), pp. 31–3, and Isa Dardano Basso, *La Ricerca del segno. Diderot e i problemi del linguaggio* (Rome: Bulzoni editore, 1984), pp. 62–5.

55 "La parole doit peindre la pensée et en être l'image. Mais la pensée est indivissible et ne peut par conséquent être pas elle-même l'objet immédiat d'aucune image: il faut nécessairement recourir à l'abstraction" (*Encyclopédie*, vol. VIII, p. 854a). Cf. "Il est donc évident que dans toutes les langues la parole ne transmet la pensée qu'autant qu'elle peint fidellement la succession analytique des idées qui en sont l'objet, et que l'abstraction y considère séparément." The discussion of the inversion of the supposedly natural order of language was also the subject of the *Lettre sur les sourds et les muets*. See Chouillet, *Formation des idées esthétiques*, pp. 151–257.

56 "L'art de decomposer nos pensées n'est qu'art de rendre successives les idées et les opérations qui sont simultanées." *Cours d'études pour l'instruction du Prince du Parme*, vol. II, *Grammaire*, in *Œuvres philosophiques de Condillac*, ed. Georges le Roy, 3 vols. (Paris: Presses universitaires de France, 1947), vol. I, p. 436a–b, and see Hans Aarsleff, *From Locke to Saussure. Essays on the Study of Language and Intellectual History* (London: Athlone, 1982), pp. 16–35. The claim, that the formation of language proceeded by the "decomposition" of an initial whole, and the subsequent reconstruction of a fully logical language from the components of the original speech-act, is a transposition to the linguistic domain of the resolutive–compositive method employed in Galilean physics.

57 "Alors nous pouvons observer ce que nous faisons en pensant, nous pouvons nous en rendre compte; nous pouvons par conséquent apprendre à conduire notre réflexion. Penser devient donc un art, et cet art est l'art de parler" (*Cours d'études*, vol. I, *Discours préliminaire*, in *Œuvres philosophiques*, vol. I, p. 403b).

58 "Notre âme est un tableau mouvant d'après lequel nous peignons sans cesse: nous employons bien du temps à le rendre avec fidelité: mais il existe en entier, et tout à la fois: l'esprit ne vas pas à pas comptés comme l'expression. La pinceau n'exécute qu'à la longue, ce que l'œil du peintre embrasse tout d'un coup. La formation des langues exigeait la décomposition; mais *voir* un objet, le *juger* beau, *éprouver* une sensation agréable, *désirer* la possession, c'est l'état de l'âme dans un même instant" (*Œuvres complètes*, vol. I, p. 369).

59 "Un sauvage dont la langue n'est point encore formée porroit confondre et exprîmer tout à la fois le prénom, le verbe, le nombre, le susbstantif et

108

l'adjectif, et dire dans un seul mot: *J'ai tué un gros ours*" ("Dissertation sur les différents moyens dont les hommes se sont servis pour exprimer leurs idées," in *Œuvres de Mr. de Maupertuis*, nouvelle édition corrigée et augmentée, 3 vols. [Lyons, 1756], vol. III, p. 444). Cf. Rousseau's observation that the earliest languages, "donnèrent d'abord à chaque mot le sens d'un proposition entière" (*Discours sur l'origine de l'inégalité*, in *Oeuvres complètes*, 4 vols. [Paris: Bibliothèque de la Pléiade, Gallimard, 1959–64], vol. III, p. 149).

60 Latin and Greek "rendent par un seul mot . . . l'état de l'âme . . . ce mot prononcé, tout est dit tout est entendu" (*Lettre sur les sourds et les muets*, in *Œuvres complètes*, vol. I, p. 369, and cf. p. 351, "Les Anciens, qui généralisaient moins, et qui étudiaient plus la nature en détail et par individus, avaient dans leur langue une marche moins monotone").

61 "Tant que ces [deux] causes agissent contradictoirement, la nation est insensée. Elle ne commence à prendre l'esprit qui lui convient, qu'au moment où ses principes spéculatifs conspirent avec sa position physique. C'est alors qu'elle s'avance à grands pas vers la splendeur, l'opulence et le bonheur qu'elle peut se promettre du libre usage de ses ressources locales" (*Histoire*, vol. V, pp. 1–2).

62 On Herder and his reading of the *Histoire*, see Pagden, *European Encounters*, pp. 172–81.

63 "Le moral ne change point le physique, mais il le contraint, et cette contrainte finit par lui ôter toute sa énergie primitive et naturelle" (*Réfutation suivie d'ouvrage de Helvétius intitulé L'Homme*, in *Œuvres completes*, vol. II, p. 379).

64 *Histoire*, vol. I, p. 41.

65 "[L]e premier instinct, le premier nœud de la société, sans lequel tous les autres liens factices n'ont point de ressors ni de durée" (Ibid., vol. VIII, pp. 210–11).

66 See Donald Kelley, *The Human Measure. Social Thought in the Western Legal Tradition* (Cambridge, Mass. and London: Harvard University Press, 1990), p. 9.

67 *Miscellaneous Reflections*, Miscellany III, Cap. I, in *Characteristicks*, vol. III, p. 151.

68 Ibid., pp. 143–6. On Diderot's relationship to Shaftesbury, see the now classic account by Franco Venturi, *Jeunesse de Diderot (1713–1753)*, trans. Juliette Bertrand (Paris: Albert Skira, 1939), pp. 64–6.

69 "Les métropoles des empires sont les foyers de l'esprit national, c'est à dire, les endroits où il se montre avec le plus d'énergie dans le discours" (*Histoire*, vol. V, p. 2).

70 "[M]étier actif, pénible, errant et dissipé de voyageur" (*Œuvres philosophiques*, p. 456).

71 "[P]orté dans l'océan sans bornes des fantaisies d'où l'on ne se tire plus" (Ibid., p. 504).

72 On this see Pagden, *European Encounters with the New World*, pp. 157–8.

73 He who travels constantly "ressemble au possesseur d'une habitation immense qui, au lieu de s'asseoir à côté de sa femme, au milieu de ces enfans, employeroit toute sa vie à visiter ses appartemens. [He carries] la tyrannie, le crime, l'ambition, la misère, la curiosité, je ne sais quelle inquiétude d'esprit, le désir de connoître et de voir, l'ennui, le dégoût d'un bonheur usé, ont expatrié et expatrieront les hommes dans tous le temps" (*Histoire*, vol. V, p. 16). On the presence of "curiosité" on this list, cf. *Pensées philosophiques*, in *Œuvres philosophiques*, p. 26: "L'ignorance et l'*incuriosité* sont deux oreillers fort doux; mais pour les trouver tels, il faut avoir *la tête aussi bien faite* que Montaigne." This is a reference to *Essais*, III, 3, but echoes a phrase from Pascal's *Entretien avec Monsieur de Saci*: "L'ignorance et l'incuriosité son deux oreillers pour une tête bien faite."

74 "[U]ne machine ou il y avait toujours à refaire" (*Réfutation suivie d'ouvrage de Helvétius intitulé L'Homme*, in *Œuvres complètes*, vol. II, p. 431).

75 "Je n'en excepte que quelques circonstances rares. A mesure que la distance de la capitale s'accroît, ce masque se détache. Il tombe sur la frontière. D'un hémisphere à l'autre que devient-il? Rien. Passé l'équateur, l'homme n'est ni Anglois, ni Hollandois, ni François, ni Espagnol, ni Portugais. Il ne conserve de sa patrie que les principes et les préjugés qui autorisent ou excusent sa conduite" (*Histoire*, vol. V, p. 3).

76 "Les expéditions de long cours [have thus] enfanté une nouvelle éspèce de sauvages nomades. Je veut parler de ces hommes qui parcourent tant de contrées qu'ils finissent par n'appartenir à aucune; ... de ces amphibiés qui vivant à la surface des eaux ... qui n'ont vraiment ni pères, ni mères, ni enfans, ni frères, ni parens, ni amis, ni concitoyens; en qui les liens les plus doux et les plus sacrés sont éteints" (Ibid., vol. X, p. 297).

77 Ibid., vol. V, p. 5.

78 "[U]n tigre domestique qui rentre dans le forêt" (Ibid., vol. V, p. 2). Cf. Voltaire's description of pirates – another group who, because of their nomadism, travel down the chain of civility – as "des tigres qui auraient un peu de raison" (*Essai sur les mœurs et l'esprit des nations*, ed. René Pomeau, 2 vols. [Paris: Garnier, 1963], vol. II, p. 376).

79 *Discours preliminaire* to the *Essai sur le mérite et la vertu*, in *Œuvres complètes*, vol. I, p. 9.

80 "Je suis maintenant bien loin du sanctuaire des sciences et des lettres que mes idées et mon style n'ont que trop pris l'empreinte de la vie errante et sauvage que je mène depuis douze ans" (Louis Antoine Bougainville, *Voyage autour du monde par la frégate du roi La Boudeuse et la flûte L'Etoile en 1766, 1767, 1768 et 1769*, 2 vols. [Paris, 1772], vol. I, pp. xxxviii–xxxix); see also Jay Caplan, *Framed Narratives. Diderot's Genealogy of the Beholder* (Manchester University Press, 1986, pp. 79–80).

81 "Rien de plus bizarre que de voir l'Europe transportée et reproduite,

pour ainsi dire, en Amérique, par le nom et la forme de nos villes; par les loix, les mœurs et la réligion de notre continent" (*Histoire*, vol. V, p. 5).

82 "L'art de lever un pan de voile et de montrer aux hommes un coin ignoré ou plutôt oublié du monde qu'ils habitent. L'inspiré est lui-même incertain quelquefois si la chose qu'il annonce est une realité ou une chimère, si elle exista jamais hors de lui; il est alors sur la dernière limite de l'énergie de la nature de l'homme et a l'extrémité des ressources de l'art" (*Salon de 1767*, in *Salons*, vol. III, p. 213).

83 *Histoire*, vol. V, p. 140.

84 "[U]ne nature toute nouvelle rest muette sous les regards de l'Espagnol" (Ibid., vol. V, p. 22).

85 Ibid., vol. V, pp. 44–5.

86 "[A]u fond de leurs cœurs le germe fatal d'une dépradation qui dût se developper avec une célérité à une fureur inconcevable, lorsque sous une autre ciel, loin de toute vindicité publique et des regards imposans de leurs concitoyens, ni la pudeur, ni le crainte n'en arrêtèrent par les effets" (Ibid., vol. V, p. 138).

87 "Environ deux siècles après la dépopulation de l'Europe en Asie [came the migration into America, and] cette révolution substitua le chaors au néant et mela parmi nous les vices et les productions de tous les climats" (Ibid., vol. X, p. 287).

88 "La différence des cultes et des nations, a familiarisé les esprits les plus grossiers avec une sorte d'indifférence pour l'object qui avait le plus frappé leur imagination" (Ibid., vol. X, pp. 10–11).

89 *Réfutation suivie d'ouvrage de Helvétius intitulé L'Homme*, in *Œuvres complètes*, vol. II, pp. 379–40. See Philippe Lacoue-Labarthe, "Diderot, le paradox et la mimesis," *Poétique, revue de théorie et d'analyse littéraires* 43 (1980), 267–81.

90 "La variété, la multiplicité des objets que l'industrie a présentés à l'esprit et aux sens, a partagé les affections de l'homme et affoibli l'énergie de tous les sentimens" (*Histoire*, vol. X, p. 11); and cf. Albert Hirschman, "Industrialization and its Manifold Discontents: West, East and South," *World Development* 20 (1992), 1225–32.

5

The aesthetics of nationalism and the limits of culture

DAVID CARROLL

> The ethics, politics, and philosophies of community . . . pursued their paths
> . . . without suspecting that an experience reputed to be "literary" or
> "aesthetic" was caught *in* the ordeal of community and was struggling with
> it.   Jean-Luc Nancy, *La Communauté désœuvrée*

> Racist theories necessarily contain an aspect of sublimation, an idealization
> of the species, the privileged figure of which is aesthetic . . . The aesthetici-
> zation of social relations is a crucial contribution of racism to the constitu-
> tion of the projective field of politics.
>   Etienne Balibar, "Racism and Nationalism"

> We "know" that the Other is in us . . . Rimbaud's "Je est un autre" is
> historically literal.   Edouard Glissant, *Poétique de la Relation*

Nationalism has never been an exclusively political question, for in theorizing the interests of the nation, in justifying actions taken in the name of national interests, in identifying with and supporting the collective entity called the nation, more has always been at stake for the people constituting what nineteenth-century theorists such as Ernest Renan called the *spiritual principle* of the nation than specific political gains or narrow economic self-interests.[1] The latter may constitute desired effects of nationalism, but the primary interests of the hypothesized collective self of the nation are always claimed to be more fundamental than politics or economics: they have to do rather with the cultural identity of the people, its sense or image of itself, its very being.

Recent political theorists have begun to focus more and more on the mechanisms and techniques, if not technologies of production, of collective identity in nationalism, rather than on its strictly historical–political manifestations. In doing so they also have tended to emphasize the cultural rather than strictly political nature of nationalism, its imaginary rather than material roots and effects. Their analyses and critiques of nationalism have provided new and important insights into what could be called the development of a critical analysis of the nationalist political imagination. At the same time, however, they have often been limited by their reluctance if not refusal to take seriously or pursue in more than a perfunctory way the problem of the aesthetic dimension of the cultural and political self-fashioning of a people or nation. In some cases this has meant that even the most critical of the analyses have left intact and even reaffirmed the specific aesthetic basis and biases of the extreme forms of nationalism being criticized. In fact, critical approaches to nationalism always risk reaffirming what they intend to criticize if they do not question and undermine the aesthetic principles and identificatory strategies inherent in the production of a collective sense of self and the making or fashioning of a people.

In a recent work on nationalism, anti-Semitism, and fascism in France, the French historian Michel Winock insists on the important role played by poets and historians after the French Revolution and throughout the nineteenth century in providing the imaginary content and mythological foundation for the principle of the French nation: "Poets and historians, of whom Michelet was undoubtedly the most influential, throughout the nineteenth century enriched the principle of the French nation with an affective content, transfigured its history into a destiny, and provided the patriotic cult [of the nation] with a mythology: that of a chosen people."[2]

Republican and antirepublican forms of nationalism may differ over which form the French people has been destined to take and what the determining historical events and cultural typologies are. They may disagree over what the people is determined to be and what it has been chosen to do. But they do agree on the basic fact that a particular form of the people, the people as a form or type, has been chosen, that its history is its destiny, that the myth of an indigenous unified people is the people. And it is poets and historians, historian-poets or poet-historians – rather than philosophers or political theorists, assuming one can always distinguish between them – who seem to have played the most important role in the elaboration of this fundamental nationalist principle and the production and enrichment of the myth.

In discussing the role played by the influential novelist and militant anti-Dreyfusard, Maurice Barrès, in the ultranationalist Ligue de la Patrie Française, Winock claims that because Barrès "did not have a systematic mind," his greatest contribution to nationalism was to supply it with an "art poétique" (*Nationalisme*, 20). The role of art is thus to fill in for the absence of philosophical rigor and in this way to root politics in aesthetics, to make it possible for a collectivity to be identified and act as a people even when the political grounds of the nation are not firmly established. My general concern in this chapter is not with the particular nature of the "*art poétique*" supplied by Barrès or any other nationalist "poet," but rather with the formative role of the aesthetic in general in the formation of nationalism. For the question of aesthetics has to be addressed directly if we are to evaluate critically both the positive and negative effects, the affective force and repressive consequences, of both moderate and extreme forms of nationalism.

Because of the strongly affective side of nationalism – setting aside the question of whether it is true or not that the number of theoretical texts written by nationalists with "systematic minds" is quite limited if not nonexistent – Winock is certainly not wrong to evoke the importance of the poetic and mythological side of nationalism, the crucial role played by art and literature in the creation of a French nationalist mythology. In fact, the different "*arts poétiques*" supplied by republican nationalists such as Michelet, on the one hand, and antirepublican nationalists such as Barrès, on the other, are not just incidental, superficial surface phenomena which have importance only because nationalist ideologues failed to give to their ideas a rigorous, systematic, philosophical coherence. On the contrary, the aesthetic dimension of nationalism could be argued to be essential to its conceptualization and implementation, the poetics of nationalism serving as the foundation for its highly coherent and often dogmatic politics, its aesthetics not just illustrative of nationalist themes or providing emotive examples when analytical argumentation was lacking, but rather the very basis of the "systematic logic" of nationalism.

In any case, there seems to exist a general agreement among contemporary political theorists of nationalism that there exists no sophisticated, coherent theory of nationalism, that nationalist thinkers, such as they are, are either very weak, inconsistent, or simply irrelevant. Benedict Anderson has called this the paradox of "the 'political' power of nationalisms vs. their philosophical poverty."[3] Ernest Gellner claims that even though ideas and belief systems, even bad ones, do count in some areas, when it comes to nationalism they do not.

> Nationalism, notwithstanding its indisputable importance, has received relatively little attention from academic political philosophers; there was not enough in the way of good doctrines and texts . . . for them to get their teeth into . . . [Nationalist] thinkers did not really make much difference . . . Their precise doctrines are hardly worth analyzing . . . Local circumstances . . . deserve study, but I doubt whether the nuances of nationalist *doctrine* played much part in modifying those circumstances.[4]

Another important analyst of nationalism, E. J. Hobsbawm, in much the same vein, argues that "the mystical identification of nationality with a sort of platonic idea of the language . . . is much more characteristic of the ideological construction of nationalist intellectuals . . . than of the actual grassroots users of the idiom. It is a literary and not an existential concept."[5] And to say that a concept is literary for Hobsbawm means that it should not be taken very seriously by the political theorist.

Though rich, then, in imaginary constructs, literary concepts, and identificatory strategies, a consensus exists among these theorists that nationalism receives poor grades in philosophical consistency and theoretical sophistication. This means for Gellner, Hobsbawm, and Anderson that the origin and roots of nationalism must be looked for "outside" the realm of "ideas" and in history and the changing social conditions of modernity, in what Hobsbawm calls an "existential concept" that has nothing to do with so-called literary concepts, assuming thus that there is a way of conclusively distinguishing between what is lived and what is only imagined, of determining where experience ends and art and literature – and the political imagination – begin.

The trivializing of aesthetics, and the lack of attention given to the "literary concepts" it encourages, are all the more surprising given that Gellner, Hobsbawm, and Anderson all stress the cultural rather than strictly economic or political basis for nationalism – at least up to a point. It all depends on what one means by culture. Gellner, for example, gives the following "makeshift, temporary definitions" of the idea of the nation:

> (1) Two men are of the same nation if and only if they share the same culture, where culture in turn means a system of ideas and signs and associations and ways of behaving and communicating.
> (2) Two men are of the same nation if and only if they *recognize* each other as belonging to the same nations. In other words, *nations maketh man*;

115

nations are the artifacts of men's convictions and loyalties and solidarities
. . . It is their recognition of each other as fellows of this kind which turns [a
category of persons defined linguistically or territorially] into a nation.

(Nations and Nationalism, 7)

Gellner points out the inadequacies of each definition in itself and
the special difficulty of defining culture, which he allows is equal to
that of defining the nation. He nevertheless makes an investigation of
what culture "does" and how "self-recognition" works his starting
points.

Paradoxically, Gellner is invoking in each case the very aesthetic
concepts, ideas, and logic at the basis of the "nuances of nationalist
doctrine" that he has claimed have not made any difference. For if
there are two themes common to the different nationalist theories
proposed by philosophers and literary ideologues, they are the
formative role of culture in the making of a people and the role of
mutual recognition and the will to unity in the construction and
defense of the nation. It is precisely the aesthetic dimensions of such
questions that in fact are crucial for an understanding of nationalism
and how it imagines and fashions a people.

If one is even provisionally and partially going to define nationalism in terms of culture, it seems legitimate to ask how one goes
about determining what culture is in the first place, what it means to
share the same culture, and how exactly culture founds the nation.
What are its origins and roots, its form, its way of including those
who make up the nation and excluding those "foreigners" who do
not and cannot be incorporated into the nation? When his own
analysis leads him to such questions, Gellner in each case skirts
them or begs them, admitting culture is "an elusive concept [that]
was deliberately left undefined" (43). Gellner does insist, however,
that nations are never the natural phenomenon nationalisms all
claim they are, and that the "Sleeping Beauty" theory of the rebirth
of the nation (and the national culture) constitutes a myth in which
the national entity exists as "an old, latent, dormant force" (48)
before its reawakening in modernity. He further claims that the
national culture is primarily an invention of nationalism, not its
origin: "Nationalism, which sometimes takes pre-existing cultures
and turns them into nations, sometimes invents them, and often
obliterates pre-existing cultures: *that* is a reality" (49).

The nation is thus always a formation, the product of a fashioning
process which is as destructive of existing cultures as it is productive
of modern culture. The cultures being defended or revived by

116

nationalism are never authentic, actual cultures. They are "often its own inventions, or are modified out of all recognition" (56). In this sense nationalism makes the nation, not the other way around, and it makes or fashions the people in terms of imaginary cultural constructs rather than letting the form taken by the people emerge "naturally" out of preexisting culture. One form of culture is thus being opposed to another; one form of "natural" aesthetic fashioning is being opposed to an "unnatural," artificial form.

Gellner thus ascribes to nationalism "a pervasive false consciousness. Its myths invert reality" (124) – that is, they distort and invert the preexisting "genuine communities" by imposing high cultural mechanisms and homogeneity on what Gellner considers the true diversity of folk or popular cultures. "High culture" is the weapon nationalism uses to control and mold the people in whose name it pretends to speak, to remold them artificially, rather than let them mold themselves naturally and genuinely. His scorn for and refusal to take seriously the "literary propagandists" of nationalism result from his displeasure at "school-transmitted culture," at "high culture" in general, as opposed to genuine "folk-transmitted culture" (36). Thus, in the name of a critique of nationalism he uses the weapons of nationalism against it, praising the authentic cultural roots of the lost community and attacking the false consciousness of the artificial, nonpopular, school and media-engendered and transmitted culture, its homogenizing language and its style (127). The "literary" or "aesthetic" dimensions of his own conception of culture and nationalism remain uninvestigated; the common roots his own defense of genuine culture and his criticism of high culture share with the "literary propagandists" he attacks and dismisses indicate an important limitation of his critique.

Like Gellner, Hobsbawm also insists on the difficulty of defining what a nation is and distinguishing a priori the nation from other entities. He argues that agnosticism is the best stance to have in treating the question of the nation, to start out believing no one, to take no definition or theory of the nation as more than an assertion, a belief, a justification of self. He insists rightly on the continually changing nature of these beliefs and justifications in history, and does not "regard the nation as a primary nor as an unchanging social entity" (*Nations and Nationalism*, 9) but rather a product of a particular historical period and a particular design. He too thus stresses the fabricated, artificial characteristics of the nation, with nationalism itself in the place of the artist or artisan: "With Gellner I would stress the element of artifact, invention and social engineering which enters into the making of nations . . . In short, for the purpose of analysis nationalism comes before nations. Nations do not make states and nationalisms but the other way round" (10).

This means that all of the "natural" bases for nationalism can be shown to be in fact artificial cultural constructs, images and figures of homogeneity, mechanisms to produce collective identification. For example, Hobsbawm argues that all national languages, rather than constituting the natural basis for nationalism, are in fact expressions and products of it.

> National languages are therefore almost always semi-artificial constructs and occasionally, like modern Hebrew, virtually invented. They are the opposite of what nationalist mythology supposes them to be, namely the primordial foundations of national culture and the matrices of the national mind. They are usually attempts to devise a standardized idiom out of a multiplicity of actually spoken idioms. (54)

Hobsbawm is of course right to attack the reactionary, mystified defense of the national language, what he calls "philological nationalism, i.e. the insistence on the linguistic purity of the national vocabulary," as a "rearguard action," for the absurdity (and danger) of the naturalization of historical and cultural products in the name of the nation is nowhere more evident than in attempts at linguistic and cultural purifications.[6]

Like Gellner, however, Hobsbawm situates nationalism in the period *after* the fall or destruction of authentic communities and cultures and considers the artificial, imaginary construction of the nation to be a replacement for the real community: "[The nation] can be made to fill the emotional void left by the retreat or disintegration, or the unavailability of *real* human communities and networks, but the question still remains why, having lost real communities, people should wish to imagine this particular type of replacement" (46). He in fact drastically limits the critical impact of his approach by not investigating the imaginary, aesthetic bases of the "real communities" whose disappearance allegedly created the possibility and necessity for imaginary constructs. As long as the communities of the prenationalist era are seen as authentic or real, as opposed to the artificiality of the national community, the ultimate basis for nationalism remains untouched by the critique of nationalism, for the model of an authentic ethnic, linguistic, geographic, or tribal community could always be evoked to support the rebirth of a people and the construction of a new, more authentic form of the nation.

Gellner's and Hobsbawm's powerful critiques of nationalism and the economic and political systems that nurture it ultimately support a form of nationalism that would be genuine and populist, not a product of a high cultural elite and the arts and media it dominates and controls but of a natural, spontaneous art of politics.

In contrast to Gellner and Hobsbawm, Benedict Anderson's *Imagined Communities* opens the way for studies that do not assume such authenticity as an alternative to the artificiality of modern nationalism. The claim that nationalism and nationness are "cultural artifacts of a particular kind" (4) leads Anderson to propose that the nation is "an imagined political community – and imagined as both inherently limited and sovereign" (6). But unlike Gellner (and Hobsbawm), Anderson, at least in principle, refuses to privilege other forms of community as original or genuine, that is, lived or directly experienced rather than imagined:

> Gellner is so anxious to show that nationalism masquerades under false pretenses that he assimilates "invention" to "fabrication" and "falsity," rather than to "imagining" and "creation." In this way he implies that "true" communities exist which can be advantageously juxtaposed to nations. In fact, all communities larger than primordial villages of face-to-face contact (and perhaps even these) are imagined. Communities are to be distinguished, not by their falsity/genuineness, but by the style in which they are imagined. (6)

The "perhaps" should not in fact be included in the phrase in parentheses, for according to the logic of "the imagined community," even the "primordial villages of face-to-face contact" must imagine their community, for community is never present in itself, even in the most immediate forms of contact. The supplementary, "artificial," imaginary process of fabrication must be seen as an integral component of all forms of community, a determining element in even the most spontaneous, immediate, genuine forms of "face-to-face" contact.

Anderson's main purpose in treating nationalism "in an anthropological spirit" as a cultural construct belonging with " 'kinship' and 'religion' " is to distinguish it from political categories such as " 'liberalism' or 'fascism' " and to stress that it is not "an ideology" (5). "What I am proposing is that nationalism has to be understood by aligning it, not with self-consciously held political ideologies, but with the large cultural systems that preceded it, out of which – as well as against which – it came into being. For the present purposes, the two relevant cultural systems are the *religious community* and the *dynastic regime*" (12). Anderson never spells out the exact differences between his notions of cultural systems, on the one hand, and ideologies, on the other, but given the examples he gives of the cultural systems that preceded nationalism and that in some sense he claims it was modeled after, there seems to be a great deal of overlapping between the two categories. For clearly what he calls cultural systems have decided ideological effects and some of the "self-consciously held political ideologies" to which he refers are rooted in cultural systems and have a specific cultural politics as one of their expressions.

Perhaps the crucial difference, then, is between what is con-sciously held – an explicit belief in liberalism or fascism and the decision to act according to that belief – and what is first uncon-sciously experienced in daily life and in social interactions with others before being affirmed as a belief or an identity. But here too the boundaries break down very quickly, and what is "originally" unconscious or what remains unconscious in self-conscious beliefs is far from determined or determinable. It would seem to me that to approach nationalism as a cultural system necessarily implies that ideology itself has an important cultural and "aesthetic" component and that cultural systems always have significant ideological effects. It is possible to draw this conclusion from Anderson's approach to nationalism in spite of his conscious efforts to affirm the contrary. Nationalism could in fact be considered a culturalist ideology, an ideology of culture which is not rooted in class distinctions *per se* but in the claim to negate and transcend them, along with all internal cultural distinctions, in order to produce the image or illusion of a unified people. At the core of the process of transcendence in the fashioning of the imagined community lies the problem of the aesthetic as a political phenomenon, of art as the model for the self-creation, manifestation, and self-recognition of a people.

But since Anderson and others treat nationalism as a specifically modern phenomenon, modern techniques of fashioning need to be identified in order to distinguish the imaginary representations of traditional religious communities and the *ancien régime* from those specific to nationalism and modern historicity. Anderson claims that the simultaneous development of the novel and the newspaper in the eighteenth century constitutes a crucial moment in the fash-ioning of a people in the form of a nation: "For these forms provided the technical means for 're-presenting' the *kind* of imagined commu-nity that is the nation" (25). They also allegedly produced in their readers, especially through the production and consumption of the daily newspaper, the feeling of being-at-one with unidentifiable others – they created the feeling of belonging to a community of readers and thus made possible an "extraordinary mass ceremony" of communal but anonymous reading, "the almost precisely simultaneous consumption ('imagining') of the newspaper-as-fiction."

Each communicant is well aware that the ceremony he performs is being replicated simultaneously by thousands (or millions) of those whose existence he is confident, yet of whose identity he has not the slightest notion. Furthermore, this ceremony is incessantly repeated at daily or half-daily intervals throughout the calendar. What more vivid figure for the secular, historically clocked, imagined community can be envisioned? . . . The newspaper reader, observing exact replicas of his own paper being consumed by his subway, barbershop, or residential neighbors, is continually reassured that the imagined world is visibly rooted in everyday life . . . Fiction seeps quietly and continuously into reality, creating the remarkable confidence of community in anonymity which is the hallmark of modern nations.   (35–6)

What interests Anderson is not what is read or how what is read is understood, but rather the repeated daily "ceremony" of reading and then disposing of the newspaper and the assurance that others have done the same, the reading of the newspaper as a secular form of a communal ritual. What is reinforced in such ceremonial consumerism is not the unity of the spiritual community in the figure of God, but the unity of the secular community in the "vivid figure" of the newspaper and its anonymous readers. The modern aesthetics of nationalism root community in anonymity, in the solitary reader identifying with other readers and somehow affirming his or her identity by the ceremonial act of reading and in this way being at one with all other readers – at least, as we shall see, with all those who read in a similar manner.

The reasons for Anderson's decision to treat nationalism as a cultural rather than ideological construct, no matter how problematical each term and the distinctions between them remain in his work, become clear in his chapter entitled "Patriotism and Racism." For in this chapter, Anderson attempts to save nationalism from its worst, xenophobic, totalitarian manifestations by linking what he considers is nationalism in its most positive cultural form – a spontaneous, patriotic love of country and willingness to give up one's life for one's country – to literature and art. In this way he opposes cultural nationalism and the genuine aesthetic products it produces to all the expressions of hate of modern, xenophobic, political nationalism, which allegedly has no aesthetic or literary expression.

> In an age when it is so common for progressive, cosmopolitan intellectuals (particularly in Europe?) to insist on the near-pathological character of nationalism, its roots in fears and hatred of the Other, and its affinities with racism, it is useful to remind ourselves that nations inspire love, and often profoundly self-sacrificing love. The cultural products of nationalism – poetry, prose fiction, music, plastic arts – show this love very clearly in thousands of different forms and styles. On the other hand, how truly rare it is to find analogous products expressing fear and loathing.   (141–2)

Culture is love of self but with malice toward none; ideology, as its opposite, would therefore be the defensive, at times paranoid elevation and defense of self and the hatred and repression of the Other.

Literature and art are presented as the "cultural products of nationalism" because they are assumed to be the natural expressions of the love and generosity of a people. This assumption is one of the most serious problems with Anderson's approach to nationalism. Another problem has to do with the way the vocabulary of culture is also treated in an unambiguous way as expressing natural phenomena, even the most ideologically loaded terms such as

> kinship (motherland, *Vaterland*, *patria*) or that of home (*Heimat* or *tanah air* [earth and water, the phrase for the Indonesians' native archipelago]). Both idioms denote something to which one is naturally tied . . . In everything "natural" there is always something unchosen . . . – skin colour, gender, parentage and birth-era – all those things one cannot help. And in these "natural" ties one senses what one might call "the beauty of *Gemeinschaft*."   (143)

According to Anderson, the very words, concepts, and feelings, which in an extremist political context would have to be considered ugly, hateful, and even racist, retain their natural innocence and "beauty" within the boundaries delimited by culture. The problem, I would suggest, is how to delineate such boundaries.

The beauty of natural sociability (of nationalism) is thus opposed to the unnatural asociability of racism, sexism, and all forms of colonialism and postcolonialism. And the difference between them lies entirely in the alleged disinterestedness of the cultural realm and thus its beauty – as opposed to the interests of politics: "Precisely because such ties are not chosen, they have about them a halo of disinterestedness" (143). Like the literature and art that are its expressions, cultural nationalism is virtually incapable of self-interest or the fear and hatred of others. The break between culture and ideology, disinterested art and the interests of politics, love and hate, beauty and ugliness, is, for Anderson, absolute. This is why he treats literature, art, and music as all being hymns of and to the nation, as national anthems or prayers, pure expressions of the nation which produce the feeling of belonging and being at one with others. "The Marseillaise, Waltzing Matilda, and Indonesia Raya provide occasions for unisonality, for the echoed physical realization of the imagined community. (So does listening to [and maybe silently chiming in with] the recitation of ceremonial poetry, such as sections of the Book of Common Prayer). How selfless this unisonance feels!" (145). Insomuch as he treats art and literature exclusively as occasions of the feeling of selflessness and unisonance, Anderson's own approach is limited by the very nationalist–aestheticist principles he criticizes when they take on a strictly political form.

When, as a further example of the community of (aesthetic) feeling, Anderson evokes what he is sure is the beauty of a poem of Charles Wolf that is "inseparable from the English language – one untranslatable, audible only to its speakers and readers" (146), it seems necessary to ask to which readers and speakers he is referring and according to what nationalist–aestheticist norms and principles beauty is being affirmed? Or when he speaks of the "eerie splendour" of phrases from a text by Thomas Browne which "can bring goose-flesh to the napes only of English-readers" (147), here too it must be asked what is at stake in such a reaction and how universal it can be claimed to be among "English-readers." Surely, if pressed, Anderson would be forced to modify this claim and concede that it could not possibly apply to all those who read English, even as their primary language or "native tongue," that something more is needed to make one respond to texts or hymns in such an emotional way than the ability to read English.

A *cultural norm* is thus being evoked to define what it is to be "English" (to be an authentic speaker or reader of English with the proper appreciation of the untranslatable beauty of the language and its poetic–patriotic expressions) and to limit access to the nationalist community of feeling, which has in fact been claimed to be open because it is allegedly based only on the ability to learn and read English. In other words, a particular notion of culture functions within Anderson's own argument as an ideological construct which establishes norms and typologies determining what it means to be a true *English* reader or speaker.

It is true, in spite of these examples, that Anderson's main point is that culture (as opposed to race) is nonexclusive, open, that anyone can eventually become part of a culture, no matter what his or her race, ethnic or social background, or national origin. "Naturalization" (and enculturation) is in principle always possible if politics does not intervene to prevent it, because, given that Anderson's general model for culture is language, languages can always be learned and "mastered," they are never the exclusive property of any one group, even if reactionary organizations such as the Académie Française have always acted as if they had the right (and the means) to control the use of French language. Language is also the ultimate basis for the feelings of unisonance and belonging to a community, not just the community of the present but the national community of the past as well. If, as he argues, "the nation was conceived in language, not in blood, [then] one could be 'invited into' the imagined community . . . Seen as both a *historical* fatality and as a community imagined through language, the nation presents itself as simultaneously open and closed" (145–6). Closed to those who were not born in the community and who do not at the moment speak the national language, the nation is in principle open to those who are "invited" into it or who meet the requirements of naturalization and eventually learn to react to collective expressions of national unity in the appropriate manner.

Even the most militant French, German, or English nationalists would agree that anyone can learn their national language and become in appearance a "native speaker," but they too would evoke a norm that would separate the authentic nationalists and "natives" from the foreign usurpers of the language, many of them not just naturalized citizens but "native sons" who are judged to be not authentically native. In fact, cultural norms associated with the practice of language always define nationalism, not the mere fact of language itself, assuming language can ever be reduced to being a mere fact. In the aesthetics of "unisonance" there is always a hierarchy of responses and a mechanism of exclusion built into the cultural norms and typologies being assumed and therefore the possibility even of a politics of cultural discrimination. Exclusion is an inherent possibility of language and culture in general.

That is one of the reasons why Anderson's separation of racism and nationalism cannot really be defended. He claims that "nationalism thinks in terms of historical destinies, while racism dreams of eternal contaminations transmitted from the origins of time through an endless sequence of loathsome copulations: outside history . . . The dreams of racism actually have their origin in ideologies of *class*, rather than those of nation: above all in claims to divinity among rulers and to 'blue' or 'white' blood and breeding among aristocracies" (149). Here too it is difficult to see the exact difference between an historical destiny determined by culture differences which have racial if not racist ramifications and the biological determination of history which has decided cultural ramifications. Though not necessarily exactly the same, cultural and biological forms of racism overlap with each other and rely on each other for support. Culturally based racisms can be even more inclusive in their definition of the inferior "race," because even those allegedly of the same "biological" race can be considered "racially" inferior if rigid norms of culture are used to distinguish between who really belongs to the nation and who does not.

By rooting racism exclusively in class differences rather than cultural distinctions, Anderson saves culture and the nationalism he equates with it – especially when it comes to the emerging nations of the Third World – and treats genuine, popular nationalism basically as an affirmative, generous, unifying force. In nationalism and "through [the native] language, encountered at mother's knee and parted with only at the grave, pasts are restored, fellowships are imagined, and futures dreamed" (154). When what is usually called nationalism is not benevolent, however, it is no longer really nationalism at all, according to the logic of Anderson's argument, but ideology, no longer a product of culture and "fond imagining" but of the hateful constructs of class and race.

Anderson thus makes a distinction between cultural or "popular" nationalism, which is "true" nationalism, and state or official nationalism, the former being benevolent, the latter, not. This is argued to be the case even or especially when nationalism is fashioned by the revolutionary leaders of the Third World who "inherit old switchboards and palaces" from the ancient dynasties, because they mobilize "popular nationalism largely after the fact and always in the language of self-defense" to accomplish their own ideological ends (161), even the massacre of their own people. If "the difference between the inventions of 'official nationalism' and those of other types is usually that between lies and myths" (161), that is, once again between ideology and authentic cultural expressions, then this means, for example, that "the policies of the Pol Pot regime can only in a very limited sense be attributed to traditional Khmer culture or to its leader's cruelty, paranoia, and megalomania . . . Far more important are the models of what revolutions have [done and], can, should, and should not do, drawn from France, the USSR, China, and Vietnam – and all the books written about them in French" (159). Ideological models are thus the perversion and at times criminal transformation and destruction of cultural practices. As in the case of Cambodia, rather than being rooted in the "truths" of myth and the authentic, indigenous imagined community, they inevitably are written in a foreign language and come from the "outside" to pervert and destroy the indigenous culture, to lie to, enslave, and even exterminate the very people they claim to be serving.

It is not just that "print-capitalism gave a new fixity to language" (44) and by doing so reduced the heterogeneity of spoken dialects and thus determined the image of a unified people and the nation, or that "*creole* communities . . . developed . . . conceptions of their nation-ness . . . *well before most of Europe*" (50). It is also that in general "print-language is what invents nationalism, not *a* particular language *per se*" (134). The general rule is that as printed language (writing) comes after spoken language, to fix it and determine (artificially) the image of the collectivity, so " 'official nationalism' – willed merger of nation and dynastic empire – . . . developed *after*, and *in reaction* to, the popular national movements proliferating in Europe since the 1820s" (86). What Anderson calls "the whole process of reactionary, secondary modelling" (87) leads to the ideological use and perversion of the popular, cultural roots of nationalism: "These nationalisms were historically 'impossible' until after the appearance of popular linguistic nationalisms, for, at bottom, they were *responses* by power-groups – primarily, but not exclusively, dynastic and aristocratic – threatened with exclusion from, or marginalization in, popular imagined communities" (109–10).

Print thus makes possible, even encourages, the abuses of power inherent in all modern nationalisms, and provides technologies – undoubtedly not confined to the print media but now provided by the media in general – to manipulate the popular, cultural roots of the nation, to transform culture into ideology. It is as if all would be well, nationalisms would remain cultural, if the popular, pre-print-capitalist roots of the nation could be rediscovered and the values associated with them revitalized, if culture could once again replace ideology, if the aesthetics of unisonance could replace the politics of power.

Such a project is of course the nationalist project in its essence. This does not mean that Anderson is wrong to point to the ideological bases of "official nationalisms" and to state that the legacies of nationalism are truly Janus-like (159), inspiring the highest form of patriotism and justifying the most atrocious crimes. It is rather that by making cultural artifacts examples of disinterestedness, love, and natural community – authentic, productive myths – he limits seriously the import of the imagined community and fails to see what is ideological in it at its very roots. He reinforces the aesthetics of nationalism at the basis of its ideological effects and reintroduces in another form the notion of the authentic cultural community he criticized Gellner for evoking – even if this community is for him also imagined and fashioned. In doing so his own approach is Janus-like, both opening up the question of the aesthetics of nationalism and closing off the possibility of treating it critically – which means treating it in something other than aesthetic or aestheticist terms, that is, in terms of the ideal of unisonance, immediacy, immanence, or authenticity at the heart of not only Gellner's and Hobsbawm's, but also Anderson's notions of culture.

The problem is that culture and ideology, popular and official, or "good" and "bad" (that is, xenophobic, racist) nationalism, cannot be distinguished absolutely from each other, for each assumes and models itself after the same aesthetic–political ideal. In "Racism and Nationalism," Etienne Balibar addresses directly the problem of the contradictory, dual identity of nationalism and the fact that "the very category of nationalism is intrinsically ambiguous."[7] This means that even though different nationalist movements in different historical situations should not be equated – "Bismarck or De Gaulle are [*sic*] not Hitler" – there is nonetheless an effect of "ideological symmetry" produced by these antagonistic forces, for there exists "a common element . . . in the nationalism of the Algerian FLN and that of the French colonial army, or today in the nationalism of the ANC and that of the Afrikaners . . . [and] this formal symmetry is not unrelated to the painful experience we have repeatedly undergone of seeing nationalisms of liberation transformed into nationalism of domination" (45–6). The exact point where "a 'normal' ideology and politics (nationalism)" is transformed into "an 'excessive' ideology and behavior (racism)," is difficult if not impossible to determine, especially since Balibar rejects solutions to the problem which either simply "oppose the two or offer the one as the truth of the other" (46). The principal question Balibar pursues is the nature and function of the "formal symmetry" common to "normal" and "excessive" forms of nationalism, not their deep ontological or political "truth" but rather how they are configured, what Anderson would call their "style."

Unlike the political theorists discussed up to this point, Balibar does not assume that "the good" always precedes "the bad," that some form of "genuine community," "authentic culture," or "popular nationalism" always precedes the ideological use of culture or "official nationalism." For such an assumption would make it necessary to determine when and how the corruption or perversion of the authentic occurred, or as Balibar puts it, when "an intolerable, seemingly 'irrational' violence enters upon the scene, *where* we are able to place that entry" (47). But it is precisely in determining the "when" and "where" of the entry of "bad nationalism" that what he calls the "dilemma of nationalism constantly dividing" is perpetuated:

There is always a "good" and a "bad" nationalism.
There is the one which tends to construct a state or a community and the one which tends to subjugate, to destroy; the one which refers to right and the one which refers to might . . . There is one which derives from love . . . and the one which derives from hate. In short, the internal split within nationalism seems as essential – and as difficult to pin down – as the step that leads from "dying for one's fatherland" to "killing for one's country" . . . No one, in my view, has wholly escaped this reinscription of the dilemma within the very concept of nationalism itself. (47)

Because Balibar considers such a split to be internal, the solution to the problem of how we are "to break out of this circle" and account for the "ambivalence of effects [which] forms part of the very history of all nationalisms" (48) is far from evident. But in Balibar's terms, it is clear that no critical response to the problem can take the form of a reinscription of the dilemma and a reassertion of another, supposedly more authentic form of nationalism, populism, or culturalism, another form of "good nationalism," even if imagined.

Like Anderson's notion of the imaginary community, Balibar insists that the nation is always a product of "a *fictive* ethnicity" rather than of the natural existence of a people or race. But he also adds that the privileged form of the "idealization of the species" necessary for racism is in fact "aesthetic," with "the aestheticization of social relations [being] a crucial contribution of racism to the constitution of the projective field of politics" (58) and therefore closely associated with or even inseparable from the aesthetics of nationalism. What interests him especially is how various peoples "institute in real [and therefore historical] time their imaginary unity *against* other possible unities" (49), for this is the mechanism within nationalism that is also at the heart of racism.

Balibar does not, however, equate nationalism and racism or derive one from the other, but he does argue that their constant interrelation in history is far from accidental and constitutes rather a "cycle of historical reciprocity" (53) in which racism is not "an 'expression' of nationalism, but *a supplement of nationalism* or more precisely *a supplement internal to nationalism*, always in excess of it, but always indispensable to its constitution and yet always still insufficient to achieve its project" (54). For this reason, the "good form" of nationalism is never totally independent of the "bad form," nationalism never free of racism (or sexism), its aesthetics never unrelated to the aestheticization of race (or gender).[8]

At the same time, nationalism, except in the exceptional case of Nazism, where "the logic of racism overwhelms all other factors, and imposes itself to the detriment of 'pure' nationalist logic" (51), should not be simply equated with the lethal imaginary mechanism within it, which is both more and less than it. At the same time, nationalism cannot do without this component. In this way "the idealization of the species" in racism constitutes not the essence of nationalism, its ultimate truth, but an irreducible possibility in the imagining and establishment of the figure of the people necessary to nationalism.

The problem is how to keep the fictive image of the people from becoming the ideal or the idealized figure of the race, how to undermine the aesthetics of nationalism before they are accomplished in the aesthetics of race. According to Balibar's argument, racism is a possibility within nationalism which can always be realized – I would even say which is always at least in part being realized – if the formative mechanisms producing the idealized subject are not challenged, their different historical, mythical, institutional, and imaginary manifestations, not confronted.

A way to end the cycle of the reinscription of the internal contradiction of nationalism within critical approaches to nationalism is to analyze how the good form of nationalism is internally related to the bad, how even the positive figure of the people needs the fiction of an Other in order to realize itself, how the aesthetics of immanence of the collectivity are also potentially the aesthetics of racial idealization and a justification for the demeaning and hatred

David Carroll

of the Other. This would not be to take the position that nationalism is inherently evil and therefore should be abolished in all its forms – assuming such a project could ever be realized and that the means to carry it out would not be as repressive and violent as the "bad nationalism" it opposes. It would rather be to attempt to imagine the nation otherwise and to recognize that ethnicity, the integrity of the national language, the naturalness of culture, and the immanence of community all constitute fictions, which means they are all in fact expressions of an irreducible nonnatural difference or "foreignness" within these allegedly pure or natural entities, no matter how original or authentic they (or their precursors and models) are claimed to be. The "challenge," as Balibar puts it, to "every 'people' is to find its own means of going beyond exclusivism or identitarian ideology" ("The Nation Form," 105). It is not just a question, then, of finding alternatives to nationalist ideology but also of undermining the aestheticist principles at the basis of nationalism and of identificatory politics in general – whether identification is with fictions of the self or with the Other.

One of the principal critical thrusts of Homi K. Bhabha's "DissemiNation: Time, Narrative, and the Margins of the Modern Nation" – in Homi K. Bhabha, ed., *Nation and Narration* (London and New York: Routledge, 1990) – is precisely to insist on the problematical, divided, conflicted status of the figure of the people in nationalism, what could be called the counterfigures not just against which the nation-self is constructed, but within the construction or figure of the nation and the people themselves. In combating the illusion of the horizontal, homogeneous space of an organic people, Bhabha points to the possibility of "another time of *writing* that will be able to inscribe the ambivalent and chiasmatic intersections of time and place that constitute the problematic 'modern' experience of the western nation" (293). He suggests ways of imagining community that do not reduce the diversity of the peoples constituting "the people" or their various historicities, their radically different experiences of space, to the homogeneity of one time and one place, one identity and one image – that do not, I would add, assume or apply an aesthetics of the nation or community.

It is not, however, a question of cultural pluralism, which reasserts the priority and dominance of the homogeneity of space and the continuity of time, as well as the specificity of each individual culture, people, and nation, within a more diversified but nonetheless integral and hierarchical space and time. It is rather a

130

question of an internal crisis in representation, narrative, art, and politics: "The people are not simply historical events or parts of a patriotic body politic. They are also a complex rhetorical strategy of social reference where the claim to be representative provokes a crisis within the process of signification and discursive address. We then have a contested cultural territory" (297). The contestation is so basic, in fact, that no culture or combination of cultures could have entered or could emerge from the crisis intact, integral. No single culture or fusion of cultures, no matter how popular or genuine, could serve as the model for the nation, therefore, for the territory and identity of each constitute the stakes of the struggle, not what is given in advance. This is why Bhabha argues that, strictly speaking, there is no such thing as "the nation itself": "The barred Nation *It/ Self*, alienated from its eternal self-generation, becomes a liminal form of social representation, a space that is *internally* marked by cultural difference and the heterogeneous histories of contending peoples, antagonistic authorities, and tense cultural locations" (299).

The Other is within the self, not outside. This means that the nation is marked within itself by the alterity of the others it is but that it attempts to imagine it is not. "Once the liminality of the nation-space is established, and its 'difference' is turned from the boundary 'outside' to its finitude 'within,' the threat of cultural difference is no longer a problem of 'other' people. It becomes a question of the otherness of the people-as-one" (301). This "other-ness" of the people or the people as Other, marginal, split, has and can have no singular, totalized, determined form or identity. It can never be fashioned as an identity or an accumulation or synthesis of identities. The origin of the crisis of the people is the origin of the people – which is why the nation is an imagined rather than "real" community, a people always a product of the aesthetic–political imagination, fashioned in and by history rather than existing as the origin of history and as a preexisting subject that gives form to history. And this is why the totalized image of the people is always the repression of the alterity in fact constituting it.

Bhabha situates the problems associated with "minority discourse and culture," the disenfranchised, and postcolonial peoples at the very core of the problem of the people, for "it is in this supplemen-tary space of doubling – *not plurality* – where the image is presence and proxy, where the sign supplements and empties nature, that the exorbitant, disjunctive times (of colonized and postcolonial peoples and women) . . . can be turned into the discourses of emergent cultural identities, within a non-pluralistic politics of difference" (305). Such a strategy not only "empties nature" and therefore rids nationalism of its claims to being the "natural" expression of a people. It also displaces the aesthetics of identity and identification at the heart of the nationalist imagining of community as well as at the basis of most critical approaches to nationalism. In other words, "the question of cultural difference as the perplexity of living, and writing, the nation" (311) cannot be resolved because it is "original" in its supplementary otherness and persistent in its opposition to closure and totalization. With such an emphasis, no single image of the people should or can be fashioned as *the image* of the people, no nation as the subject of a unified narrative or in the form of a completed work can be imagined as community, and no aesthetics can complete its work on or as the political and guarantee the immanence or "unisonality" of the community. The work of the nation, or the nation as a work, is interrupted, deferred, and complicated, the imagined community "undone" or "unworked," displaced, opened, and deformed or "unformed" in the very process of taking form. There is not, then, good nationalism and bad nationalism but always nationalism internally divided against itself.

Bhabha's approach to the problem of nation as an imagined community and of the image of the people supporting it recalls Jean-Luc Nancy's *La Communauté désœuvrée* (Paris: Christian Bourgois, 1986). In it, Nancy opposes the traditional notion of community (whether religious, metaphysical, or political in form), which takes the form of "beings producing by their essence their own essence as their work, an absolute immanence of man to man" (14), to a community that has not been formed or fashioned into a work, that does not work on or as the people to mold them and express their essence. Nancy thus attacks all notions that society in general (or the nation in particular) emerged only with the disappearance or destruction of a genuine form of community:

Gesellschaft did not come, with the State, industry, or capital, to dissolve a preexisting Gemeinschaft. It would undoubtedly be more accurate to say, cutting short . . . all the mirages of the origin or of "the old days," that Gesellschaft – "society," the disassociating association of forces, needs, and signs – took the place of something for which we have neither a name nor a concept, of something that originated at the same time in a much more ample form of communication than that of the social space . . . Society was not made on the ruins of a *community* . . . So that community, far from being what society allegedly lost or broke up, is *what comes to us* – questions, expectations, events, imperatives – *from society.* (34)

In other words, all assumptions of the original community that were lost, the authentic culture that was destroyed, the organic, unified people that no longer exists, are all projections of society – and this is true whether the lost community is imagined as being one's own or that of an (or the) Other. It is precisely society's inability to deal with its own internally divided nature that is the origin of its projections of what it once was and once again could be. Nationalism would have to be considered one of the most important of the political names given to such a projection of community, the one that in modernity could be argued to have been the most frequently institutionalized.

The question Nancy asks is how it is possible to think (and imagine) community without nostalgia, "neither [as] a work to be produced nor a lost communion but the space itself and the spacing [*espacement*] of the experience of the outside, of the outside-of-self" (50). The basis of the imagined national community in such a context could no longer be, therefore, an integral people, whether racially, politically, or culturally defined, a native language, an authentic culture or tradition. Whether nationalism could resist the "suspension of immanence"(53) implied in such an approach to community and imagine itself otherwise, as the experience of alterity rather than of self, remains, however, to be seen. Certainly both Bhabha's and Nancy's insistence on the original alterity of community, on the experience of what is "outside-of-self," would necessitate that critical approaches to nationalism do more than trace the fall from authenticity of the imagined national community (and thus its possible return), its corruption in the hands of politicians and educators, artists, journalists, and other representatives of modern "high culture" (and thus its possible purification) – that is, do more than criticize community in terms of an ideal of lost immanence represented by authentic culture or an aesthetics of the integral, organic aesthetic–political work.

Perhaps no writer, critic, or political theorist has insisted more on the internally divided, originally heterogeneous nature of the nation and the national language(s) and culture(s) than the Martiniquais writer Edouard Glissant.[9] It might seem at first that the defining terms of Glissant's notion of "Caribbean discourse" – namely, creolization and *métissage* – are diametrically opposed to and would in themselves negate all possible ideas or fictions of the nation, the national culture, and national identity. In other words, where there exists the creolization of discourse and culture, there apparently can exist no unique national language, no single national literature or culture, no specific sense of national identity. There would seem to be no grounds on which to construct any form of nationalism at all.

Creolization is such a radical "deterritorialization of languages" (*Poétique de la Relation*, 17), it is so opposed to the notion of a unique root for any language or culture (27), so much "an explosion of cultures" and thus opposed in all ways to the "thinking of the One" (46), so fundamental, so exemplary a "mode of mixing [of languages)" (103), that it would seem difficult if not impossible to construct out of such multiplicity the sense of linguistic unity or cultural identity which appear to be basic requirements for nationalism. Creolization would thus seem to mark the limit of nationalism; where European nationalism ends (especially in the ex-colonies), creolization begins – or rather, where there is creolization, there "true" nationalism has ended.

But such is not of course the case, because Glissant is a nationalist of sorts, a very different kind of "Caribbean nationalist," however, one for whom the defense of the nation, of the national language and of culture, takes the form of a defense not of their uniqueness but of what he calls "la Relation." What he is defending in his notion of nationalism is not the pristine identity of the one but the active, internal relations of the one with the other. Glissant's *Poétique de la Relation* thus constitutes a counteraesthetics of nationalism or a poetics of counternationalism, one that defends the specific and the particular in the name of internal difference and otherness. His nationalism is rooted not in exclusivity or exclusion, but rather in the opening to the Other, in the active and productive interaction of peoples and cultures where "all identity extends into a relation with the Other" (23).

Glissant's position does not constitute a form of multiculturalism, however, but what he calls cross-culturalism. It does not culminate in the idealization of self or Other and thus the separation of languages and "cultural" identities – each ideally in its own pristine place, a place uncontaminated by other places and languages – but rather in their constant contact and reciprocal transformation. For "without contact with other languages," and the same must be said for cultures, "a language appears, perhaps in the long term, condemned to a real impoverishment" (126). To attempt to protect a language or culture by cutting it off from the influences of other languages and cultures allegedly in order to strengthen it and establish or reestablish its identity – assuming "defenses of the national language" could ever achieve this goal – is on the contrary to weaken it, deaden it, destroy it.

It is not the content of other languages and cultures that keeps a language or culture alive, but rather the process of relating, the new relations themselves. If the Other is always-already in us, and if we "know" this to be the case (39), then there can be no simple sense of individual or cultural identity, no closed, totalizing aesthetics or politics of nationalism of any sort, that does not, either affirmatively or negatively, deal with the Other in dealing with the self. Glissant's *Poétique de la Relation* is a daring attempt to recast nationalism and its aesthetics without either subsuming national, cultural particularities into a universal sense of "Man" (and thus negating them through abstraction) or denying the right of other languages or other cultures to exist (and negating them through negation).

Creolization constitutes then not the end of nationalism but rather the end of the recourse to "unique origins" and any form of genealogical descent that allegedly would guarantee "racial exclusivity." It opposes any notion of roots posited as the essence of an individual, race, or people, and, paradoxically, represents the end of the category of "the creolized" itself. "To assert peoples are creolized, that creolization has value, is to deconstruct in this way the category of 'creolized' that is considered as halfway between two 'pure' extremes . . . Creolization as an idea means the negation of creolization as a category" (140–1). Since there are no "pure extremes," there can be no notion of a pure median term, a halfway category that is neither one nor the other. What could be called Glissant's generalized idea of creolization thus supports an argument neither for assimilation nor for cultural isolationism or protectionism, whether explicitly proclaimed as in *apartheid* or practiced without official acknowledgment as in most Western cultures. In undercutting itself as a category, the ideal of creolization "is not primarily the glorification of the composite nature of a people," but rather "the unceasing process of transformation" of a people (142).

Because they are relational and antiteleological, Glissant's poetics of creolization thus constitute a movement neither toward universal unification nor toward a rediscovery of origins and roots. They work "against the monolingual imperialism inherited from the West" – which I am not convinced is inherited only from the West – which is based on the equation "one people, one language," because they acknowledge that "a people can also signify the dramatic lack of fulfillment of a language" (150). At the same time they refuse the temptation of folklore, for "literature cannot 'function' as a simple return to oral sources of folklore" (151). Nomadic, rhisomic (*Poétique de la Relation*, 23), the poetics of creolization (of "the Relation") affirm the complexity of the relation between language and people, language and tradition, language and place, language and identity. "This is what I call cultural identity," asserts Glissant: "An identity on its guard, in which the relationship with the Other shapes the self without fixing it under an oppressive force" (*Caribbean Discourse*, 169). Such a notion of a fundamental, internal nonoppressive relation with the Other could certainly be considered optimistic, perhaps even utopian. But at the same time, it highlights not the resolution of conflict but the struggle involved in all cultural relations, the necessity for identity to be always on guard, not only in order to protect itself from being destroyed by dominant, mono-linguistic, and thus oppressive cultural forces, but also, and ultimately more important, in order not to eliminate or diminish its relations with others.

The creolized poetics of Glissant, therefore, lead not to an increased national or regional sense of cultural identity, a linguistic or cultural nationalism of minority peoples or languages to counter those of the Western world, but to a politics of resistance to "the imperialism of monolinguism," of the imposition of a single language on postcolonized and postcolonizing peoples. This resistance is proclaimed in the name not of one people or language, or unisonance, but of multilinguism, defined in the following way:

Multilinguism is the passionate desire to accept and understand our neighbor's language and to confront the massive leveling force of language continuously imposed by the West – yesterday with French, today with American English – with a multiplicity of languages and their mutual comprehension. This practice of cultural creolization is not part of some vague humanism, which makes it permissible for us to become one with the next person. It establishes a cross-cultural relationship, in an egalitarian and unprecedented way, between histories that we know today in the Caribbean are interrelated. (249)

The creolized, multilinguistic counterpoetics of nationalism advocated here thus support an idea of a nation which is a cultural composite, a multinational, cross-cultural, nonexclusive nationalism, delimited only by what Glissant calls in his *Poétique de la Relation* "an open border" (45).

The poetics of the Relation do not, therefore, provide an alternate way of knowing or representing a culture or people; they are not a poetics of national identity. Rather they are rooted in the impossibility of such representation, given the complexity of cross-cultural influences and of the various trajectories which lead to various cultural confluences and the different senses and forms of the collective or individual self in the self. The poetics of Relation, as not *the Other*, but as an other of thinking, imagine what cannot be conceptualized, and what is imagined is the complexity of the dynamic process of the construction of identity itself, the openness of the reciprocal process of the Relation. The individual or collective self is never established, predetermined, or determined; neither is the Other. The poetics of the Relation thus mark the end of all typologies: of the chauvinistic, nationalist typologies of self and the mystifying and mystified typologies of the Other.

The defense and illustration of the Relation constitute also a defense and illustration of the particularity of each culture in relation with others, the defense of "the right (of each culture) to opacity, which is not its imprisonment in an impenetrable autarky, but its subsistence in an irreducible singularity . . . The thinking of self and the thinking of the Other become obsolete in their duality in this context. Every Other is a citizen, no longer a barbarian" (204). Or put another way, the barbarian is a fiction of the traditional nationalist who argues on behalf of a predetermined, natural, collective self, the nationalist who treats others as barbarians and attempts to put an end to all relations that limit the alleged autonomy of the self, the nationalist who pretends that all such relations are external and insignificant, that the nature of the self is to preexist them and to return to itself as itself before or outside all contact with others. All aesthetics of nationalism (of unisonance) are rooted in such fictions of self and Other.

Glissant's greatest contribution to our understanding of the aesthetics of national identity may be to have helped us imagine the potential critical effects of alternate imagined communities and alternate ways of imagining. His poetics do not fall back on a "good" imagined community for support, on "good" notions of the nation to combat "bad" ones. They rather demand that imagination and a hybrid and critical notion of poetics or aesthetics work for other ends than the institution of national identity and the experience of unisonance. The ends of the poetics of Relation cannot be determined but are constantly being produced and transformed by the process of relating itself. The poetics of Relation thus mark the limits of cultural identification and undermine the aesthetics supporting and forming the various nationalisms (and critical approaches to nationalism) which depend on or advocate identificatory procedures as the means of "fashioning the people." In the poetics of Relation the otherness of the people is "figured" as the nonfigurable, and what Bhabha calls the "'double and split' time of national representation" (*Nation and Narration*, 295) is considered to be an irreducible component of the representation of the imaginary community called the nation. The poetics of Relation present us with the possibility of forms of nationalism in which "the question of community and communication [is thought and presented] without the moment of transcendence" (304), that is, as a counter to the aesthetics of unisonance and of the original imagined community and its culture.

Notes

1 Renan's much cited and yet frequently misunderstood definition of the nation is the following:

> No, it is no more soil than it is race which makes a nation. The soil furnishes the substratum, the field of struggle and of labour; man furnishes the soul. Man is everything in the formation of this sacred thing which is called a people. Nothing [purely] material suffices for it. A nation is a spiritual principle, the outcome of the profound complications of history; it is a spiritual family not a group determined by the shape of the earth. We have now seen what things are not adequate for the creation of such a spiritual principle, namely, race, language, material interest, religious affinities, geography, and military necessity. What more then is required?

> Renan then immediately answers his own question: "Two things, which in truth are but one, constitute this soul or spiritual principle. One lies in the past, one in the present. One is the possession in common of a rich legacy of memories; the other is present-day consent, the desire to live together, the will to perpetuate the value of the heritage that one has received *in an undivided form*" ("What is a Nation?," trans. Martin Thom, in Homi K. Bhabha, ed., *Nation and Narration* [London and New York: Routledge, 1990], pp. 18–19; my emphasis). For an excellent analysis of the double and contradictory legacy of Renan, see Joël Roman's introduction to the recent French edition of Renan's essays on nationalism entitled *Qu'est-ce qu'une nation? Et autres essais politiques* (Paris: Presses Pocket, 1992).

2 Michael Winock, *Nationalisme, anti-sémitisme et fascisme en France* (Paris: Seuil, 1990), p. 14. All translations from the French, unless otherwise indicated, are my own. Subsequent references are given in the main text.

3 Benedict Anderson, *Imagined Communities: Reflections on the Origin and Spread of Nationalism* (London and New York: Verso, 1991), p. 5. All subsequent references will be given in the main text.

4 Ernest Gellner, *Nations and Nationalism* (Ithaca, NY: Cornell University Press, 1983), pp. 123–4. All subsequent references will be given in the main text.

5 E. J. Hobsbawm, *Nations and Nationalism since 1780: Programme, Myth, Reality* (Cambridge University Press, 1990), p. 57. All subsequent references are given in the main text.

6 And this, I would add, is the case not just when the "purification of French" is undertaken by an institution such as the Académie Française. It is also and more surprisingly true in cases like the recent one in France where a petition signed by intellectuals and writers such as Régis Debray, Michel Serres (a recently elected member of the Académie), and Philippe Sollers was circulated in which the above pledged themselves to the struggle against the invasion of the French language by English expressions and the attack on French culture represented by degraded (nationalists of the turn of the century would have said "barbaric") American practices. Such an action highlights the way in which what I am calling the aesthetics of nationalism and the cultural politics of language supporting them are taken as natural phenomena even by artists and writers who were once and perhaps still consider themselves to be on the left.

7 In Etienne Balibar and Immanuel Wallerstein, *Race, Nation, Class: Ambiguous Identities*, Balibar's essays translated by Chris Turner (London and New York: Verso, 1991), p. 45. This collection includes another of Balibar's essays, "The Nation Form," to which I shall also refer. Subsequent references are given in the main text.

8 Balibar argues that "the phenomenon of 'depreciation' and 'racialization' which is directed simultaneously against different social groups which are quite different in 'nature' (particularly 'foreign' communities, 'inferior races,' women and 'deviants') . . . [represents] *a historical system of complementary exclusions and dominations which are mutually interconnected.* In other words, it is not in practice simply the case that an 'ethnic racism' and a 'sexual racism,' exist in parallel; racism and sexism function together and in particular, *racism always presupposes sexism"* (49).

9 Given the similarity of the critical projects of Glissant and Bhabha and the latter's interest in developing a "theory of cultural hybridity," it is surprising that Bhabha, in *The Location of Culture* (London and New York: Routledge, 1994), a collection of essays on the problems of identity, culture, and national affiliation from a "postcolonial perspective," makes no reference to the work of Glissant. In this chapter, I shall be referring to *Le Discours antillais* (Paris: Seuil, 1981), translated by J. Michael Nash as *Caribbean Discourse: Selected Essays* (Charlottesville: University Press of Virginia, 1989), and *Poétique de la Relation* (Paris: Gallimard, 1990).

139

6

Peripheral visions: class, cultural aspiration, and the artisan community in mid-nineteenth-century France

NEIL MCWILLIAM

Sometime around 1820, Pierre Deruineau, an apprentice scenery painter, left the provincial town of Angers to undertake the *Tour de France*. This circuit round the nation had become a well-established ritual, allowing the novice artisan to mature into an accomplished craftsman by working alongside a variety of masters and observing the differing techniques practiced in the regions. As he looked back on his experiences thirty years later, Deruineau waxed lyrical on the moral benefits to be gleaned from what he presents as a form of proletarian Grand Tour. Not only does travel offer the young worker an opportunity to challenge the preconceptions inbred by small-town life, it also seemingly opens up a dazzling itinerary of cultural events, at which he acquires new confidence in his own judgment by rubbing shoulders with the *"grand monde"* for whom the arts and learning are a form of birthright:

we find him at big meetings and public festivals, mixed in among the elegant and well mannered crowd, in the midst of intellectuals and artists of every sort. Full of enthusiasm, he visits monuments and public buildings, where, despite the difference which sets him apart from the upper crust, he feels the same enthusiasms or antipathies as they; he has the same feelings and the same views; he joins the crowd around works of art and criticizes or admires them with judgment which is always upright and so, more often than not, is correct and true.[1]

And, indeed, upon arriving in Paris, Deruineau tells us that he embarked on a frenetic round of visits to galleries, theatres, and public monuments. Yet beneath the breathless account of his initiation into the ways of the world, one soon senses a rather different story of demoralization, diffidence, and isolation. For want of anything better to do, one learns, the young man began to haunt the working-class taverns of the *barrière*, liminal territory both socially and geographically, where he consorted not with the art-world elite, but with laborers who sought in cheap wine and popular song some relief from the fatigues of the workplace. Though he paints a picture of genial sociability and innocent pleasure, Deruineau also acknowledges a darker side, populated by men who find in the oblivion of drink some escape from the misery of everyday life. He confesses, too, that the cultural riches of the capital left him confused and lonely, his moral sense eroded, deep in debt and pining for his family. "Every day in Paris," he complains, "youth encounters traps held out to their inexperience. The passions give themselves over to pleasure with uncontrollable power. The idle ways one so quickly takes up encourage every vice; good sentiments are stifled and soon one loses all shame."[2]

This is, of course, a familiar tale of the treachery of urban life and the vulnerability of the young worker brought up against the moral isolation and material limitations of his state. What is striking, though, is the tenacity with which Deruineau holds on to the myth of the enriching value of culture, and the opportunities it affords for social assimilation, even as the narrative of his Parisian experience so radically subverts his claims. Significantly, we learn little of his working life, though a sustained polemic against the apprenticeship system and its suppression of natural aptitude suggests his own disenchantment. In a redemptive fantasy, Deruineau claims that the progress achieved since his own youth has secured a new meritocracy in which all men are citizens and brothers, and recognition of the nobility of labor has slowly penetrated every level of society.[3] It is, perhaps, the shared spaces of culture, rather than the fragmented territory of the workplace, which stand as implicit testimony to this claim for class solidarity – a claim which Deruineau's own story effectively contradicts.

This brief vignette of frustrated expectation and undiminished hope highlights the contradictions which so often accompanied popular efforts to gain access to the consecrated circuits of art and literature. At a time of accelerating socioeconomic change, which simultaneously eroded traditional artisanal practices and laid the foundations of a politicized working class, the issue of cultural identity took on crucial symbolic force. As the philosopher and historian Jacques Rancière has so vividly demonstrated, mid-nineteenth-century France witnessed a startling challenge to inherited patterns of discrimination which had relegated workers to an unreflective ritual of physical tasks and discounted their capacity for speculative thought or ideated sensation.[4] For Rancière, the stirrings of cultural aspiration, testified in the burgeoning of popular educational projects and in workers' initiation to the power of the word as a medium for asserting and exploring their own subjectivity, challenged the segregation of thought from action which, since the time of Plato, had served to license the exclusion of all but a cultivated elite from legitimate participation in political discourse.[5] Sanctioned by the masses' alleged brutishness – their inability to reason or to dream – this act of denial invested in the cultural realm an image of impaired affectivity which disqualified the worker from participation in the life of the polis.

The confidence which Deruineau expresses in his aesthetic judgment – significantly rooted in a sense of spiritual communion with his social superiors – can thus be read as a *prise de conscience* which destabilizes far more than consecrated notions of the relationship between culture and class. Similarly, Rancière has insisted, the proliferation during the 1830s and 1840s of worker-poets writing in an idiom which owes more to the giants of Romanticism than to the vernacular of the *menu peuple* represents a challenge to social and symbolic hierarchies which has too often been underestimated. For Rancière, the very act of writing out of one's class, of undertaking a "voyage of apprenticeship into the land of the other's culture,"[6] disrupts the boundaries between labor and leisure, hand and brain, language and silence along which the distinctions between power and subjection had been policed. From such a perspective, the aspiration to culture of the weaver or bricklayer, whose evenings were spent composing hexameters, forms part of "a spontaneous movement of deprofessionalization which was establishing a distance between the worker and his trade while abolishing the distance between specialist knowledge and amateur culture."[7]

Yet the ambivalence of Deruineau's experiences should encourage some caution, not because his case is in any way exceptional but through the very frequency with which we encounter tales of aspiration undermined, of hope deferred or dissipated altogether. The coming of age around 1840 of a generation of artisans for whom an active interest in literature or the arts often complemented an equally active commitment to social and economic change testifies to a desire for recognition not simply as a political constituency buttressed by sheer force of numbers, but as an ethical power capable of revivifying the cultural health of the nation. Committed to winning the respect of the affluent classes as moral equals, artisan intellectuals affected an earnestness of tone which infuses their cultural production and encouraged intolerance towards more unruly plebeian pleasures which reinforced pejorative bourgeois stereotypes. As Rancière has remarked, the strategy was less one of militant confrontation than of presentation of the worker as an exemplary figure whose bid for cultural and political enfranchisement was inspired by love and a spirit of social solidarity.[8]

Such a strategy was fraught with difficulties, however. Challenging the segregation of art and labor exacted a high cost on the individual worker, while initiation in "the sacred, forbidden and fascinating language of the other"[9] could all too easily degenerate into empty mimicry, the forms and protocols of high art themselves abstracting out the political imperative through which this alien language had first exerted its delusive appeal. As we shall see, the ambivalence which marks Deruineau's cultural initiation exemplifies a more fundamental dilemma which confronted the aspiring plebeian intellectual. Though many artisans achieved a degree of public recognition for their literary and artistic production, their exertions often intensified an already punishing daily routine and brought about an uncomfortable hybridity which isolated them from their fellows while denying all but the most limited access to dominant social groups. The assertion of subjectivity, as an act of political empowerment as well as of personal enrichment, thus questioned the social ontology of subjection, but in doing so risked inflicting upon the artisan intellectual contradictory identities which ultimately exacerbated the pressures of moral and material existence.

In challenging denigration of the worker as pariah and representing himself as a paragon of moderation and refined feeling, the artisan had necessarily to contend with bourgeois intellectuals' mounting preoccupation with *"le peuple"* and with popular culture.[10] Inflected by concern at the impact of the capitalist free market on artistic production, these debates interrogated the status of the worker both as cultural consumer and producer. In the process, they prompted a radical reassessment of art as a form of labor and of labor as a form of art. It was within these boundaries that popular initiatives for cultural recognition were framed. As we shall see, the dream which sustained the nights of labor spent on sonnets and short stories could also transfigure the workbench into a site of creative fulfillment in its own right. Rather than antinomies, the one vitiating the successful accomplishment of the other, mental and manual work were refigured as potentially complementary moments of popular self-realization. Yet the fragile attempts made by an artisan elite, fast losing ground to mechanization and deskilling, to win recognition as a distinctive cultural constituency ultimately served to compound their impotence as a social force rather than enhancing their capacity for common action and defense.

I

In 1850, the same year that saw the appearance of Deruineau's memoirs, the jewelry engraver and socialist activist Pierre Vinçard published a brief pamphlet with the suggestive title *L'Artiste et le peuple.* During the course of a polemical assault on visual artists for repudiating their social responsibilities, Vinçard draws a striking analogy. "Who is more like the artist than the worker?," he asks. "Both are the children of their works, both are condemned to a permanent battle against injustice and prejudice, they are brothers through labor and suffering. They both have many martyrs, and the same feelings have often made their hearts beat as one."[11]

Though shaped by his desire to pursue his indictment of contemporary art, the comparison Vinçard draws was not entirely unfamiliar under the July Monarchy and Second Republic. On one level this derives from an inclusive notion of labor common at the period, which could happily describe intellectuals as *"ouvriers de la pensée"* or identify factory owners and manual workers as belonging to the same class of *"producteurs."*[12] Indeed, it was only recently that the term *"artiste"* had come to refer more or less exclusively to individuals engaged in creative pursuits, and had lost its residual connotations of artisanal activity.[13] This association was underlined by recognition that many of those who gained their living as professional artists were drawn from humble backgrounds,[14] typically adapting such family pursuits as stone-cutting or wood-carving to more lucrative and prestigious ends.

Yet the association between artist and worker runs much deeper than this in radical discourse of the 1830s and 1840s. It is perhaps most strikingly encapsulated in two works by Antoine Etex, a painter and sculptor with socialist leanings, who in the 1845 Salon exhibited *Mort d'un homme de génie incompris* (fig. 6.1), an austere allegory which apparently takes up the theme of the romantic outcast popularized in such texts as Vigny's *Chatterton* of 1835.

Fig. 6.1 Antoine Etex, *Mort d'un homme de génie incompris*, 1845

Four years later, under the Second Republic, the work was published as a lithograph by Célestin Nanteuil carrying the inscription *La Délivrance, ou la mort du prolétaire* (fig. 6.2). Now adorned with a decorative border, in which artisanal tools and agricultural implements are juxtaposed with the painter's palette and the writer's quill, the print conflates mental and manual labor and, through reference to the 1845 image, equates the suffering artist with his proletarian brother. Evoking the more familiar forms of the *pietàs*, Etex's anonymous martyr, with his rugged though emaciated body and firm, muscular arms, bespeaks the plebeian rather than the aesthete.

It was the depredations of free-market competition which provided radicals with the common denominator equating artist and worker. Just as they accused the capitalist of assaulting the dignity of labor by replacing the skilled craftsman with untrained operatives paid only subsistence wages, so the effect of cultural mercantilism was judged every bit as corrosive on the dignity – and integrity – of the artist.[15] Within the profession itself, competition was blamed for frustrating any possibility of forging a progressive public art by obliging artists to sell themselves to the highest bidder, whatever the cost in self-respect. Thus, in 1849, the manifesto of the newly founded *Comité central des artistes* bemoaned the "painful and ignominious labor of the proletarian" endured by all of those exposed to the "isolation, competition and selfishness" of a cultural marketplace controlled by the caprice of the private buyer.[16]

Working-class radicals shared this diagnosis, though they were more inclined to reproach artists for colluding with the market and abnegating broader responsibilities of social leadership. The indictment was central to critiques of the Salon exhibition published during the 1840s in *L'Atelier*, a journal produced by a group of artisan intellectuals sympathetic to the Christian socialist philosopher Philippe Buchez. The ostentatious moral severity qualifying their judgments left little room for indulgence of stylistic virtuosity; instead, deficiencies in subject matter came under sustained assault, and were squarely attributed to the corrupting commercialization of the arts. As the journal's anonymous correspondent reports on his visit to the 1844 exhibition: "What we saw is less a gallery of paintings than a bazaar; – it is not talent which is wanting, but thought. – Yes, of course, the style is capable, the concepts daring, the ideas ingenious, but the mercantile spirit makes itself felt throughout . . . at every step, caprice, fantasy and frivolities are offered to attract weak minds."[17]

Fig 6.2 Célestin Nanteuil, after Antoine Etex, *La Délivrance, ou la mort du prolétaire*, 1849

Whatever allowance they might make for the artist's subjection to commercial forces beyond his control, working-class radicals were quick in trying to turn the perceived deficiencies of high culture to their own ideological advantage. While immorality and weak-mindedness had become familiar tropes in contemporary investigations of the popular classes, artisanal commentators inferred from the state of the arts a moral debility from which the people themselves were allegedly exempt. To this degree, the worker lay claim to a privileged clarity of vision which enabled him to penetrate the moral meaning of art in a way that was denied to his social superiors. It was on such grounds that the writers in *L'Atelier* presumed to judge the Salon, asserting that the uncorrupted popular gaze was most sensitive to the fundamental moral significance of art.[18] This militant moralism thus exploited perceived deficiencies within the arts to underline the discrepancy between the people's proclaimed ethical superiority and their material oppression. More than this, it accused the nascent culture industry of deliberately attempting to vitiate popular integrity through the deceptive illusions of art. The shameless display of nudity in the Salon, the prurient indulgence of fantasy in the boulevard theatres, the coarse vulgarity of carnival – all fell foul of the journal's censorious tone.[19] The novel was particularly isolated as a threat to popular virtue:

What is it that has made our daily task sometimes seem harsh, our humble state repugnant, and our deprivation painful if not these provocative depictions of a refined and elegant world, where fantasy alone is the supreme law, where the heat of passion excuses everything, where obstacles disappear before the daring protagonist? Ah! Away from us, away from our wives and children these corrosive glorifications of the wasted days of the world's privileged! Let us not teach our loved ones to blush at their humble state; let us spare them such an experience.[20]

This high-minded dismissal of cultural contamination positioned the worker – urban as well as rural – as a final refuge of probity in a society increasingly alienated from fundamental moral "truths" by the corrupting force of material wealth. Such essentializing, endlessly reinforced by artisan intellectuals, found a powerful echo in the romantic populism of figures such as Michelet and George Sand, with their emphasis on the reliability of the people's native instincts.[21]

Such efforts to project the popular classes as possessing a moral vigor which legitimized their claims for enhanced political authority encountered powerful opposition amongst conservative opinion, however. Here, too, the issues at stake involved not only the political and artistic enfranchisement of the people, but also reflected distaste at the emergence of an increasingly commercialized cultural market-place. Figures on the Legitimist right were particularly apprehensive of what they saw as an incipient industrialization of culture, which threatened to subject the professional artist to the whim of a debased popular taste. Regarding the lower orders as vulnerable to the perverting influence of obscene or inflammatory works, due "to their intrinsically impressionable and volatile natures,"[22] conservatives regarded cultural control as a strategic element in maintaining deference for established hierarchies. As the social investigator Antoine-Honoré Frégier remarked in his 1838 study of the *"classes dangereuses"*: "it is by strengthening the power of intelligence in the laboring man that we will silence the brutal instincts that tempt him and reduce him to the state of ignorance in which he is plunged."[23] It is inherent moral debility, exacerbated by noxious cultural influ-ence, which Frégier blames for the worker's ignorance, rather than the material restrictions of his economic state.

Such a diagnosis acquired increasing urgency with the expansion of elementary education and encouraged initiatives to ensure that access to culture should moralize the working classes rather than exacerbate their insolence and depravity. Proposals were made for the establishment of popular libraries to counter the corrupting influence of commercial "cabinets de lecture," wholesome festivities organized by the authorities were recommended, and strict controls over the theatre urged on those in power.[24] Nor were the visual arts neglected in this projected rehabilitation of popular taste. Writing in *L'Artiste* in 1842, the critic Ulysse Ladet remarked favorably on the growing number of workers patronizing the Louvre, an experience he presented as sowing the seeds of a moral instruction which would gradually extend throughout the lower orders: "These lessons, picked up haphazardly and by chance, ripen in the shadows; they give the people a gentler tone; they spread myster-iously from one person to another, seeping into even the most rebellious personalities until one finds their beneficial signs even where one would least expect such a discovery."[25]

It was such a conviction of the efficacy of visual art as a medium for popular instruction that had inspired the banker and philanthro-pist Benjamin Delessert to sponsor a competition for moralizing imagery in 1836.[26] The winning project, a series of twelve episodes by the lithographer Jules David portraying the contrasting consequences of *Vice and Virtue*, effectively distilled bourgeois fears and fantasies of lower-class life. Its dramatization of the bad worker's inexorable decline from dissipation to criminality and inevitable retribution at the hands of the law is offset by a familiar parable of probity rewarded in which the diligent and thrifty apprentice gains his employer's confidence, marries into the firm, and wins promotion as an affluent and respected member of the bourgeoisie.

Rather than arousing the suspicion of its intended audience, the contradiction embodied in such a fiction, with its reliance on the familiar *deus ex machina* of the socially exogamous liaison, shadows a profound and debilitating tension implicit in much artisanal commentary on culture and morality. The very celebration of the working class as paragons of virtue amidst an acquisitive and egotistical bourgeoisie locked subordinate groups into an ethical structure incompatible with their social and political objectives. In basing claims for greater justice on the people's imputed moral responsibility, radical artisans and socialist theorists necessarily endorsed standards of conduct – and notions of popular deviation from such standards – which seriously compromised any radical questioning of prevailing ideological norms. At its most insidious, assimilation of such values encouraged a plebeian moralism which itself colluded in denigrating aspects of proletarian behavior while failing to question the socioeconomic pressures sustaining particular cultural options. In the words of the communist *La Fraternité de 1845*:

Workers, how many things we need to change in ourselves. Let each of us seriously examine his conscience and ask what needs reforming in his tastes, his pleasures, his relationships, and in the way he uses his time. Let us dedicate everything we eliminate from our present behavior which is idle, useless, or vicious to the life of the mind . . . Are you resigned to living forever the brutalizing life that the world offers you today? Do you renounce, then, the complete development of your being? . . . Learn at last how to raise yourselves from your intellectual lethargy, your shameful degradation.[27]

Underscoring such remarks is the unspoken conviction that in some sense it is the worker himself who is answerable for his abasement, rather than the oppressive economic circumstances which govern his life. The mechanics of social change thus come to depend less on resisting those forces sustaining oppression from above than on an internal struggle against moral failings compromising claims to superior virtue. Radical artisans appealed to the artist in helping to eradicate these deficiencies, calling for instructive literature and imagery specifically directed at the people.[28] It is in this spirit that *L'Atelier* argues in 1844 that "It is the goal of the fine arts to improve us as individuals; they must inspire us with love for our fathers, charity, gentleness, family concord, chaste and pure love; they must excite in us a horror of selfishness and of all of those vices which undermine societies and families; in a word, they must help us to fulfill our duties."[29]

In line with such priorities, it was works extolling Christian charity, such as Ary Scheffer's *Christ consolateur*, or patriotic evocations of national glory, like David d'Angers's *Joseph Bara*,[30] which attracted most favorable comment amongst progressive artisans. Beneath the republican coloring of such preferences, there lay a more fundamental assimilation of social values – and a conviction in the arts' ability and duty to inculcate them – which transcended overt dissent from dominant cultural discourse. Though, like many on the left, artisan radicals condemned contemporary art for elevating form over content, they nonetheless shared with their political antagonists a conviction in the artist's responsibilities toward the moral well-being of the nation. They failed to understand that competing on the same moral ground as their adversaries was so politically disabling as to frustrate any persuasive strategy for cultural renewal.

II

The nub of this paralyzing contradiction was lived out in the anomalous, testing, and often painful existence of the artisan intellectual, a figure trapped between two worlds, risking isolation in both. It is in the lived relationship between the artisan and the institutions of culture – which he tried either to infiltrate or to shape to his own needs – that the limitations of art and learning as a force for empowering the worker and offsetting his material frustrations emerge most vividly. The mid nineteenth century witnessed an efflorescence of artisanal commentary in journals such as *L'Atelier* or *La Ruche populaire*,[31] and saw the astonishing emergence of worker-poets as a conspicuous literary force,[32] yet what remains most striking is the abiding difficulty encountered in reconciling mental and manual labor. Rather than being a springboard, all too often culture acted as a snare, trapping the worker in a mesh of conflicting representations of himself, of his place within the artisanal community, and of his standing as an adopted member in the "republic of arts." Finding a voice was no easy matter for a class which had assumed silence as its natural state, and needed to overcome a debilitating sense of inadequacy to represent itself in a language which could be heard and understood by others.[33] The point is well made by Agricol Perdiguier, a carpenter who played a pivotal role in reforming the *compagnonnage* system of journey-men's guilds in the mid century. "Misery breeds timidity," he claims. "In front of the rich, who often disdain them, the poor speak rarely, afraid of speaking badly and making what they call a muck of things [*des cuirs*]. This fear paralyses them, and it is only with their equals that they sparkle and express themselves spontaneously."[34]

To speak and be heard all too often involved mimicking the voice of another culture. Lamartine and Hugo were models every bit as potent for the aspiring worker-poet as the more vernacular and approachable Béranger. However ambivalent they might be towards the moral exhaustion of established forms, workers adopted them instinctively as enjoying a cultural legitimacy to which they them-selves could lay claim by association. For their champions, this stylistic refinement could be read as evidence of a personal nobility which endured the material pressures of the worker's life to reach out in a gesture of conciliation to his social superiors.[35] Poetry's artificiality as a form of discourse, which allowed it to disguise the real differences of everyday speech – differences rooted in the social experience of the worker's life – recommended it to a figure such as Olinde Rodrigues, former Saint-Simonian and editor of a collection of workers' verse in 1840: "Through the irresistible attraction of its language, poetry is indeed ideally suited to prepare a reconciliation between all classes. Overcoming the gap in rank and position, it can raise to the highest levels of the social pyramid the most pressing and authentic needs, the most legitimate claims of those numerous classes who make up the base of the social edifice."[36]

Yet gaining acceptance as a cultural intermediary between classes involved embracing one's divided state rather than nurturing any ambitions to transcend it. Inherent in the contract negotiated across the social divide was a clause which extended recognition of the artisan's cultural accomplishments on the strict understanding that he should remain firmly in his allotted place. Only by doing so, it was claimed, would he retain an independence so crucial in distin-guishing him from the jaundiced professional writer. Only at his bench could he preserve the freshness and imagination which the rituals of metropolitan existence obscured from his bourgeois counterpart. Only as a worker, reconciled with his state, could he capitalize on the solace and redemption which art could provide in an otherwise harsh existence. As Victor Hugo intoned from the Olympian heights to the cobbler turned poet Savinien Lapointe: "Continue, monsieur, in your double role: your task as worker and your apostolate as thinker. So, take courage and patience: courage for great hardships and patience for small ones. And then, when you have finished work each day, sleep serenely. God is looking over you."[37]

Stoical acceptance of one's lot, rather than any more aggressive questioning of the social order, was, then, the price to pay for recognition by the outside world. For celebrities such as Hugo, Lamartine, or Sue, each with their favored proletarian voice, as for a publicist such as Rodrigues, popular literary aspirations acquired legitimacy – and hence visibility – only to the degree that they served to articulate a social outlook as harmonious as the rhetorical forms in which they were couched. The edifying value of the "poète-ouvrier" was thus implicitly invested in a perceived symmetry between the life and the work, the founding virtues of the one informing the other and sanctioning its recognition as a worthy, if indelibly curious, token of popular sensibility. Personal ambition or political antagonism tainted this ideal disinterestedness, which commentators readily saw as drawing sustenance from the challenge of material deprivation. As a plebeian surrogate for the suffering romantic, the appropriate demeanor was one of patience, piety, and resignation.[38]

Within the working-class community itself, cultural aspirations seemed at once a necessary relief from the rigors of everyday life and a dangerously destabilizing force, upsetting the individual's capacity to deal with material oppression and isolating him from his work-mates and family. The popular press continually returned to the theme, warning the ambitious young worker from being seduced into abandoning his toolkit for the pen or paintbrush. It was Antoine Etex who, in 1847, took up the call in *La Ruche populaire*, counseling all but the most gifted to accept their preordained place in society at the risk of meeting only poverty and despair. His advice to the proletarian family is clear:

As far as you are able, make your children into serious, knowledgeable, outstanding workers; inspire in them a love of goodness and beauty; make them understand that all useful work elevates the soul much more than the idleness of so-called thinkers who drain their families for so long before finally dishonoring them; tell them that useful work strengthens body and soul at the same time; that the best thing is to excel in one's father's trade, to try to be the best, as in any walk of life.[39]

Cautionary tales to this effect also appeared in the journal. In a short story pointedly entitled "Une Vie perdue," Pierre Vinçard detailed the destiny awaiting the presumptuous worker impatient with his lot. His hero, Georges, an orphaned carpenter befriended by his workmate Urbain, announces his decision to abandon the workshop and become a journalist. Motivated by what Vinçard describes as "an imperious need to make a name,"[40] Georges abandons his pregnant mistress, sells himself to the gutter press, and is later found dying from starvation in a squalid apartment on the Ile de la Cité by the faithful Urbain, whose wise counsel Georges had so disdainfully refused. As the two men embrace in reconciliation, the prodigal carpenter expires in his comrade's arms.

This brief melodrama not only asserts the superior integrity of labor, but also reveals popular suspicion of the vitiating influence of capital upon culture, in which any professionalized activity – and journalism above all others – was regarded as inherently corrupting. To this degree, artisan writers and artisan journalists especially held on to the notion of manual work as offering the plebeian intellectual an independence denied their more established professional superiors.[41] Yet the paradigm of an integrated existence in which the worker was exhorted to "take up the plane having set aside the pen"[42] proved hard to sustain. Even as they commended the mason Charles Poncy for having remained true to his class and calling following the success of his poetry, the artisanal contributors to *La Ruche populaire* canvased for financial assistance on his behalf, arguing: "Society would not be fulfilling its duty if it delayed in elevating our author to the place he merits. God brought him into the world to do something other than lay bricks on mortar."[43]

The implied tension here between mental and manual labor continually threatened to overwhelm the paradigm of the artisan intellectual, the purity of whose vision was rooted in love of his craft. The brute fact was that work was more often physically extenuating and mentally deadening than it was ennobling and poetic. Labor as an impediment rather than a spur to creativity flew in the face of the sanitized myth of the worker's harmonious existence favored by established figures such as Victor Hugo or Eugène Sue.[44] Yet even the stalwarts of *L'Atelier* or *La Ruche populaire* occasionally gave voice to the frustration born of a double existence, each facet of which served to undermine the other. Neither fulfilled as a worker nor enjoying the moral and material circumstances to realize his ambitions as an artist, the artisan finds his cultural aspirations a source of frustration and torment rather than consolation. As the carpenter Gabriel Gauny ruefully remarked: "An active imagination invents for itself an easy position in an ideal world, so richly restful, so full of treacherous beauty that upon return from this fantastic voyage reality is odious, and our social surroundings are so many unforgiving dungeons made all the worse by our imagination's horror at its fall."[45]

For Gauny, the workshop itself was an "enfer sans poésie," intolerable in its reduction of the individual to the unthinking level of an automaton, unyielding in its sapping of all intellectual and physical vigor with which the worker could seek solace in his moments of leisure. There is, then, no escape. Imagination exacerbates the worker's sense of his own demoralization, yet a life without imagination is unthinkable. The treachery of imagination is a necessary, though dispiriting, consolation to the misery of labor, whose pressures it inevitably makes all the harder to bear.[46]

Yet the commitment to education sustained in the artisanal press implied that there was, indeed, some way out. If not in constructing a mental refuge through the consolations of poetry, then at least through professional instruction, the worker could, it was implied, hope to reap real rewards by enhancing his competence and, hopefully, gaining in prestige. The humble draughtsman, for example, could, with application, win recognition as a professional artist and achieve celebrity in the Salon:

The artisan whose profession relates to the arts of drawing can give life to his chisel, his burin or his brush by learning the secrets of the figure, of ornament, and of perspective. Perhaps he will discover a serious vocation; perhaps he is destined to play a part in the promised future renewal of art. Instead of the insipid and trivial works which are currently displayed, perhaps he will show us a truly popular work of art which, in recording great thoughts and actions, will make them imperishable.[47]

This is a noticeably contingent account, hedged with qualifications. The visual arts did, of course, offer a rather less arduous route to social ascent than literature, if only because of the emphasis upon drawing which linked many manual crafts with painting and sculpture. Acquisition of these skills in institutes such as l'Ecole gratuite de dessin brought young Parisian artisans into contact with aspiring artists in a shared pedagogical space.[48] Yet such common foundations could sustain a career spent as a sculptor's anonymous *praticien* or a humble house painter just as well as it could provide a privileged elite with the key to public celebrity in the Salon.

A revealing, if unintentional, insight into the moral and material circumstances which mediated the worker's destiny is provided in a discussion of professional training published in 1859 by Anthime Corbon. In the course of a polemic against narrowly specialized apprenticeships, Corbon – formerly a leading light on *L'Atelier* and a deputy under the Second Republic – tells the contrasting stories of two former workmates. The first, a painter-decorator, displayed extraordinary versatility; an accomplished draughtsman, he assists professional architects with their plans, gives geometry lessons to his comrades, designs furniture and textiles, assists sculptors on bas-reliefs and painters on mural decorations. He exhibits an architectural drawing at the Salon as well as a landscape, which was warmly praised by Corot and Daubigny, and snapped up by a collector even before the exhibition's opening. And yet, still, he remains an artisan, his talents largely unrecognized and unrewarded. By contrast, a printer with whom Corbon had once worked had enjoyed far better fortune, winning recognition on his Salon debut and since emerging as a major figure in French art. Corbon is quite certain of the secret of his friend's success: "Such was its power, his sense of vocation overcame all obstacles, such at least was his strength of will."[49] It was this lack of determination which Corbon blames for the versatile decorator's failure:

This man, this friend, obviously had a true artistic vocation. But material need, overwhelming timidity and perhaps also a lack in energetic determination, frustrated its fulfillment. It was doubtless really heartbreaking for him. Yet this does not stop him from doing what is asked of him very well. If he had been able to follow his vocation as a painter, art would have gained and so would the artist himself, but no one would ever have imagined that there were so many varied skills within him.[50]

Corbon uses the decorator's tale to illustrate his conviction in the innate versatility of most workers, but his story also displays the burden of unfulfilled potential, the artisan's inhibition before the institutions of high culture, and the disabling silence which afflicts him when confronted by the world beyond the workshop.[51] Though he mentions in passing that the decorator has never made any money, in a paradoxical way he remains more of an ideal for Corbon than the successful printer, since in his failure he ostensibly confirms Corbon's thesis that work well done brings its own rewards.[52]

Such a conclusion conveniently overlooked the overwhelming practical obstacles that confined the artisan to his labor, like it or not. As Corbon's erstwhile associates on *L'Atelier* had to admit, any form of training, vocational or otherwise, made financial demands that few were able to meet. The price of paper, pens, and geometric instruments was a real disincentive to workers hoping to attend evening classes at les Arts et métiers or l'Ecole polytechnique,[53] and take-up of such initiatives seems to have been limited.[54] Indeed, the overwhelming physical demands of the working day, which could be fourteen hours or more in length, meant that any leisure pursuits had to be snatched from the brief respite the worker was allowed to restore his depleted physical strength. Under such circumstances, as Perdiguier pointed out, the worker had "difficulties keeping his eyes open and his mind alert," and little guarantee that his intellectual exertions would bring any tangible return.[55] The very logic of the market, with its increasing reliance on unskilled operatives performing a limited range of repetitive tasks, envisaged rest and remuneration as little more than the minimum required to sustain the individual's labor power. Far from providing the worker-intellectual with a material independence which guaranteed his artistic integrity, labor rather monopolized the time and sapped the energies upon which cultural aspirations relied. As Charles Noiret, a hand-loom weaver from Rouen, remarked in 1836:

Since his profit is inadequate, the worker must work fifteen to eighteen hours a day: he then has neither time nor means to develop his intelligence, something he doesn't even think of, so much is he ground down by misery. To win these things, the privileges, prohibitions and monopolies which burden the industry would have to be progressively removed, something which will not happen in a hurry.[56]

Noiret was typical in regarding popular intellectual emancipation as contingent on economic transformation, and in common with most radical workers favored cooperative associations as the solution to moral and material exploitation. Indeed, an enterprise such as *L'Atelier*, in which contributors pooled their talents in anonymously published articles, itself pointed to the benefits of association.[57] In an environment where the labor process increasingly fragmented the worker, reducing him to little more than a set of isolated gestures dictated by the overall logic of production, collective artistic labor symbolized a rediscovery not only of individual integrity, but of the organic bonds uniting the artisanal community. Commitment to cooperative work fostered an idealization of such past artistic undertakings as the cathedrals, where a unity between artist and artisan, laborer and master, ostensibly enhanced the work and ennobled the worker.[58] By contrast, the threat of isolation symbolized at once the greatest impediment to intellectual advance and, in a tragic paradox, one of its greatest consequences in dividing the worker from his fellows.

As Agricol Perdiguier was to emphasize, ignorance was born of isolation. In a dialogue on poetry included in his *Livre du compagnonnage*, a worker who has written a number of poems oblivious to the basic rules of versification expresses dismay on learning his error: "Oh! if only I'd known," he complains, "I wouldn't have made so many, but I would have made better ones. Oh! poor orphans of fortune, we are so tied down! There are so many obstacles standing in our way and so many difficulties in breaking them and taking a few steps forward."[59] The autodidact's disenfranchisement was blamed for frustrating any efforts to master the language of a culture whose codes remained out of reach. Yet acknowledgment of the authority of such codes – a willingness to accept consecrated values on their own terms – helped to handicap the artisan, distanced him from the vernacular culture of his own class, and condemned him to the often condescending recognition of social superiors for his impersonation of a language which was not his own. It could condemn him, too, to isolation within his own community, where his interests and aspirations could inspire bemused incomprehension or smouldering hostility. The radical campaigner Flora Tristan noted the often harsh treatment visited on the worker-intellectual during her *Tour de France*,[60] and her observations are vividly confirmed by the Rouennais tinsmith Charles Beuzeville who in 1844 complained of the moral hardships suffered by poets such as he:

In the midst of their fellows, they are like strangers speaking a foreign language, whose feelings are continually hurt without it even being noticed. Unless he enjoys widely recognized success, the worker-poet is treated as conceited by some, as mad by others, and as naïve by all. He is thus obliged to isolate himself; and, since talent is merely the result of inspiration following the rules of art and directed by a constant observation of the human heart and mind, which he must satisfy, his enforced isolation becomes one of the obstacles which he must overcome to make himself understood by anybody.[61]

There is, perhaps, just a little too much here of the romantic outsider, of the *"génie incompris,"* for Beuzeville's remarks to carry complete conviction. Yet, his insistence on the impoverishment of his artistic inspiration by the internal exile he suffers within his own class suggests the humiliation of the misfit rather than the imperious disdain of the self-proclaimed superior.

The dilemmas and discomforts of the artisan, squaring up to a culture which exacted such a high moral cost on individual workers, form part of a broader crisis in perceptions of labor and hierarchies of production which marked the mid nineteenth century. As unskilled workers threatened to displace established artisans, as the production line supplanted the craftsman, as female operatives colonized the masculine sphere of the workplace, so artisans attempted to assert their professional distinction from the casual laborer as a means of defending their traditional status as members of a popular elite. Education played a crucial role in this process.[62] So too did claims to a cultural mastery which differentiated artisans from the unlettered proletariat and cast a reflected glory on the craft-based milieu from which they emerged. The overt radicalism affected by so many of these artisan-intellectuals was thus strongly qualified by a conservative impulse to preserve traditional differentials from the incipient threats of industrialization.

This rearguard action emerges most strongly in the brief renaissance of the *compagnonnage* movement, with its carefully preserved history and esoteric rituals, which surrounded the various crafts it embraced with a mystique designed to elevate them above the demeaning regime of the factory and the dispiriting routine of the machine-hand. To this degree, isolation was an objective, rather than an unfortunate side-effect, of cultural aspiration. Yet it was an objective only imperfectly achieved, since it merely exacerbated the ambivalent status of a group struggling to preserve an identity which was inevitably compromised by the pace of economic change. The worker-intellectual was almost inevitably consigned to the periphery, a marginality which reinforced his impotence. Yet if cultural assimilation offered no real basis for social renegotiation, other strategies did suggest themselves. If the artisan could not be an artist in traditionally ordained terms, he could attempt to reverse the equation, to claim that work itself was a form of art – a process of self-realization which transcended the material procedures and practical consequences of purposive labor. To lodge such claims for work was to position the craft skills of the artisan as an unalienated form of production akin to the creation of the artist. More importantly, such skills clearly demarcated a regime of labor-as-art from the monotonous regularity endured by the unskilled operative.

III

The sapping of popular creativity by reliance on the machine attracted increasing comment during the course of the century. A by-product of the machine was the man-machine, deprived of initiative, technically illiterate, skilled in only the most rudimentary gestures, and alienated from a productive' process in which he had little emotional investment or practical insight. As the author of a professional drawing manual remarked in 1863: "More and more, mechanical automation is replacing the hand. Workers' creative potential is no longer exploited. One would at least hope that they would know how to read the language of industry that is drawing, but they have learnt only how to copy clumsy models."[63]

Both practically and symbolically, drawing was an integral element in elevating the artisan and securing claims for the creative status of traditional craft skills. As a conceptual aid to carpentry, metalwork, stone carving and the like, drawing provided the theoretical underpinning to manual realization, investing in the worker an executive responsibility which implied an ability to think through problems abstractly and find practical solutions. Drawing was thus the visual manifestation of thought applied to craft – hence the disdain for its misuse as a debased mechanical aid requiring little theoretical insight.[64] For the *compagnon* Agricol Perdiguier, drawing united the artisan not only with the medieval mason but also with the great artists of the past, Raphael and Michelangelo, whose cartoons, he claimed, served the same function as the worker's portfolio of geometric plans.[65] Drawing at once testified to the artisan's responsiveness to beauty[66] and to a venerable tradition of mathematical knowledge, credit for which had been usurped by established *savants*' more recent claims to have systematized practical geometry.[67] Rather than being treated merely as a necessary tool allowing the craftsman to pursue his trade with efficiency and skill, drawing acquired an almost metaphysical status as birthright, guarantor of social eminence, and guardian of the integrity of labor. In the words of Perdiguier:

Drawing gives us the courage to undertake all sorts of work, and the facility to complete it successfully by the most economical and reliable means; drawing attracts the admiration and regard of the community at large as well as the respect and benevolence of the workers we employ. Drawing, in a word, is the soul of carpentry.[68]

The promotion of the artisan as a vernacular equivalent to the artist, possessing a body of theoretical knowledge embodied in objects which retained the particular mark of their maker, lay at the heart of *compagnonnage*. The flowering of this long-established workers' movement in the mid nineteenth century testifies to the value invested in craft as a response to deskilling, while the conflicts which set its constituent groups against each other for much of the period betray their anxieties in the face of economic change.[69] Beyond the practical assistance the *compagnons* offered to young artisans accomplishing the *Tour de France* in terms of shelter, pastoral care, and professional placement, they upheld an ideology of labor which implicitly elevated craft skills to the status of art. Not only did they provide drawing instruction – the carpenters ran six schools in the Paris area in 1850, while figures such as Perdiguier offered private lessons[70] – they further undertook to initiate novice artisans into tricks of the trade that only an experienced professional could teach.[71] In this respect, the institutions and practices of *compagnonnage* bear more than a passing resemblance to artistic apprenticeship. Perdiguier's description of drawing schools, in which benevolent artisans oversee students' first steps in geometry and architectural draughtsmanship, as well as supervising practical exercises in carpentry, recalls the academic principle of "émulation." His evocation of these "écoles mutuelles d'arts, de sciences et de fraternité" stresses popular solidarity rather than competitive individualism: "The teachers, generally chosen from amongst the most enlightened *compagnons*, direct all their attention to their many pupils, who themselves, in their generous regard for each other, exchange advice: knowledge is held in common."[72]

The principle of professional continuity, central to Beaux-Arts training, was exemplified in the prize objects which decorated the drawing schools and the "salles des modèles" in branch offices (or *cayennes*), which could be studied by itinerant apprentices, whose *Tour de France* itself bears some comparison to the academic rite of passage in the *Prix de Rome*. These exemplary objects, known as "*chefs d'œuvre*," fulfilled a variety of functions, one of which was to serve as reception pieces confirming the artisan's mastery of his trade. Again, analogies with the academic "*morceau de réception*," abolished during the Revolution, are quite vivid. Yet, in its multiple manifestations, the *chef d'œuvre* went far beyond this limited warranty of competence to map out an elaborate aesthetic of labor, ironically rooted in the gratuitous expenditure of time and skill.[73]

Almost by definition, the *chef d'œuvre* was an exercise in the mastery of difficulty for its own sake. The miniature scale generally employed or the fanciful nature of the object produced ensured that these bravura displays of ingenuity enshrined the disinterested process of their own manufacture. Whether modeled by a single individual, or by a group of craftsmen working together, the *chef d'œuvre* was essentially intended to do no more or less than dazzle the informed observer by its accumulation of technical problems effortlessly solved, its elegant display of artistry reveling in its own confident superiority (fig. 6.3). Though in a number of celebrated instances *chefs d'œuvre* were produced in order to arbitrate between rival groups of *compagnons* operating in a contested locality, more often than not they served either as a material record of individual skill or as a focus for collective identity, to be paraded through the streets on public holidays or at religious festivals. As the imagery of *compagnonnage* itself confirms, the *chef d'œuvre* played a key role in the personal and collective self-definition of the artisans who formed the movement, emblematizing the intellectual accomplishment and manual dexterity to which its members lay claim.[74]

As an ostentatious display of nonpurposive labor, the *chef d'œuvre* represented a symbolic defiance of the logic of capitalist production. Its very complexity announced the extravagant expenditure of time invested in its construction – a carpenter's baldaquino could take anything up to twenty years to complete, incorporating many thousand individually crafted elements.[75] Its disinterested production implied an independence from the cash nexus – in 1889 the maker of an elaborately carved walking stick, completed some twenty-five years previously, declined the offer of 1,000 francs from a prestigious umbrella maker, merely to display the *chef d'œuvre* in his shop window.[76] Finally, its ingenuity conferred prestige and commanded respect – such was the fame of a boot elaborately decorated with mythological scenes in silk thread, that under the Second Empire Napoleon III invited its maker, the cobbler Pierre Capus, to an audience at the Tuileries.[77] The *chef d'œuvre* asserted the worker's apparent control over his own destiny: it represented an independence from constraints of time and money and thereby pointed to the superior social standing of its producer. It epitomized, too, a privileged relationship between artisan and object, in striking contrast to the alienation reputedly experienced by the unskilled laborer in his dependence on the capitalist entrepreneur. As an exercise in work for work's sake, the *chef d'œuvre* aspired to the condition of art, its maker to the status of artist.

Fig. 6.3 *The Berryer: chef d'œuvre* presented to the lawyer Berryer by the Compagnons Passants Charpentiers du Devoir, Bons-Drilles du Tour de France (Soubises) in 1845

Yet the obsessive, almost neurotic quality of the *chef d'œuvre* betrays the delusive nature of such ambitions, caught as they were in the powerful countercurrent of economic change. The assertion of work as art which they embodied presupposed the survival of specialized crafts as central activities in the modern world, an assumption inexorably undermined by the gradual shift to mass production. Indeed, it is striking that those political theorists most wedded to the ideal of unalienated labor as a universalized form of art – most notably Fourier and Proudhon – were least able to envisage the consequences of mechanization for traditional working practices.[78] Beyond this, the aestheticization of labor implicitly invested in the artisan a degree of autonomy and public credit unavailable in the more regulated organization of the capitalist enterprise. Under such a regime, it was the entrepreneur who was celebrated for the excellence of his products, rather than those whom he employed.

This tension between recognition and invisibility surfaces as a central concern in 1863, in the reports published by the workers' delegations to the previous year's International Exhibition in London. Claims to artistic standing are lodged by a number of delegations, both through the language they employ in evaluating examples of their craft displayed at the show and in the references they draw upon in establishing their professional pedigree.[79] While ornamental sculptors cite Ghiberti, Cellini, and Jean Goujon in deploring the fragmentation which has relegated their own speciality to a lowly artisanal status,[80] bronze workers evoke Phidias and Michelangelo, and affect a tone which privileges the worker's individual temperament and imagination, rather than his manual skill.[81] In common with other groups, they express resentment at their exclusion from established artistic institutions and call upon the state to extend its patronage as a means of enhancing the public reputation of art workers.[82] Libraries, museums of decorative art, drawing schools – in effect an artisanal counterpart to the Ecole des beaux-arts: such measures are prescribed as a means of safeguarding the worker's status and allowing the refinement of his craft.[83]

Yet, even as such solutions are presented, a lurking suspicion remains that the very structures ever more tightly embracing such trades preclude the reassuring myths of the artist-artisan. The bronze workers reserve special praise for the chasing work of the French craftsman Antoine Vechte, remarking, "he has not allowed his name to be hidden by his bosses, and has signed his own work,"[84] yet such an act of naming, of laying claim to one's work as an emanation of oneself, flew in the face of a planification of labor which was increasingly accused of denying the individual a creative identity, an investment in the product of his own hand. For decorative sculptors, this suppression of independent initiative was blamed upon an increasing specialization which condemned them to mere imitation in which "one is no longer oneself" and "imagination becomes an error, originality a crime."[85] Yet, as the jewelry workers understood, comprehensive appropriation of the commodity by the manufacturer or retailer abstracted out the material process of production embodied in the craftsman himself:

If the true creator of a piece – in other words the worker or designer – is disqualified from exhibiting and being credited with any glory it may merit, then at least let it go no further than the manufacturer. When we see the shopkeeper – the intermediary between the customer and the manufacturer, who is himself not the true producer – when we see this merchant competing over the merit of a work which he has not made and would be incapable of making, then we feel ill at ease in the judgment we pass on objects that we know full well were made – and will be made – in factories entirely foreign to the exhibitor.[86]

It is the realization that they are in fact implicated in the conflict between capital and labor which ultimately cuts across the delegates' rhetoric of the artist-artisan. Not that one defeats, or supplants, the other; rather, they coexist in an awkward, irreconcilable tension. Old habits die hard. Yet over and over, disinterested appraisal of artistic excellence and technical skill is brought short by a litany of grievances over pay, working conditions, and unemployment.[87] All of a sudden, the "*artiste*" becomes an "*ouvrier*," rewarded and treated as such. The old nostrums of workers' associations, familiar from the pages of *L'Atelier* and the debates of 1848, are endlessly revived, but the space they once apparently offered, satisfying the worker's aspirations to elevate his craft to the refinement of art while meeting his personal aspirations for cultural self-improvement, seem increasingly vague and anachronistic.

IV

The unstable union between art and labor fashioned to sustain political aspiration and personal self-worth was central to the image of the earnest, respectable worker savaged by Paul Lafargue in his classic Marxist polemic *Le Droit à la paresse*, published in 1880. In this searing "Réfutation du 'Droit au travail' de 1848," Lafargue

165

gleefully demolishes the ethical structure which an earlier generation of artisans and theorists had elaborated to justify popular
participation in the life of the polis. Dismissing the workers'
"morbid passion for labor," he maintains that "all individual and
social miseries"[88] derive from their misguided complicity in an
economy which benefits an idle minority at the price of mass
suffering and exhaustion.

Lafargue's iconoclasm is far removed from the measured tones of a
Perdiguier or the high-mindedness of *L'Atelier*. We are dealing here
with a different generation, a different ideology, a different order of
discourse. The very language of irony and invective conveys a
truculent aggression impatient with the deference implicit in much
of the rhetoric of the incipient workers' movement. With his radical
inversion of values, duties, and pleasures, Lafargue has no time for
the aestheticization of labor let alone the standards of a culture
founded on measure and moderation. The censorious tone of the
outraged artisan, shocked by the Salon nude or the rumbustious
vulgarity of carnival, gives way to a Rabelaisian fantasy of culture as
violence, dissonance, and subversion. Legislators and army officers
are conscripted into miming humiliating parodies of their erstwhile
roles, Gambetta and Cassagnac are reduced to sideshow acts, providing the warm-up for a *"Farce électorale"* in which former
deputies, dressed in motley, perform grotesque dances and wipe
their backsides with election manifestos.[89] Spectacle thus not only
symbolizes social inversion, it also consolidates it through relegating
former rulers to the marginal status of burlesques.

Within Lafargue's robust vision of culture as social catharsis,
carnival becomes a paradigm for insubordination and a swaggering
exposure of art's edifying pretensions as nothing more than a
hypocritical confidence trick designed to maintain received inequal-
ities. Tapping into a tradition whose moral implications the *Atelier-
istes*, had explicitly condemned, Lafargue evokes a demotic culture
of *charivari* and excess more akin to the casual sadism of Contat's
cat massacre or the whiff of rebellion at *mardi gras*[90] than to the
artisans' earnest world of carefully wrought verse and conscientious
craftsmanship. Lafargue celebrates a satirical outlook whose very
savagery drowns out the calls for harmony and restraint inherent in
the language of high culture. The putative bonds between art and
labor are violently ruptured in a gesture which denounces the
ethical foundations of their union as sustaining, rather than attenu-
ating, the age-old division between hand and brain.

Notes

I should like to thank Katie Scott and David Solkin for the invitation which led me to undertake this piece, and to Ruth Harris, Olga Grlic, and former colleagues at the University of East Anglia for their helpful comments on an earlier version. All quotations from French texts have been translated by myself.

1 P. Deruineau, *Souvenirs d'un ouvrier . . . peintre en décors* (Angers: Bource et Maige, 1850), p. 11.

2 Ibid., p. 20.

3 "Il ne peut plus y avoir désormais parmi nous d'autres titres, d'autres distinctions que ceux que donnent le mérite et la vertu. La société française n'est donc plus formée de classes, mais de citoyens, mais de frères participant aux mêmes droits, jouissant des mêmes avantages" (Ibid., p. 64).

4 For the fullest exploration of this position, see Jacques Rancière, *La Nuit des prolétaires. Archives du rêve ouvrier* (Paris: Fayard, 1981).

5 See Jacques Rancière, *Le Philosophe et ses pauvres* (Paris: Fayard, 1983) and his "La représentation de l'ouvrier ou la classe impossible," in Philippe Lacoue-Labarthe and Jean-Luc Nancy, ed., *Le Retrait du politique* (Paris: Galilée, 1983), esp. pp. 93–5.

6 Jacques Rancière, "Ronds de fumée (Les Poètes ouvriers dans la France de Louis-Philippe)," *Revue des sciences humaines* 61.190 (April–June 1983), 34.

7 Jacques Rancière, "Good Times or Pleasure at the Barrière," in Adrian Rifkin and Roger Thomas, ed., and John Moore, trans., *Voices of the People: The Social Life of "La Sociale" at the End of the Second Empire* (London and New York: Routledge and Kegan Paul, 1988), p. 51.

8 Rancière, "Ronds de fumée," 43.

9 Ibid., 33.

10 See M. Agulhon, "Le Problème de la culture populaire en France autour de 1848," *Romantisme* 9 (1975), 50–64.

11 Pierre Vinçard, *Les Artistes et le peuple* (Paris, 1850), p. 7.

12 On the abstract nature of understandings of labor around 1848, see William Sewell, *Work and Revolution in France: The Language of Labour from the Old Régime to 1848* (Cambridge University Press, 1980), p. 267. On artists, writers, and intellectuals as *"producteurs,"* in the context of artisanal discourse of the 1840s, see Auguste-Antoine Giraud, *Réflexions philosophiques sur le Compagnonnage et le tour de France* (Paris: Allovard, 1846), p. 53.

13 See G. Matoré, "Les Notions d'art et d'artiste à l'époque romantique," *Revue des sciences humaines* (April–September 1951), 120–36.

14 As is claimed by the communist Edouard Hervé ("De l'art," *L'Intelligence, Journal de la réforme sociale* [July 1838], 14), "Presque tous sont sortis des rangs du peuple, presque tous ont partagé sa misère, ses angoisses de chaque jour dans le monde, où tout est froid, compassé et de convention."

15 See, for example, the remarks on "cette classe d'artistes que j'appellerais volontiers la classe ouvrière" in a discussion of the art market and administrative policy in Laurent de Mars, "Salon de 1838," *L'Intelligence* (April 1838), 14. See also the response to Saint-C[héron], "De la position sociale des artistes," *L'Artiste* 1.4 (1832), 50–3, signed "Un Artiste." This challenges the claim made by the former Saint-Simonian that the free market offered the artist a degree of independence denied by the more hierarchical system obtaining under the *ancien régime* ("[L'artiste] n'est plus un valet, mais peuple, il n'attend son salaire que de son travail et des productions libres de son génie," 53). Instead, the anonymous correspondent responds that "L'artiste est un peu comme le prolétaire qui a payé au prix de la misère toutes les conquêtes de sa liberté," 81.

16 Anon., "Manifeste du Comité central des artistes," *La Voix des artistes* 1 (August 15, 1849), 1. On the organizational implications of such a perspective, see Neil McWilliam, "Art, Labour and Mass Democracy: Debates on the Status of the Artist in France around 1848," *Art History* 11.1 (March 1988), 64–87.

17 Anon., "Salon de 1844," *L'Atelier* 4.7 (April 1844), 109–10. On the damaging impact of commerce on literature, see, for example, the anonymous review of Lachambeaudie's *Fables* in the communist *La Fraternité* (August 1846), 171–2.

18 See Anon., "Salon de 1844," *L'Atelier* 4.7 (March 1844), 55.

19 See, for example, the anonymous review article "Marines. Poésies de M. Ch. Poncy, ouvrier maçon, de Toulon," *L'Atelier* 2.9 (May 1842), 71; Anon., "Des fêtes publiques," *L'Atelier* 3.11 (July 1843), 99–100; Anon., "Le Carré des fêtes aux Champs-Elysées," *L'Atelier* 7.11 (August 1847), 553.

20 Anon., "De l'instruction de l'ouvrier," *L'Atelier* 4.2 (November 1843), 23–4.

21 On the notion of popular creativity, see, for example, George Sand, "Arts," *La Cause du peuple* 2 (April 16, 1848), 26–7, reprinted in G. Sand, *Questions d'art et de littérature* (Paris: Calmann-Levy, 1878), pp. 231–2. On "instinct" as a shared characteristic of the people and the genius, see Jules Michelet, *Le Peuple* (1846; Paris: Hachette, 1974), pp. 184–6. More generally, on romantic populism, see Alain Pessin, *Le Mythe du peuple et la société française du XIX siècle* (Paris: Presses universitaires de France, 1992).

22 See, for example, Fortunat, "Du colportage des mauvais livres," *L'Ange gardien* 1 (1848), 466–9.

23 Antoine-Honoré Frégier, *Des classes dangereuses de la population des grandes villes et des moyens de les rendre meilleurs* (1838; Paris: J.-B. Baillière, 1840), p. 363. See also Frégier's observation: "ce qui manque le plus aux classes pauvres, c'est le sentiment vrai de leur situation, et la force de s'y conformer," quoted in René Parize, "Savoir de soumission ou savoirs de révolte? L'Exemple du Creusot," in Jean Borreil, ed., *Les Sauvages dans la cité. Auto-émancipation du peuple et instruction des*

prolétaires au XIXe siècle (Paris: Presses universitaires de France, 1985), p. 92.

24 On "bibliothèques populaires," see, for example, Emile Bères, *Les Classes ouvrières, Moyens d'améliorer leur sort sous le rapport du bien-être matériel et du perfectionnement moral* (Paris: Charpentier, 1836), pp. 237–9; on festivals, see ibid., pp. 243–4; on control of the theatre, see, for example, Frégier, *Classes dangereuses*, p. 410.

25 Ulysse Ladet, "De l'influence des beaux-arts sur la civilisation," *L'Artiste* 3.1 (1842), 83.

26 On the 1836 competition, for which Delessert offered a 2,000 franc prize, see J. Janin, "Salon de 1839," *L'Artiste*, 2.2.24 (1839), 339.

27 Quoted in Rancière, *La Nuit des prolétaires*, p. 276.

28 On literature, see, for example, the communist Albert La Ponneraye, "Le but que tout écrivain doit se proposer, c'est d'éclairer et de moraliser les masses," *in Mélanges d'économie sociale, de littérature et de morale*, 2 vols. (Paris: pub au Dépôt, 1835), vol. II, pp. 97–101.

29 Anon., "Salon de 1844," *L'Atelier*, 55.

30 See Vinçard, *Les Artistes et le peuple*, p. 8, on Scheffer, David d'Angers, and Rude's *Marseillaise*.

31 See Armand Cuvillier, "Les Journaux ouvriers en France avant 1840," in *Hommes et idéologies de 1840* (Paris: Librairie M. Rivière, 1956), pp. 87–94, and, more particularly, A. Cuvillier, *Un Journal d'ouvriers: L'Atelier, 1840–1850* (Paris: Editions ouvrières, 1954).

32 See Edmond Thomas, *Voix d'en bas. La Poésie ouvrière du XIXe siècle* (Paris: F. Maspero, 1979); Edgar Leon Newman, "The New World of the French Socialist Worker Poets: 1830–1848," *Stanford French Review* 3.3 (1979), 357–68.

33 See Jacques Rancière "Savoirs hérétiques et émancipation du pauvre," in Borreil, ed., *Les Sauvages dans la cité*, pp. 37–8.

34 Agricol Perdiguier, *Le Livre du compagnonnage* (Paris: Pagnorre, 1841), 2nd edn (2 vols.) vol. II, p. 105n2.

35 Though see Michelet's rejection of worker-poets' imitation of established poetic forms in *Le Peuple*, p. 159.

36 Olinde Rodrigues, ed., *Poésies sociales des ouvriers* (Paris: Paulin, 1841), p. iii.

37 Quoted in E. Dolléans, *Féminisme et mouvement ouvrier, George Sand* (Paris: Editions ouvrières, 1951), p. 15. See also Béranger's remark to the mason Charles Poncy: "Se faire de la littérature un poste pour déserter son métier c'est faire croire qu'on méprise la classe dans laquelle on est né, c'est no plus vouloir être peuple; et ce peuple, comment le relèvera-t-on si, dès qu'on s'en distingue par quelque rare talent, on se hâte de s'en séparer? Si cela vous est possible, mon enfant, restez maçon, sans rien négliger pour devenir grand poëte." Cited in a review by the button-maker Lombard of "Préface aux Poésies de Poncy, par Georges [*sic*] Sand," *La Ruche populaire* 5 (May 1844), 149.

38 See, for example, Alphonse Viollet, *Les Poètes du peuple au XIXe siècle*

(1846; Geneva: Slatkine, 1980) with its negative assessment of the work of socialist print-worker Eugène Orrit (p. 125) as opposed to the admired Christian resignation of Théodore Lebreton. Orrit's early death, like the celebrated fate of worker-poet Hégésippe Moreau, is explicitly linked with his inappropriate ambitions, both political and artistic. On worker-poets in general, Viollet remarks, "loin de s'emporter contre la rigueur de leur sort, ils se montrent calmes, patients, résignés, parce qu'ils espèrent" (p. iii).

39 Ant.[oinel E.[tex], statuaire et peintre, letter dated "Paris, ler janvier 1847," *La Ruche populaire* 9 (January 1847), 18. Etex concludes: "Courage, donc, travailleurs, aimez vos travaux, votre vie est plus libre, votre rôle est plus noble et plus beau; du calme, de l'ordre, de la résignation." See also the attack on artistic vocation as "une maladie morale . . . une passion malheureuse, alimentée par l'orgueil et la paresse," in Henri Leneveux, *Almanach-manuel d'apprentissage. Guide pour le choix d'un état industriel* (Paris: Passard, 1855), p. 27. A typographer and republican free-thinker, Leneveux was associated with *L'Atelier* before 1848 and founded la Bibliothèque des connaissances utiles, a series of cheap pamphlets in which this manual appeared.

40 Pierre Vinçard, "Une Vie perdue," *La Ruche populaire* 2 (June 1841), 17. For a further example of this genre, involving a worker aspiring to become a visual artist, see Hippolyte Voileau, "Théophile Renaud," in *Souvenirs et nouvelles* 2 vols. (Paris, 1859), a short story written around 1847–8.

41 On suspicion towards professionalized culture, particularly journalism, see L. F. Kuhn (dessinateur lithographe), "Cur non," *La Ruche populaire* 2 (November 1841), 6–11.

42 Ibid., 10.

43 Anon., "Poncy," *La Ruche populaire* 5 (March 1844), 81. In the same issue, Léon Leroy extols the "indépendance" and "liberté" conferred by Poncy's labor; see his review of *Le Chantier*, pp. 89–95. See also Jules Vinçard's review of Poncy's earlier collection, *Marines*, in *La Ruche populaire* 3 (May 1842), 12.

44 On the independence afforded by his work as a cobbler, see the introduction by Eugène Sue to Savinien Lapointe's *Une Voix d'en bas* (Paris: Bureau de l'imprimerie, 1844), p. x.

45 Gabriel Gauny, "Opinions," *La Ruche populaire* 2 (April 1841), 18.

46 On the repression of creativity by labor, see C. Debeaux, commis en soieries, "Réponse au Globe," *La Ruche populaire* 2 (October 1841), 21. A similar point emerges in a text by a disciple of Pierre Leroux dedicated to the glorification of labor: Joseph-Pierre-Basile Robert du Var, *Histoire de la classe ouvrière*, 4 vols. (Paris: Michel, 1845–50), vol. IV, p. 436. The issue of workers' negative representation of labor is explored by Jacques Rancière in "The Myth of the Artisan: Critical Reflections on a Category of Social History," in Steven Kaplan and Cynthia Koepp, ed., *Work in France: Representations, Meanings, Orga-*

nization and Practice (Ithaca, NY: Cornell University Press, 1986), pp. 317ff.

47 Anon., "De l'instruction de l'ouvrier," *L'Atelier* 4.2 (November 1843), 24.

48 On l'Ecole gratuite and drawing tuition in mid-century Paris, see Anne Middleton Wagner, *Jean-Baptiste Carpeaux: Sculptor of the Second Empire* (New Haven and London: Yale University Press, 1986), pp. 29–62.

49 Anthime Corbon, *De l'enseignement professionnel* (Paris: Librairie Germer Baillière, 1859), p. 47

50 Ibid., p. 46.

51 A more negative presentation of the worker's frustrated artistic vocation is presented by Robert du Var, *Histoire de la classe ouvrière*, vol. IV, p. 436, a position that conflicts with the author's eulogy of the nobility of labor.

52 Corbon himself corresponds to the versatile decorator in his own professional trajectory, in which he was apprenticed to a weaver before becoming in turn a sign painter, a surveyor, a print worker, a wood carver, and a stonemason. Elected to the Assembly in 1848, he briefly returned to wood-carving under the Second Empire. Having renounced the radical beliefs he shared with his former colleagues on *L'Atelier* he became a professional publicist, joining the daily *Le Siècle* in 1863.

53 Anon., "De l'instruction de l'ouvrier," 24.

54 See Georges Duveau, *La Pensée ouvrière sur l'éducation pendant la Seconde République et le Second Empire* (Paris: Domat-Montchrestien, 1948), p. 287. He argues that "bibliothèques populaires" enjoyed a similarly restricted success (p. 289).

55 Perdiguier, *Livre du compagnonnage*, vol. II, p. 104. On the restraints imposed on the worker's intellectual development by the physical demands of labor, see also Agricole Perdiguier, *Biographie de l'auteur du Livre du compagnonage* [sic] (Paris: Pagnorre, 1846), p. 7.

56 Charles Noiret, *Mémoires d'un ouvrier rouennais* (Rouen: François, 1836), p. 49. The textile industry in Rouen at this period was still largely based on outworking and small workshops operating on piece rates.

57 See Anon., "De l'association dans les travaux intellectuels," *L'Atelier* 4.3 (December 1843), 38–41.

58 See, for example, Perdiguier, *Livre du compagnonnage*, vol. II, pp. 176–7, 181.

59 Ibid., vol. II, p. 140.

60 See the remarks quoted in Thomas, *Voix d'en bas*, p. 74.

61 Quoted in Viollet, *Les Poètes du peuple*, p. 207.

62 See Alain Faure's introduction to *Agricol Perdiguier, Mémoires d'un compagnon* (Paris: Librairie du Compagnonnage, 1977), p. 28. On the defensive nature of craft valorization, see Michelle Perrot, "On the Formation of the French Working Class," in Ira Katznelson and Aristide R. Zolberg, ed., *Working-Class Formation: Nineteenth-Century Patterns in Western Europe and the United States* (Princeton University Press, 1986), p. 82.

63 J. Fauché, *De l'enseignement oral du dessin industriel*, cited in Yves Deforge, *Le Graphisme technique, son Histoire et son enseignement* (Paris: H. Champion, 1981), p. 225.

64 See Perdiguier, *Livre du Compagnonnage*, vol. I, p. 119.

65 Perdiguier, *Biographie*, p. 88. On the unity of theory and practice represented in medieval working practices, see Pierre Vinçard, *Histoire du travail et des travailleurs en France*, 2 vols. (Paris: P. Vinçard, 1845), vol. I, pp. 267–8.

66 See the discussion of Simonin's *Traité de la coupe des pierres ou art du trait* in P. Barret and J.-N. Gurgand, *Ils voyagaient la France. Vie et traditions des Compagnons du tour de France au XIXe siècle* (Paris: Hachette, 1980), p. 238.

67 See Perdiguier's attack on Monge and other theorists in the *Biographie* (p. 89), where he reproaches the *savant* for obscuring workers' prior claims to technical innovation: "ne nous dénigrez pas, ne faites pas de nous d'absurdes machines; ne nous dépouillez pas de la pensée, ne nous contestez plus la légitime possession du capital scientifique qui est à nous."

68 Perdiguier, *Livre du compagnonnage*, vol. I, p. 139.

69 On tensions within *compagnonnage* under the Restoration and July Monarchy, see, for example, J.-P. Bayard, *Le Compagnonnage en France* (Paris: Payot, 1990), pp. 124–30, and Emile Coornaert, *Les Compagnonnages en France du moyen âge à nos jours* (Paris: Editions ouvrières, 1966), pp. 65ff. On *compagnonnage* more generally, see Cynthia M. Truant, *The Rites of Labor. Brotherhoods of Compagnonnage in Old and New Regime France* (Ithaca: Cornell University Press, 1994).

70 On the carpenters' schools and Perdiguier's lessons, see Coornaert, *Compagnonnages en France*, p. 258.

71 On these "*tours de main*," see Roger Lecotté in the exhibition catalog *Le Compagnonnage vivant* (Paris, Hôtel de Sully, May–July 1973), p. 11.

72 Perdiguier, *Livre du compagnonnage*, vol. I, p. 155.

73 On the various circumstances which could lead to the production of *chefs d'œuvre*, see Roger Lecotté, *Chefs d'œuvre de compagnons* (Paris: Chêne-Hachette, 1980), pp. 16–28.

74 A partial introduction to the imagery of the movement is provided in Roger Lecotté, *Essai pour une iconographic compagnonnique. "Champs de conduite" et "Souvenirs" du Tour de France* (Paris: Hachette, 1948). This has been more recently extended by Laurent Bastard, "L'Iconographie compagnonique der XIXe siècle" in *Le Compagnonnage, chemin de l'excellence* (Paris: Musée des arts et traditions populaires, 1995–6), pp. 63–101.

75 The collectively produced baldaquino of the Compagnons Passants Charpentiers du Devoir in Paris was begun in 1866 and completed only in 1884. See Bayard, *Le Compagnonnage en France*, p. 316.

76 See *Le Compagnonnage vivant*, p. 19. The stick is now in the Musée du compagnonnage, in Tours.

77 Ibid., p. 18. The boot is also in the Tours museum.
78 For a discussion of Fourier's notion of labor as art in a regime of *"travail attrayant,"* see Neil McWilliam, *Dreams of Happiness. Social Art and the French Left, 1830–1850* (Princeton University Press, 1993). On Proudhon, see James Henry Rubin, *Realism and Social Vision in Courbet and Proudhon* (Princeton University Press, 1980), pp. 49–51, and the conclusion to McWilliam, *Dreams of Happiness*.
79 For a similar analysis, relating to the 1867 Paris exhibition, see Daniel Willbach, "Work and its Satisfactions: Origins of the French Labor Movement, 1864–1870" unpublished Ph.D. dissertation (University of Michigan, 1977), 215–33 and to Leora Auslander, *Taste and Power. Furnishing Modern France* (Berkeley: University of California Press, 1996), pp. 231–42.
80 *Délégations ouvrières à l'Exposition universelle de Londres en 1862. Rapports des délégués sculpteurs ornemanistes, des délégués de la marbrerie et des délégués tabletiers ivoiriers* (Paris, 1863), p. 3.
81 *Rapport des délégués du bronze, ciseleurs, tourneurs et monteurs* (Paris, 1863), pp. 28, 9.
82 Ibid., p. 38.
83 See, for example, ibid., p. 40 and *Rapports des délégués sculpteurs ornemanistes, des délégués de la marbrerie et des délégués tabletiers ivoiriers*, p. 11.
84 Ibid., p. 9. A similar point is made in the *Rapports des délégués sculpteurs ornemanistes, des délégués de la marbrerie et des délégués tabletiers ivoiriers*, p. 20. On Vechte, see Whitney Walton, *France at the Crystal Palace. Bourgeois Taste and Artisan Manufacture in the Nine-teenth Century* (Berkeley: University of California Press, 1992), pp. 153–4.
85 Ibid., p. 6. See also the complaint of the "monteurs de bronze" in *Rapport des délégués du bronze, ciseleurs, tourneurs et monteurs* that the better their work, the more invisible it is to the viewer.
86 *Rapport des délégués bijoutiers* (Paris, 1863), p. 3. A similar point had been made as early as 1844 in a report on the industrial exhibition by Pierre Vinçard, "De l'exposition en 1844," *L'Union* 2.7 (June 1844), 2. See also Doré, *L'Art, le capital et la patente* (Paris, 1848), pp. 13–15.
87 See, for example, *Rapport des délégués du bronze, ciseleurs, tourneurs et monteurs*, pp. 59–62.
88 Paul Lafargue, *Le Droit à la paresse* (1890; Paris: Mille et une nuits, 1994), pp. 121, 123.
89 Ibid., pp. 147–8.
90 See Alain Faure, *Paris carême-prenant. Du carnaval à Paris au XIXe siècle* (Paris: Hachette, 1978), pp. 114ff. on the links between carnival and political unrest in 1831 and 1848.

7

The war of tradition: Virginia Woolf and the temper of criticism

DANIEL COTTOM

You will understand that as I write this a war is being fought, and as I write this the war is over. There is nothing to disturb you in these contradictory words. You, too, have confided ink to paper, finally beginning your letter to that friend kissed by distance and transformed into a promising abstraction . . . only to find that by the time you came to a close, the world you were addressing had changed once again. Revision was still possible, the margins left room for scribbled addenda, or you may have decided just to throw the damn thing away so you could start afresh; but whatever you did, you knew there was no way to get around this impossible time of writing, which is never so simple as even to let its beginning be named by the date when the first line is struck on a page. As Charles Lamb put it, "But what security can I have that what I now send you for truth shall not before you get it unaccountably turn into a lie?"[1]

I must trust that you know all this as well as I do. And so you must be aware that I cannot hope to direct your attention to this war without addressing others. If I can attribute the beginning of this chapter to the fall of 1990, when I began to make notes for it, I might just as well refer to other times, with any selection among them having no more significance than the outcome of a lottery – and certainly no less. You have read your Borges; or if you have not, I can refer you to a figure loitering in the grim lobby of a dormitory in East Lansing, Michigan during another war, one the powerful enchantments of the media had yet to transform into a "syndrome," which in turn would be said to have been cured by the high-tech butchery of this impossible time, in which a war is now being fought and now is over. There may have been such an occasion, and this chapter may have had its beginning at the time when this student of literature walked over to look at the list of randomly ranked birth dates just then posted on the wall so he could learn his chances of toiling on in school, serving a term in prison, seeking refuge in Canada, or heading into battle.

"An adverse drawing might mean mutilation, a varied infamy, death," says the narrator of "The Babylon Lottery."[2] Taking a cue from this story, I could go on to mention other events, this or that time, each having something of the lottery about it; but there is no getting over the suspicion that doing so would be pointless. One might as well ask Virginia Woolf actually to produce the images to which she called her readers' attention when she wrote in *Three Guineas*, "Also consider these photographs. They are pictures of dead bodies and ruined houses."[3] Woolf included other photographs in this book, and she did not think the destruction considered here was meaningful only as a symbol, negligible as a historical event. Taking these circumstances into account, I have to believe that her omission of these photographs was an attempt to clarify something in them. Although it might seem perverse to say so, Woolf knew that what she was concerned to show us in these images of the Spanish Civil War would only be muddled by their reproduction within her book. As if anticipating the critique of documentary photography in the photomontages Martha Rosler made between 1967 and 1972, which combined images of embattled Vietnam with pictures from *House Beautiful*, Woolf knew better than to let photographs of the Spanish Civil War try to speak for themselves.[4]

"Great wars are strangely intermittent in their effects," Woolf noted elsewhere;[5] and certainly the time of other forms of art, such as photography, is no simpler than the time of writing. Woolf's decision was something of a gamble, then, something like a deliberate act of censorship, and just maybe a silent outburst of pure rage. One way or another, she figured the pictures would have said "this dead body" or "this ruined house" too simply, as I might have said "this war" or "this date"; and so the real battle would never have been joined.

In *Three Guineas* Woolf was concerned, *inter alia*, with the relation between anger and criticism, which is also the topic of this chapter. War seems almost immediately to come to mind when this topic is raised, as does censorship, which is as closely associated with the art of warfare as it is with art in general. And censorship, too, may be identified too hastily if we think it sufficient to wag a finger at government office holders, codes, and practices, all of which then appear to be related to warfare only by chance. Like

Woolf, William Blake knew better. He could hear the chilling rage of Urizen in the voice of reason: "For we have Hirelings in the Camp, the Court, & the University: who would if they could, for ever depress Mental & prolong Corporeal War."[6] No wonder Woolf recalled his example in her late essay, "Thoughts on Peace in an Air Raid" (1940), when she was contemplating the historical conditions that might lead women to suppress their own thinking on war in particular and politics in general.[7]

In its ordinary acceptance, in which it refers to the deliberate destruction or withholding of information, censorship does not begin adequately to represent the limits to "free speech," which is generally taken to be its opposite term. Currently, for instance, it cannot come anywhere close to grasping the phenomenon we witness when Henry Kissinger is hailed by the media as an "elder-statesman," a "distinguished diplomat," an "expert in foreign affairs." When these sorts of panegyrics are applied to this indivi-dual, the erasures necessary to produce such language could not be more obvious or odious; but how many in the media will be complaining about censorship?

The case is similar with war monuments, the works of art made to lend dignity to our frenzied butchery. As with the tomb of the Andronici in *Titus Andronicus* or Maya Lin's *Vietnam Veterans' Memorial* (1982) in Washington, DC, the only names they mention and the only figures they represent are "our own," and yet no one can hope to file suit under the Constitution to protest such practices. (This point was made by Chris Burden with his sculpture, *The Other Vietnam Memorial* [1991], which is designed to remind us that the names of millions of Vietnamese killed in this war have been ritually suppressed.) In keeping company with the ordinary notion of censor-ship, the First Amendment proves as hapless in this instance as when it comes to defining the difference between violence and legitimate speech. Thus, we learn that Barbara Foley had no right to be so angry when she tried to stop the leader of the so-called Nicaraguan Democratic Forces, Adolfo Calero, from spreading his lies about the Nicaraguan *contras* whom he had led (with the clandestine support of the Central Intelligence Agency and other government bodies);[8] meanwhile, his record of stilling voices by killing the bodies whence they emerged did not appear to strike Northwestern University as an infringement of free speech; and meanwhile, the Department of Defense would continue to sponsor research on our campuses as if the military engagements of the

United States had never been known to trifle in the least with anyone's rights.

You have heard all this many times before – for instance, when June Jordan protested the appearance of William Shockley, the famous exponent of scientific racism, at Yale University in 1975.[9] You know all this as well as I do, and yet I must think there is something we are still overlooking here, something we are surveying and repressing, mapping and missing, all at once. For if we cannot get past the ordinary notion of censorship, it hardly matters that we can condescend to it, recognizing how inept it is at making the discriminations that would be necessary to lead us to truth. The grace of a lie, like the aesthetics of a monument to war, cannot be judged in isolation from its political duties. If Immanuel Kant's sense of aesthetics demands that we find war sublime, there are many curious reasons motivating it, but none we can enter via the traditional gateway of censorship and free speech.[10] And what I say of censorship I may say as well of wars and lotteries: that after we are sure we have all seen the same pictures, known the same words, and so shared the same experiences, there is still something we are overlooking, something that goes to the very heart of our conception of virtue.

Traditionally, temperance is accounted one of the four cardinal virtues. In thinking about criticism and critical tradition, what we tend to overlook (even as it stares us right in the face) is that where we see the cardinal virtues of temperance, courage, justice, and prudence, we must also orient ourselves to a compass in which temperance may figure as anger, courage as a brutal declaration of war, justice as the irrational outcome of a lottery, and prudence as the grace that seeks to render acts of censorship sublime. In short, in these cardinal virtues we must also see what Blake called "the four iron pillars of Satan's Throne."[11]

To come to this recognition is to propose a different understanding of tradition – which is also, at the same time, a return to tradition. A consideration of the relation between anger and criticism may become an exemplary exercise in this respect. For from the time of Plato's *Republic* (in which lotteries, censorship, and warfare figure prominently) to the recent essay in which David Wojnarowicz happily envisioned the incineration of Senator Jesse Helms, thereby calling forth the panicked wrath of the National Endowment for the Arts,[12] the relation between anger and criticism has spelled out the polities we imagine for ourselves. However it is formulated, this relation appears fundamental to the chances we can expect of life, the battles we are led to fight, and the regulations through which we entertain experience. As they establish our sense of tradition, these issues of anger and criticism tell us what we can hope to arrive at through the impossible time of writing.

Of course, in what is most commonly pronounced in the name of Western critical tradition, anger is simply outlawed. As in Platonic discourse, it is said to show a lack of self-mastery, a groveling of the individual's higher self before his or her base passions, a failure of temperance or cultural tempering. So Kant noted that it must interfere with the freedom of the mind, without which one cannot hope to establish the vital possibility of a "censorship of taste."[13] This anger is then a solecism that marks the absence of a harmony one must desire – what Matthew Arnold, in *Culture and Anarchy*, called "sweetness and light."[14] Just as it can be counted on to sneer at dialectic or critical thought, so must anger mock the making of art, its cacophonous outbursts distracting us from what ought to be an imperative universality, as when William Wordsworth wrote of the "scorn and condemnation personal / That would profane the sanctity of verse."[15]

In this way of thinking, if art is not to run headlong toward its own destruction, its creators either must bridle themselves or, as Horace recommended in his *Art of Poetry*, look for a prudent critic to pull them back from the volcano's edge. Such anger is by no means the only danger artists and critics must avoid; but when they are possessed by anger, gripped by this madness, they are running wild and yet straight into the narrowest of cages. To those observing this spectacle, words like *distorted* or *warped* will come to mind and tell of anger as anamorphosis, an all-too-familiar perversion that can be corrected only through an all-too-rare form of reflection, the very reflection anger would seek to smash. Or a self may have been so upset that it has disappeared or completely split off from the figure acting intemperately, as when we describe individuals "beside themselves" with anger. Therefore, in the contemporary United States, we judge more severely crimes committed "in cold blood," and we construct an exception to the constitutional right to free speech based upon the category of "fighting words." These are utterances considered to be such a provocation to anger as actually to constitute an act of violence in and of themselves – although the deathly palaver of Professor Henry Kissinger, the racist and homophobic rantings of Senator Jesse Helms, or the half-in-love-witheaseful-war eloquence of those dear to the CIA, such as Adolfo Calero or George Herbert Bush, will not be judged to fall under this category, which is notorious in legal circles for its obscurity, as well it might be.[16]

In cases allowed to have extenuating circumstances, some pardon may await people in an angry condition, but precisely because these individuals are seen as pitiably disturbed. At the very least, they will be considered troubling neighbors, difficult to have around, an embarrassing reminder of noisome and squalling infancy, wild animality, or ancient blundering chaos. More importantly, their anger is likely to associate them with stubbornness, fanaticism, unholy zeal, and violent menace. For according to the tradition we are following here, to be ill-tempered is to be dangerously narrow or limited, hopelessly enthralled by the moment, and so unable to rise above the song and dance of the passing show to reach the timeless realm of transcendence, which is the sole dwelling place of a truth forever young. Eternally in contrast to such failure will be the example of Socrates, whose jailer, in the act of handing him his poison, said he was certain the philosopher would not be mad at him.

This tradition would have it that those who are angry are unable to do justice to any subject. Insufficiently reserved, overrunning their own boundaries, they act with the warmth of a consuming fire. Like Bertha Mason in Charlotte Brontë's *Jane Eyre*, they must blacken and destroy whatever they touch. Their anger is indiscriminate, like the flailing about of someone tumbled into an alien element; or if we speak more in contempt than in sorrow, it is the moral equivalent of a riot, at once threatening to others and destructive to the individual suffering the anger, which will always have been misguided. This was a point appreciated by Arnold when he noted that Charlotte Brontë's mind contained "nothing but hunger, rebellion, and rage"; the more broad-minded critic was forced to conclude, "No fine writing can hide this thoroughly, and it will be fatal to her in the long run."[17] In fact, this critical tradition would have it that anger in general may be markedly feminine, temper more often than not a temptress, as when Cicero recommended against an unseemly tone in discourse: "Sharp exclamation injures the voice and likewise jars the hearer, for it has about it something ignoble, suited rather to feminine outcry than to manly dignity in speaking."[18] Instead of Socrates, large-browed and serenely seeking truth, we have Xanthippe, the scold.

To be sure, this critical tradition has always had its ironies, as when Arnold took his catchphrase, "sweetness and light," from Jonathan Swift – hardly a model of dispassion either as poet or critic, and a man who freely admitted as much. ("[W]hat I do," he wrote in a letter to Alexander Pope, "is owing to perfect rage and resentment."[19]) In the same century, Samuel Johnson was destined to become a critical model even though he proclaimed anger to have a devout role to play in criticism, and even Kant showed a sneaking sympathy with this emotion when he described the conditions under which he believed it would be *"aesthetically Sublime."*[20] As such examples would indicate, the eighteenth century may have been an especially fine time for critical hostility; but Socrates had worked himself around to a comparable irony a couple of millennia earlier. In the *Phaedo*, he was willing to allow that with the exception of the true philosopher, a type so rare as possibly to be without instantiation on this mortal earth, men called temperate may be so only "because they are intemperate." (So, too, many centuries later, Hegel would follow him in remarking upon a moment when Reason, thinking itself enlightened, finds that "the function of 'measure' is immoderation."[21]) No wonder Socrates arrived at a point in *The Republic*, while reflecting on the dismaying historical fate of philosophy, when he could not help but lose his temper.[22]

A related case would be noted by authors such as Cicero and Quintilian, who insisted that anger had no proper role in public discourse – "An impudent, disorderly, or angry tone is always unseemly, no matter who it be that assumes it"[23] – even as they remarked that anger spontaneously aroused within an orator could lead to an especially effective speech, one that might seem divinely inspired. These and a host of similar passages throughout the centuries make it clear that we must speak of a familiar irony by the time we come to figures such as Swift and Johnson. We have no call to feel surprised when we stumble over expressions of anger from them or from other writers of their era, such as Pope, who urged critics to purge themselves of anger, spite, fury, and spleen and yet carved out an exception to this rule when he turned to those responsible for blasphemous writings: "These Monsters, Criticks! with your Darts engage, / Here point your Thunder, and exhaust your Rage!"[24] (As his editors inform us, these lines were written in seeming nostalgia for the Licensing Act of 1663, which was designed to censor nonconformist and heretical works but which had been allowed to lapse after 1695.) Nor should we be surprised when writers of the nineteenth and twentieth centuries imitate their forebears by complaining of anger even as they out-Herod Herod in their own inflamed practice.

If any notice is taken of it within the history I have summarized here, this familiar irony is treated as just that: a bemusing aspect of criticism to which we have easily accommodated ourselves. It appears to be in but not of criticism, a violence that should be shunted aside by the same gesture that recognizes it. (As in the old joke: "But aside from that, Mrs. Lincoln, how did you like the play?") The irony of angry counsel against anger is then considered a mere figure of speech, as the saying would have it, and as such is dismissable from the terrific patriarchal thrust of tradition. It is sublimated into something like Arnold's sweetness and light, as in Augustine's accommodating explanation that the anger of God "is not a disturbing emotion of His mind, but a judgment by which punishment is inflicted upon sin."[25] Those who fail to overlook this irony must be ill-educated, or worse, "political" and therefore intellectually discreditable. The latter reproach can also be directed to artists, as in John Lockhart's truly vicious and mythically killing review: "We had almost forgot to mention, that Keats belongs to the Cockney School of Politics, as well as the Cockney School of Poetry."[26]

Lockhart, it will be said, is a notoriously unrepresentative figure. We will be assured that we need not concern ourselves with anger of this sort since it arises only in uncommon or freakish circumstances, like those addressed by Pope in his "Essay on Criticism" or by Arnold in his 1873 preface to *Literature and Dogma*, in which he replied to the cavillers who had presumed to observe that Christ and St. Paul were not above using harsh invective on occasion. In the tradition of Augustine, Arnold argued that these moments were exceptional – "such weapons can have no excuse at all except as employed against individuals who are past hope or institutions which are palpable monstrosities."[27] Following this logic, Arnold claimed that he himself would never reply "to any literary assailant" because "in such encounters tempers are lost, the world laughs, and truth is not served."[28] When he nonetheless found himself accused of personally insulting F. W. Newman, whose work he had critiqued in "On Translating Homer," he could only profess dismay that his intentions had been so misunderstood.[29] And with this posture of dismay, too, we are supposed to be familiar, for it is a logical corollary to the irony of angry counsels against anger. We hear it echoing and reechoing down through the ages to the present day, as when bell hooks, than whom there can be no critic more different from Arnold, professed a similar surprise at the fact that many readers of her first book, *Ain't I a Woman: Black Women and Feminism*, "would interpret the direct, blunt speech as signifying anger."[30]

But some, like bell hooks, will not let the matter rest there. In many feminist writings over the last three decades, as in works by other politically identified critics, the relation between anger and criticism has been interpreted differently than Arnold would have had it. When Adrienne Rich published an essay on Anne Bradstreet in 1966, raising a question about her poetry – "Where are the stress-marks of anger, the strains of self-division, in her work?" – she was not looking for flaws but for something like transcendence in the name of anger.[31] Similarly, when Sandra M. Gilbert and Susan Gubar sought to uncover the "covert authorial anger" of women authors,[32] they were seeking something very like a universal truth. This is the direction epitomized by the title of Julia Lesage's essay, "Women's Rage," in which she called for expressions of women's "own just rage" – expressions of an "authentic rage" that would no longer have to suffer the frustrating censorship of "displacement."[33]

Although writings like these are often attacked on the grounds that they betray what other critics imagine tradition to have been, they do nothing of the kind. For even as they privilege what critical tradition had seemingly outlawed, they continue to share the conception of anger promoted within that tradition. For Lesage, as for Plato, anger is a force of self-revelation. The self revealed by this means may be good or bad, and it may be more or less alert to its own condition, depending on one's argument; but there remains this assumption that the force of anger does reveal something of the self. If many would seek to ward off this force, seeing it as the enemy of propriety, harmony, and universality, others would woo it, believing it is sure to convey a hungering sense of authenticity, revolt, or personal identity. In either case, one maintains this psychological conception of anger, in which it erupts in truth by breaking through mechanisms of censorship. Thus, whether approvingly or disapprovingly, anger is described in terms of its supposed impatience toward its objects, contexts, and origins. This impatience, then, seems to guarantee a compelling revelation even in those cases where one wants to trump this with another statement presumed to be of greater consequence (as when Arnold is confident that their anger does tell us something about his opponents, albeit something not at all to their credit). Anger is a weakness, or it is a strength; a loss of self-control, or a righteous assertion of self; an incoherent cry, or a pure surge of meaning – and so on. What persists through such differences is the basic premise of anger as a force that breaks through regulating forms to reveal a hidden, inward, disruptive truth.

Yet through their very fidelity to this tradition of criticism, hooks, Rich, Gilbert, Gubar, and Lesage have contributed to the making of a great difference in it. They have recognized that the anger generally assumed to be outlawed by critical tradition has never been so. They have been able to show that the familiar irony of angry counsels against anger was always constitutive rather than exceptional, marginal, and dismissable.[34] These latter characterizations are figures that now betray the tradition they served to invent. Recalling Socrates' dictum that children, women, servants, and inferior sorts of free men are especially prone to intemperance – and perhaps remembering also that the state's prospective opponents in warfare are not even brought into this discussion – critics now may see those deemed philosophically competent as the truly outlandish cases, these outlawed figures as the censored reality.

In this realization they develop the example suggested by Woolf in *A Room of One's Own*: the case of Professor von X, who is the author of the "monumental work entitled *The Mental, Moral, and Physical Inferiority of the Female Sex*" (53).[35] Already angered at having been turned away from an Oxbridge library for reasons attributable to her sex, Woolf's protagonist ("call me Mary Beton, Mary Seton, Mary Carmichael, or by any name you please – it is not a matter of any importance" [6])[36] is further enraged when she encounters the writings of Professor von X, along with works by many others like him, in the British Museum. It does not take long for her to control her own feelings, but she is left with a question:

How explain the anger of the professors? – why were they angry? For when it came to analysing the impression left by these books [about women] there was always an element of heat. This heat took many forms; it showed itself in satire, in sentiment, in curiosity, in reprobation. But there was another element which was often present and could not immediately be identified. Anger, I called it. But it was anger that had gone underground and mixed itself with all kinds of other emotions. To judge from its odd effects, it was anger disguised and complex, not anger simple and open.   (*Room*, 54–5)

In this passage, Woolf's protagonist rises above the anger for which her sex traditionally was faulted, and she turns the tables on the representatives of learning by finding – through a meditative, impressionistic, but quite definite analysis – that it is they who have been driven by this ignoble motive. This is not the end of the matter. For if anger can be found underwriting the monuments of tradition, and this anger is not at all exceptional and dismissable, then something has happened to the very conception of this term. Traditionally – or in what had seemed to be tradition – it was assumed that anger showed itself in words, as in other kinds of behavior, through certain signs of disorder, disharmony, disfigurement, rebellion, or riotousness. Thus, in proceeding through this essay, some readers will have rushed to the conclusion that anger is definitely visible in the language of certain passages while in others the author is more calm and objective. However, if anger now strikes us in the very monuments that had been taken to represent the opposing qualities of order, harmony, and the like, then the psychological foundation of this term, its supposed basis in truth-telling and self-revelation, has been discredited. Consequently, anger becomes difficult to diagnose, perhaps even impossible to know. Oddly enough, as soon as one notices the anger of the professors ("or patriarchs, as it might be more accurate to call them"), one must wonder if it really makes any sense to call them angry. "Possibly they are not 'angry' at all." (*Room*, 58).

Woolf's protagonist is brought to realize that the issue of anger is the issue of what one will *call* anger. Anger has often been associated with calling names, as distinct from doing justice; but angry or not, we are always calling names, at once hurling them into and summoning them from out of the world – or what we call the world. So Woolf's protagonist makes fun of her own "sonorous phrases about 'elemental feelings,' the 'common stuff of humanity,' the 'depths of the human heart,' and all those other phrases which support us in our belief that, however clever we may be on top, we are very serious, very profound and very humane underneath" (*Room*, 159).

Anger does not declare itself, as critical tradition – or more accurately, a traditional image of critical tradition – would have us assume. Nor does it define and evaluate itself, as one might be led to believe by the form of Plato's dialogues, in which the philosopher is always so fortunate in getting those with whom he speaks to stipulate the premises he wants. (But then these dialogues make a very different impression if one recalls the crucial exception that haunts all these other exchanges: the failure of Socrates to obtain the premises he wants when he is put on trial and arguing for his life. In the *Apology*, Socrates suggests that the slim difference of thirty votes by which he was condemned would have turned out differently if he had had another day to make his case, as would have been true in other cities, or if the long-contemplated bringing of these charges against him had been delayed just a little longer, thus allowing him to die a natural death. "I have little time left to tell what I know," says the narrator of "The Babylon Lottery";[37] and we all know it is just a question of time . . .)

Anger is a word over which people fight, or (if they hate the hostilities entertained by their governments) it is a word over which they may refuse to fight. In either case, issues commonly associated with the topic of anger and criticism – issues of war, censorship, and turns of fortune, as in the workings of a lottery – will be seen to dwell within the very conception of anger, which no longer can be viewed as exclusively, or even especially, a matter of individual psychology. That is why Woolf bothered to note that if Jane Austen "had lain as a child on the landing to prevent her father from thrashing her mother, her soul might have burnt with such a passion against tyranny that all her novels might have been consumed in one cry for justice."[38] What Woolf suggests is that even in matters of life and death, we cannot liberate the thesis of anger from its hypothesis; we cannot divide its premises from its always extravagant promises; we cannot think of it apart from the lottery, the warfare, and the censorship in which it has its only truth. As surely as language belongs to our social being, rather than being anyone's individual possession, so do our emotions; and lotteries, wars, and acts of censorship in various forms (including every recourse of style, such as contradiction, paradox, and irony) are indissociable from all that we feel. As Catharine R. Stimpson, in writing about Woolf, has succinctly put this point about tradition, "a statement is often what the state has meant."[39]

Lotteries, wars, and censorship are not simply external to our emotions, acting upon them from without, but are intrinsic to any possible conception of emotion. Therefore, like any lottery you can name, anger is a matter of historical turnings and thus a question of rhetoric and politics, and it must be judged accordingly if we are to have any hope of knowing what we say we know. That is why many works of contemporary criticism have sought, in Brenda R. Silver's words, "to remove anger from the exclusive realm of the emotions and internal states: to move anger away from guilt, neurosis, or depression, and into the purview of cognition, external behavior, social relations, and politics."[40] As I write this chapter, which is not free of anger, I do not write off anger when I affirm the desirability of this movement.

Although Virginia Woolf is among those that I follow in coming to this point, it might be objected that I show myself here to be more akin to Professor von X, a figure intent on disguising undeniable emotion. After all, Woolf herself might be seen as having partaken to some extent of the Professor's disposition, despite her elaborate mockery of this character. We may remember that her protagonist in *A Room of One's Own*, like Arnold, criticized Brontë for writing "in a rage." She saw her predecessor's work as having been "deformed and twisted" as a consequence of this emotion: "Now, in the passages I have quoted from *Jane Eyre*, it is clear that anger was tampering with the integrity of Charlotte Brontë the novelist" (120, 121, 127). Woolf also failed miserably in her conclusion, in 1929, that the woman writer "is no longer angry."[41] Judging by these instances and others, in which her aesthetics could not tolerate what she took to be signs of an unredeemed personal urgency, some have viewed Woolf (and not without reason) as lamentably idealist in certain aspects of her art;[42] similar objections, or worse, might be made to my own reasoning here. If a war is now being fought, readers might say, bombs are not blossoming in this professor's backyard; while individuals and entire populations are being censored, he is writing as freely as he ever has; at a time when fortune's hostages are finding themselves consigned to battle, flight, jail, or the grave, he is unmolested; and so it is all very well for him calmly to discourse of anger as a question of rhetoric and politics. To such readers, my playing with distinctions may seem a clever game (or perhaps I flatter myself, perhaps not even that); but however I work it out, what I have written may well be seen as entirely irrelevant to what I have supposed to be my topic. Say what I will, those who are angry will know what they feel. If not always, then often, there is no disputing about anger; in James Baldwin's words, "Rage can only with difficulty, and never entirely, be brought under the domination of the intelligence and is therefore not susceptible to any arguments whatever."[43]

Inevitably, in the scathing sense of the term that Audre Lorde called upon in "The Uses of Anger," my words will appear to some readers as nothing more than "academic rhetoric."[44] There is simply no getting around the fact that some will be angry with me, and they will not always be the ones I would love to enrage. For all my contention that anger is not a matter of truth-telling, self-revelation, and the overthrow of censorship, I may be told that I am being absurd, people know anger when they feel it, they have to fight against great odds to express it, and so anyone taking a position such as mine is denying the undeniable.

And this objection does make sense. As Kant said, critics must accept the fate of cooks, who cannot expect their work to please people just because an argument or theory says they ought not to turn up their noses at it.[45] Nevertheless, as I believe Woolf knew, the real question here is not whether anger is undeniable. There is no contradiction in saying that it is often so while maintaining that we can conclude nothing from this fact, if fact we would call it. Anger may be undeniable, but the point here is that what cannot be denied cannot be asserted. Hence the famous and profound stupidity of the comment about pornography that Justice Potter Stewart pronounced in the case of *Jacobellis* v. *Ohio* (1964). "I know it when I see it."[46] No matter how attached we feel to our perceptions, emotions, sensations, ideas – call them what you will – they are subject to communication and thus surrendered to our experience over time, which lends itself only too generously to the conviction of certainty. ("Sluttish time," Shakespeare called it as he wrote about "wasteful war," thus criticizing the place of anger in critical tradition even as he helped to reinforce its identification with women.[47]) For all her impatience with academic rhetoric, Lorde was well aware of these temporal considerations, as she made clear when she recorded her response to the dim-witted sympathy a white listener offered after Lorde gave a reading of her "Poems for Women in Rage": "I do not exist to feel her anger for her."[48]

"Our lives are not debatable," said Jordan,[49] and on this point she was right and will always have been right. Like you, like Jordan, I would dare anyone to tell me I am not furious when I know precisely and undeniably what I feel. Yet in troubling myself to say as much, I will have allowed uncertainty to be present, in the very possibility of which I unsay what I believed myself to be saying. As so many popular songwriters have noted in the name of love, anger demands more than we can say. Its demands are beyond anyone's saying because one's own anger will always have been at the mercy of its recognition by and responsibility to others. Hence Peggy Kamuf's comment on *A Room of One's Own*: "No 'one' figures there who is not already many and no ownership guarantees there an undivided property."[50]

Daniel Cottom

"Possibly they are not 'angry' at all," Woolf has her protagonist remark of the professors before going on to analyze the rhetorical shifts by which "her own" art and anger are bound up with "other" people both alive and dead, both real and imaginary, and with disparate and changing phenomena such as literary theories, family traditions, economic structures, and educational institutions that she is not allowed even to enter. She takes this course because she knows that what we call anger is a fantastic, unpredictable historical construction from which nothing can be predicated with anything like complete assurance. Because it is built of warring identifications, it is liable to disappear and seem never to have existed at the very moment when we try to address it. In this way Woolf's protagonist goes beyond the familiar irony of angry counsel against anger to gesture toward the notably slippery truth – "the pure fluid, the essential oil" – that she had hoped would emerge after "what was personal and accidental" in her impressions had been strained off (*Room*, 42). When imagining how her audience must be criticizing her narrative, picking it apart and adding to it, even as I am doing here, she comes to the conclusion that truth "is only to be had by laying together many varieties of error" (*Room*, 183). And despite her insistence on what is undeniably true, Jordan showed the same conviction when she troubled herself to explain what should never have needed any explanation, what should have been forever known as soon as it was seen: the obscenity of William Shockley and of anyone who would claim his views deserve even the slightest respect.

Those who would outlaw anger from criticism and those who would privilege it share the same fantasy that anger might be *uncalled for*, without reason or calculation, as if it somehow might appear in advance of its objects, contexts, and origins, like the hands of an angry God thrashing our submissive souls. Within this fantasy, the only frustration of anger – the angriness of anger, as it were – is that its precedence goes unnoticed. It wants to have been first: not a response, not a movement already subject to equivocation, not the eternally provoking belatedness built into the shuttling assertion and denial of tradition, but truly *uncalled for*, like the divine sign of Socrates' *daimon*. In contrast, the hell of this anger must resemble the Monty Python routine in which a man strides into a firm that specializes in arguments, pays a fee for its services, and then finds himself embroiled in contradictions before he can even get started on what he had to say. ("You're not arguing, you're just contradicting

188

me!" "No I'm not!" "Yes you are!" "No I'm not!") The merciless humor relies upon our recognition that rhetorical impasses are an irreducible aspect of communication, which leads us in our every utterance toward the possibility of such a farcical contretemps, which in its turn may result, lo and behold, in dead bodies and ruined houses.

Thus, to imagine anger as a breaching of censorship, as a speaking of the unspeakable, is not to imagine communication but an apocalyptic release from the violent conditions of communication. The desire is then to forget the demands by which we know history – to repress or censor them through the immediacy of one's anger – even though these demands are bound to disturb this desired immediacy as surely as they will shatter the fantastic continuity desired in the ravishing name of tradition. As Wojnarowicz has said in recounting fantasies in which he would murder cops, politicians, religious leaders, and others whose existence promised violence to his own, such as certain lovers of art ("I remember times getting picked up by some gentle and repressed fag living in a high-rise apartment filled with priceless north american indian artifacts and twentieth-century art who was paying me ten bucks to suck on my dick"), one wants a gesture that will completely erase any offense against our being, expunge it, so that it will never have been; but "no one gesture can erase it all that easily."[51]

Its long and complex history shows that we gain a lot through the fantasy of an apocalyptic release from the violent conditions of communication – perhaps most notably, a capacity for disavowal that may be crucial in strengthening people to imagine and fight their way out of oppression. In such gains, however, we too often forget that God is pleased to dine with those on both sides of any war one may care to name. As Nancy Armstrong and Leonard Tennenhouse have noted, "violent events are not simply so but are called violent because they bring together different concepts of social order."[52] The fantasy of apocalyptic release from the violent conditions of communication, then, finally asks less of our imagination than we ought to ask and so allows us to get off too easily. It is then that we end up seeing, always with such dismally predictable surprise, the Old Priest writ large in the New Presbyter, or the object of anger in anger's very own self-representation. With the predictable irony that struck Karl Marx in the provision for liberty in the French constitution of 1848, the word shows itself to be other than itself.[53]

So you have heard all this before. John Milton recognized the complex rhetoric and politics of anger when he made his reply to the *Eikon Basilike*, which was supposedly written by Charles I, the deposed and soon-to-be headless monarch, in the aftermath of England's civil war. Replying to the argument that Charles had not wanted to convene a parliament because he judged its prospective members to be unreliable, Milton said that while these men "were indeed not tempered to his temper," they were not unreasonable on that account. Milton could come to this conclusion because he construed the king's "temper" as "his will" – a will that in its "glozing words and illusions" actually consisted of "rage and . . . violence";[54] and while we need not necessarily agree with Milton's interpretation, it cannot be denied save through political calculations such as those involved in the organization of states, wars, lotteries, and critical texts like his own. For no matter how often we go beyond it, the familiar irony is always lying in wait, even in the case of the famous proponent of free speech whose *Eikonoklastes* and *Defensio Populi Anglicani* were to be ceremonially burned by the decree of Charles II in 1660. We may remember that Milton spent some time licensing books for his government and so allowed himself an "exception" to his ideals, one that might have been surprising had it not been dismally predicted by the exceptions to free speech written into his *Areopagitica*.

Having read Milton intensely if idiosyncratically, Blake dealt with the irony of angry counsels against anger when he scribbled in the margins of the Bishop of Llandaff's *Apology for the Bible* (1797). Bishop Watson's *Apology* was a reply to the second part of *The Age of Reason*, which Thomas Paine, Blake's friend, had written in the wake of the revolutionary wars recently fought in America and France. Bishop Watson had previously published, among other works, a sermon meant to justify God's wisdom in having made men both rich and poor; and in commenting on the beginning of this good shepherd's latest work, Blake wrote,

If this first Letter is written without Railing & Illiberality I have never read one that is. To me it is all Daggers & Poison. The sting of the serpent is in every Sentence as well as the glittering Dissimulation Achilles' wrath is blunt abuse Thersites' Sly insinuation Such is the Bishops If such is the characteristic of a modern polite gentleman we may hope to see Christs discourses Expung'd.[55]

Like Milton before him and Woolf, Lorde, Jordan, and Wojnarowicz after him, Blake argued that anger could be identified only in the context of differing desires, conflicting wills, and words expunging each other – in short, in the contested dimensions of politics through which our cultures take shape and our histories are written and rewritten. He himself was once tried for sedition on account of words he was alleged to have uttered; and he knew that whatever else we may be and whatever else we do, we are fighting words. That is, we are fighting words as we are living history, in the doubled sense of these phrases, which divides and multiplies and ravishes us and so impassions us to go on. Blake was able to draw this lesson from classical and biblical literature, from contemporary theology, and, of course, from his ongoing attempts to figure out good strategems for communication. ("At a Friends Errors Anger Shew / Mirth at the Errors of a Foe."[56]) He could not know that post World War Two US constitutional law would argue otherwise, enforcing upon its people the theory that anger is psychologically localized and localizable; but the preoccupations of his writings suggest that an angry vision of the histories of law and war contributed to his recognition that we are always fighting words, despite what institutionalized legal and military practices would claim to be undeniable.

Through their very insistence on a pure and uncompromising anger, this is the recognition at which writers such as Rich and Lesage have also arrived. Proclaiming their anger, they establish that there is no formal way of measuring the presence, influence, or value of anger in a text. More generally, by representing anger as a compelling eruption of truth, they establish that it is no such thing.

Rich's notion of anger might have seemed simple enough when she characterized Woolf's tone in *A Room of One's Own*: "It is the tone of a woman almost in touch with her anger, who is determined not to appear angry, who is *willing* herself to be calm, detached, and even charming in a roomful of men where things have been said which are attacks on her very integrity." Rich wrote this essay in 1971, at a time when she judged much contemporary writing by women, despite Woolf's prediction, to be "charged with anger." In the above passage Rich values the anger of which she writes, and thus far she is revisionary while yet seeming quite traditional in her treatment of anger as a revelatory emotional outburst that a reader can confidently identify in someone's words. Her next sentence, however, may be even more revisionary: "I think we need to go through that anger, and we will betray our own reality if we try, as Virginia Woolf was trying, for an objectivity, a detachment, that would make us sound more like Jane Austen or Shakespeare."[57]

The interesting suggestion is that women "need to go through that anger," for it is here that Rich's historical and political judgment fights against the traditional inheritance – the ancestral voices prophesying war – that she, like the Woolf of whom she wrote, could not hope entirely to distinguish from the voice she called "her own." A "need" that is in opposition to a "betrayal" is a need given at least as much by calculated political aspiration as by spontaneous psychological essence; an anger one is recommended "to go through" cannot be an anger that carries within itself its own truth or revelation of the self; and an anger addressed as "that anger," in implicit contradistinction to others, not only does not pretend to universality but effectively insists on its polemical difference. It is thus that the name of anger in Rich's criticism turns into an utterly changed word even as it is being written: it is thus that it goes to war.

We should not be surprised, then, to find that Rich brought up the relation between rhetoric and politics when she returned to the topic of anger in a later essay, "Disloyal to Civilization: Feminism, Racism, Gynephobia" (1978). Declaring herself angry at the "abstractly correct language wielded by self-described political feminists," she added, parenthetically, that she too had pronounced the word "racism" in this stultifying way. Her conclusion about racism might also apply to the name of anger. "We have to go on using the word, however."[58] Once in possession of this recognition, we may remember that the author of *A Room of One's Own* had already raised the disturbing historical question, in "Professions for Women," "Ah, but what is 'herself'?" We would then find that in the same essay she anticipated Rich's comments about the relation between criticism and "her own" feelings. The problem of "telling the truth about my own experiences as a body," Woolf said, "I do not think I solved."[59]

A similar drama is played out in Lesage's essay on "Women's Rage," in which the author's seeming attachment to anger as an authentic, self-possessed, and immediate force is belied by other elements in her argument, as when she declares a "need to promote self-conscious, collectively supported, and politically clear articulations of our anger and rage." This passage and others related to it take note of undeniably urgent emotion while simultaneously demanding our attention to "theory."[60] The effect might seem to be an appeal to contradictory conceptions of anger, but it is more accurate to speak of differing gestures through which Lesage, like the others I have named, was trying to come to terms with the divisive political implications, identifications, and possibilities historically bound up in the name of anger. Lorde, for instance, ended her address on anger by calling upon "our power to examine and redefine the terms upon which we will live and work,"[61] effectively insisting that the opposite of anger should not be seen as self-possession but as cowering submission.

When these critics addressed anger, they lost track of the very term, but not because of some form of censorship imposed by themselves or others. They lost track of it because it was bound to turn into issues involving the relations between aesthetics and politics, war and consciousness, fortune and subjectivity, among other things, in which the name of anger was no longer able to bear the complexity of the historical differences through which human destinies have been defined. "Possibly they are not 'angry' at all," says Woolf's protagonist, because the critical thinking with which she dismantles what had seemed to be tradition cannot leave the name of anger intact. Indeed, the very words that I have had to treat here as if they might be synonymous – anger, rage, spleen, intemperance, hate, and all the others, including words translated from foreign tongues and diverse cultures – actually testify to wildly incompatible conceptions of art, science, nature, anatomy, and destiny.

An influential tradition would have it that where historical differences such as these become apparent, we must speak of competing conceptualizations addressing the same object. If Aristotle thinks revenge the defining motive of anger while Samuel Johnson would speak of piety, we have conflicting opinions and thus a better and worse judgment; but we are supposed to rest assured that the boundaries of tradition can accommodate these differences until time has enough time to sort out the truth of the matter. However, it is of the essence of tradition not to have been what it is imagined to have been – it is only by this means that it can subsume historical differences under the ultimate reasoning of time – and the same holds for anger. Friedrich Nietzsche made this point when he described the Christian whose conception of God's wrath, like Augustine's, may be transformed to an impression of beneficence in scarcely the blink of an eye: "If he previously thought he saw warnings, threats, punishment, and every kind of sign of divine anger in all occurrences, so now he *reads* divine goodness *into* his experience."[62]

When we address anger, we point to and establish its place in the same gesture. Despite David Hume's claim that a man "in a fit of anger, is actuated in a very different manner from one who only thinks of that emotion," we cannot cut our distinctions so finely –

unless, like Hume, we support them by way of assumptions about rigid hierarchical distinctions between philosophers and plebeians, men and women, and white Europeans and other races.[63] Angry or not, we call names, at once hurling them into and summoning them from out of the historical conflicts in which we are fighting words. One's anger is never in a room of one's own. So the "young airman up in the sky," writes Woolf, "is driven not only by the voices of loudspeakers; he is driven by voices in himself – ancient instincts, instincts fostered and cherished by education and tradition."[64] And so the protagonist of *A Room of One's Own* insists that the name by which she is called "is not a matter of any importance." She knows that while they go by formally indistinguishable names and even bear some of the same characteristics, her Brontë is no more Arnold's than Blake's Jesus is Milton's; and so she knows that it would be a mistake to place too much emphasis upon the name supposed to be "her own."

Why, then, does there remain this issue of anger and criticism? What draws these words together, establishing what must seem a continuing historical problem in their relation, despite all the differences (in texts, bodies, sexualities, histories, cosmogonies . . .) forcing them apart? This is a question of ravishing tradition: a question of the understanding we have trusted to be at work in the impossible time of writing even as we have had to expect all that we address to suffer unpredictable metamorphoses. Woolf commented on this question in relation to the problem of artistic evaluation when she wrote,

Are not reviews of current literature a perpetual illustration of the difficulty of judgment? "This great book," "this worthless book," the same book is called by both names. Praise and blame alike mean nothing. No, delightful as the pastime of measuring may be, it is the most futile of all occupations, and to submit to the decrees of the measurers the most servile of attitudes. So long as you write what you wish to write, that is all that matters; and whether it matters for ages or only for hours, nobody can say.   (*Room*, 184)

Open even the slightest space between artist and critic and it is as if we glimpse, as on a dimly remembered stage, forms terribly dividing and proliferating, weapons forged in a storm of fire, helpless leaf and vine shrieking in witness to the fall of a lark's song into a gaping human mouth, which swallows it and promptly spews forth ungrateful and vengeful children, squabbling lovers, lying and impious philosophers, an endless horde of interchangeable figures writhing in the blood-streaked *vomitus* of history. In the English language, this sense of things is embodied in the very name of criticism, which suggests that we cannot dream of distinguishing thoughtful analysis from disparagement. It is as if criticism of its very nature must be censorious and censoring, not merely fault-finding with Momus but perversely inventing flaws – as if all critics were the "hypercritics" of whom John Dryden complained.[65] The seemingly immemorial *animus* between critics and the figures of whom they write, what does this tell us if not that any response to art other than the encomium of stunned silence must be a malediction, a grievous offense, even a theft of the artist's soul? Hence the traditional accusation that if we scratch a critic, we will find an artist *manqué*: "Thus the corruption of a poet is the generation of a critic."[66] A historical suspicion, and yet one's own, is that any act of criticism is an intolerable and profoundly self-lacerating periphrasis. As John Ashbery puts it, "To praise this, blame that, / Leads one subtly away from the beginning, where / We must stay, in motion."[67] It is as if there is something fundamentally repulsive in the act of criticism, in the absence of which we could all be such great friends, with the contretemps of time never coming between us – time, that infernal creation of critics, who surely are the ones who invented before and after, the artwork and the commentary, the besieged integrity of the artist and the terribly cutting demands of art. Some such image of time appears to have been worked into the very structure of human emotions.

This will never do. (Or "Here let me pause a moment, for the sake of making somebody angry," as Thomas De Quincey would have it.[68]) Whether we like it or not, measuring will go on; and in the contemporary United States, as I have been concerned to suggest, the political dimensions of the critical imagination have been marked out most compellingly by the history of the civil rights, antiwar, feminist, and gay and lesbian rights movements. When Wojnarowicz, for example, expresses a fear that our current rituals of death lead people away from "a relatively simple ritual of life such as screaming in the streets,"[69] a professorial reader may hear an echo of James Joyce's *Ulysses*, in which one of the names of anger is God, who in turn is identified as a "shout in the street";[70] but this echo will be almost indistinguishable within the clamoring memories of all the public demonstrations carried out over the last four decades, right up to the recent ones organized by ACT UP, in which individuals have gathered into crowds in order to define their integrity against the forces of society and state murderously arrayed against them. "I have always viewed my friends," writes Wojnarowicz, "as checkpoints in a series of motions of resistance to the flood of hyenas in state or religious drag";[71] and one may recall the photographs of distinguished male leaders in outlandish costumes of power that Woolf included in *Three Guineas.*

Currently, the anger of those who claim not to be political in their criticism and art, the anger that defines this claim for them, has arisen in response to public movements of protest, resistance, and rebellion. For instance, it is an injury to their absurd pride that infuriates the members of the recently organized National Association of Scholars and those who sympathize with them, such as Donald Kagan, the Yale dean who was appalled that people might want to prevent Shockley from speaking at his university. They cannot bear how these movements have shown that the determining locus of aesthetics is not the room of anyone, whether artist or critic. It is as if they are maddened by the thought that crowds marching in the streets may know perfectly well something that their minds in their imagined isolation cannot bring themselves to admit, that neither art nor criticism has ever dwelt in a room of its own. There may still be a future in imagining a tradition that says otherwise, since such people certainly seem to be thriving in and out of academe, despite their whining about a supposed persecution at the hands of enemies; but for as long as it has been around, this imaginary tradition of theirs has functioned as the power of censorship for the very people who claim to represent the principles of free inquiry. It censors the way well over 100,000 Iraqis may have been slaughtered in the Gulf War as a result of what is called objective scholarly research, much of it carried out in universities; it censors exploited human flesh under an image of universal human spirit, as if it were discreditable that art and criticism will never be able to transcend the example of those who put their bodies on the line in Selma or rioted in Chicago or filled the streets of Washington, DC because they dared to revise the reigning definitions of temperance, courage, justice, and prudence; it censors the way art and criticism have been historically made, communicated, institutionalized, taught, and employed; it censors the truth of how people come to enter universities, ludicrously picturing their environment of choice as a godlike lottery that shows no special favor toward any kinds of persons – but really, there is a limit to the patience I can be expected to show in addressing these matters.

But if I may try your patience just a bit longer: like wars and acts of censorship, lotteries are never simple things. Thus, in referring to the "company" said to be responsible for the Babylon lottery, Borges's story concludes with the narrator mentioning the "vile" conjecture "that it is indifferently inconsequential to affirm or deny the reality of the shadowy corporation, because Babylon is nothing but an infinite game of chance."[72] Earlier, the narrator had made reference to Platonic tradition, but here he seems to have been attending more to a passage in Kant's *Critique of Judgment* describing games of chance:

But the affections of hope, fear, joy, wrath, scorn are put in play by them, changing their roles at every moment [indem sie jeden Augenblick ihre Rolle wechseln]; and they are so vivid that by them, as by a kind of internal motion, the entire activity of life in the body [das ganze Lebengeschäft im Körper] seems to be promoted, as is shown by the mental vivacity excited by them, although nothing is gained or learnt thereby. But since the game of chance is not a beautiful game [Aber da das Glückspiel Kein schönes Spiel ist], we will here set it aside.[73]

Whether or not Borges was actually aware of this passage when he was bringing his story to a conclusion, it is as if his tale is predicated upon this moment in Kant's text, in which games of chance are said to be unbeautiful because they stimulate sensation without attending to reason. (Schopenhauer similarly found card-playing to be "quite peculiarly the expression of the miserable side of humanity."[74]) Borges raised the stakes from "unbeautiful" to "vile" by extending the image of the game from the evening parties of which Kant wrote ("hardly any of them can be carried on without a game") to the whole of a state's existence; but in doing so he was still following Kant, since the crucial distinction between taste and sensation in the *Critique of Judgment* is based upon the need to dispense with the general possibility that beauty might be heteronomous, answerable to no design except that of chance, as in the lottery of pleasures to which Plato's "democratic man" submits himself.[75] In other respects, Borges's vertiginous fiction might seem as different as different can be from Kant's deliberate exposition of a compelling rule of subjective universality in aesthetic judgments; but the appeal of both texts derives from the way they subsume the undeniable urgencies of political differences under the all-encompassing name of chance, which is utterly indifferent to them. Like Kant's *Critique of Judgment*, "The Babylon Lottery" comes to a conclusion in which this all-encompassing image of chance is nominally rejected, but not before this image has served its purpose, which is to carry the question of political demands away with it when it goes. The enchantment of his tale lies in the way Borges imagines a carnivalesque state of political abandon; and however unlikely it may seem, this is also the enchantment of Kant's work. The fictional and the critical text both impress us with a sense that nothing is to be gained or learned by any political feelings, among which the exemplary case is anger. In both works, the concept of chance unites what this anger would divide and censors what it would demand.

Like Kant's *Critique*, the tale that Borges wrote makes room for feelings such as disgust, which are presented as a matter of personal idiosyncrasy, but not for feelings involved in political commitments. "Like all men in Babylon," the story begins, "I have been a proconsul; like all, a slave; I have also known omnipotence, opprobrium, jail":[76] given such changes in roles from moment to moment, there can be no question of anger. However, in making this criticism, I assume I do not need to tell you that this is a brilliant story, one well-nigh perfect in suggesting the impossible, which is a moment of peace long enough to give us time fully to appreciate the farcical vileness that our history would have to appear to be from a divine standpoint (or from the infinite point of the Aleph in Borges's story of that title). It is as if I could bring us to an assured understanding by identifying the time when I came to this conclusion (9:10 a.m. on June 21, 1991), now that a war is over and the war goes on, as you read this, here in Babylon.

Notes

Because of legal considerations, I have had to alter some of the passages in this text referring to Henry Kissinger and other public figures. One of my concerns in this chapter, of course, is to address the predictable demand for, and irony of, such changes.

1 Charles Lamb, "Distant Correspondents," *Elia*, in *The Works of Charles and Mary Lamb*, ed. E. V. Lucas, 7 vols. (London: Methuen, 1903), vol. II, p. 104.

2 Jorge Luis Borges, "The Babylon Lottery," trans. Anthony Kerrigan, in *Ficciones*, ed. Anthony Kerrigan (New York: Grove Press, 1962), p. 68.

3 Virginia Woolf, *Three Guineas* (London: Hogarth Press, 1943), p. 60.

4 For an account of Martha Rosler's series, which was entitled "Bringing the War Back Home: House Beautiful," see Brian Wallis, "Living-Room War," *Art in America* (February 1992), 105–7. In "'No More Horses': Virginia Woolf on Art and Propaganda" (*Critical Essays on Virginia Woolf*, ed. Morris Beja [Boston: G. K. Hall, 1985], p. 159), Jane Marcus

has argued that in the light of the photographs Woolf did include in *Three Guineas*, the omission of the Spanish Civil War photographs signifies that "[w]e are meant to put the patriarchal horse before the Fascist cart." (Marcus's entire essay is an important context to my argument here.) Diane Gillespie continues this line of analysis in " 'Her Kodak Pointed at his Head': Virginia Woolf and Photography," in *Virginia Woolf: Themes and Variations*, ed. Vara Neverow-Turk and Mark Hussey (New York: Pace University Press, 1993), pp. 33–40, in which she relates Woolf's omission of these photographs to John Tagg's argument about the way documentary photography may feminize its supposed objects of knowledge.

5 Virginia Woolf, "Four Figures," in *Collected Essays*, 4 vols. (New York: Harcourt, Brace, and World, 1967), vol. III, p. 193.

6 William Blake, preface to *Milton*, in *The Complete Poetry and Prose of William Blake*, ed. David V. Erdman, rev. edn. (New York: Doubleday, 1988), p. 95.

7 See Virginia Woolf, "Thoughts on Peace in an Air Raid," in *Collected Essays*, vol. IV, p. 174: " 'I will not cease from mental fight,' Blake wrote. Mental fight means thinking against the current, not with it."

8 The incident in question occurred on April 13, 1985. Calero had been invited to give a talk at Northwestern University. Because she took the stage before Calero arrived and urged the audience not to let him speak – a plea that some in the crowd were to succeed in fulfilling – Barbara Foley was formally reprimanded by Northwestern University and ultimately was denied tenure.

9 See June Jordan, "On the Occasion of a Clear and Present Danger at Yale," *Civil Wars* (Boston: Beacon Press, 1981), pp. 90–5.

10 See Immanuel Kant, *Critique of Judgment*, trans. J. H. Bernard (London: Macmillan, 1931), p. 127 (1.1.28).

11 Blake, *Milton*, in *Complete Poetry and Prose*, p. 128.

12 David Wojnarowicz, "Post Cards from America: X-Rays from Hell," in *Tongues of Flame* (Normal, IL: University Galleries–Illinois State University, 1990), p. 106. *Tongues of Flame* is the catalog for an exhibition of Wojnarowicz's art organized by Barry Blinderman; "Post Cards" was originally published in the catalog for *Witnesses: Against Our Vanishing*, a show by various artists concerned with the AIDS epidemic. This exhibition was held in 1989 at Artists Space in New York City, with the accompanying catalog having been partially funded by the National Endowment for the Arts. Ostensibly, the furor resulting from the show was caused by Wojnarowicz's invective against Helms, Cardinal O'Connor, and others (such as Congressman William Dannemeyer, whose death by a push from the Empire State Building Wojnarowicz took pleasure in imagining). However, comments made by Helms and others (such as John Frohnmayer, the head of the NEA) made it clear that homophobia, sexual prudery, and a reactionary aesthetics were among the more important motivations.

Wojnarowicz was also involved in a battle over censorship when he sued the Reverend Donald Wildmon, who heads something called the American Family Association, after Wildmon blew up details from his artworks (depicting naked bodies and sexual activity) and included them in his publications. Wojnarowicz won a court order enjoining Wildmon from any further appropriations of his work.

See also David Wojnarowicz, *Close to the Knives: A Memoir of Disintegration* (New York: Vintage Books, 1991), in which "Post Cards" is reprinted along with other writings.

13 Kant, *Critique of Judgment*, pp. 140n, 149 (1.1.29).

14 Matthew Arnold, *Culture and Anarchy*, in *The Complete Prose Works of Matthew Arnold*, ed. R. H. Super, 11 vols. (Ann Arbor: University of Michigan Press, 1965), vol. V, p. 80. In this quotation Arnold was referring specifically to Brontë's *Villette*.

15 William Wordsworth, *The Prelude* (1850), in *The Prelude: A Parallel Text*, ed. J. C. Maxwell (Harmondsworth: Penguin, 1972), p. 439 (11: 60–81).

16 This obscurity has not been alleviated by recent attempts in some universities to institute rules against "hate speech," which often depend upon the notion of "fighting" words.

17 Matthew Arnold, *The Letters of Matthew Arnold to Arthur Hugh Clough*, ed. Howard Foster Lowry (Oxford University Press, 1932), p. 134.

18 Cicero, *Rhetorica ad Herennium*, trans. Harry Caplan (Cambridge, MA: Harvard University Press, 1954), p. 195.

19 Jonathan Swift, in a letter to Alexander Pope (June 1, 1728), in *The Correspondence of Jonathan Swift, D. D.*, ed. F. Elrington Ball, 6 vols. (London: G. Bell and Sons, 1911), vol. IV, p. 34. Arnold took the phrase "sweetness and light" from Swift's *Battle of the Books*; on this point, see the discussion by Sandra M. Gilbert and Susan Gubar of Swift's splenetic figure, "Goddess Criticism," in *The Madwoman in the Attic: The Woman Writer and the Nineteenth-Century Literary Imagination* (New Haven: Yale University Press, 1979), p. 33.

20 See, for instance, the remark quoted in James Boswell, *The Life of Samuel Johnson* (New York: Random House, 1952), p. 618: "Being angry with one who controverts an opinion which you value, is a necessary consequence of the uneasiness which you feel"; and Kant, *Critique of Judgment*, p. 141 (1.1.29).

21 G. W. F. Hegel, *The Phenomenology of Mind*, trans. J. B. Baillie (New York: Macmillan, 1931), p. 579.

22 Plato, *Phaedo*, in *The Dialogues of Plato*, trans. B. Jowett, 2 vols. (New York: Random House, 1937), vol. I, p. 452 (69a); and *The Republic*, in *Dialogues*, vol. I, p. 796 (7: 5361).

23 Quintilian, *Institutio Oratoria*, trans. H. E. Butler, 4 vols. (Cambridge, MA: Harvard University Press, 1961), vol. IV, p. 171.

24 Alexander Pope, "An Essay on Criticism," in *The Poems of Alexander Pope*, ed. E. Audra and Aubrey Williams, 6 vols. (New Haven: Yale

University Press, 1961), vol. I, p. 304. Of course, the reader who hesitates over the first line quoted here – "These Monsters, Criticks! with your Darts engage" – meets a syntactical ambiguity, in which "Monsters" may appear to be in apposition to "Criticks." Whether intentionally or not, this ambiguity allows Pope to get his own dart into critics even as he joins them and points out their proper quarry. This point is of some interest to my discussion of "familiar ironies" in critical tradition.

25 Augustine, *City of God*, trans. Marcus Dods (New York: Modern Library, 1950), p. 515.

26 John Lockhart, "Cockney School of Poetry," in *Keats: The Critical Heritage*, ed. G. M. Matthews (New York: Barnes and Noble, 1971), p. 109.

27 Matthew Arnold, preface (1873) to *Literature and Dogma*, in *Complete Prose Works*, vol. VI, p. 154.

28 Matthew Arnold, "On Translating Homer," in *Complete Prose Works*, vol. I, p. 169.

29 See ibid., vol. I, pp. 170–1. Also, for a similar comment with which he replies to the accusation that he has attacked Christianity, see Arnold's preface to the Popular Edition (1883) of *Literature and Dogma*, in *Complete Prose Works*, vol. VI, p. 142.

30 bell hooks, "When I was a Young Soldier for the Revolution: Coming to Voice," *Talking Back: Thinking Feminist, Thinking Black* (Boston: South End Press, 1989), p. 15.

31 Adrienne Rich, "The Tensions of Anne Bradstreet," in *On Lies, Secrets, and Silence: Selected Prose, 1968–1978* (New York; W. W. Norton, 1979), p. 22.

32 Gilbert and Gubar, *Madwoman in the Attic*, p. 77.

33 Julia Lesage, "Women's Rage," in *Marxism and the Interpretation of Culture*, ed. Cary Nelson and Lawrence Grossberg (Urbana: University of Illinois Press, 1988), p. 422. On this subject see also Jane Marcus, *Art and Anger: Reading Like a Woman* (Columbus: Ohio State University Press, 1988).

34 Compare Stephanie H. Jed's description of how one may find, in the writings of fifteenth-century Florentine humanists, "two diametrically opposed representations of the philologist" – the cool, unemotional scholar and "the enraged Castigator of errors" – which cooperate with each other despite their seeming opposition. See Jed, *Chaste Thinking: The Rape of Lucretia and the Birth of Humanism* (Bloomington: Indiana University Press, 1989), p. 21.

35 Virginia Woolf, *A Room of One's Own* (New York: Harcourt, Brace, and Company, 1929). All page numbers are included within the main text.

36 Of the names Woolf gives here, Mary Beton is identified as an aunt who bequeathed her the five hundred pounds a year that enabled her to be independent, Mary Seton as a science teacher who is a resident of the women's college of which Woolf writes, and Mary Carmichael as a contemporary author whose first novel, while only modestly successful, shows the potential for better things. These names derive from "Mary

Hamilton," the traditional English ballad that tells of a woman about to be executed for infanticide – certainly an interesting association in terms of the argument of *A Room of One's Own.*

37 Borges, "The Babylon Lottery," in *Ficciones*, p. 69.

38 Woolf, "Four Figures," in *Collected Essays*, vol. III, p. 194. In this passage Woolf was comparing Austen to Mary Wollstonecraft.

39 Catharine R. Stimpson, "Woolf's Room, Our Project: The Building of Feminist Criticism," in *Virginia Woolf*, ed. Rachel Bowlby (London: Longman, 1992), p. 165.

40 Brenda R. Silver, "The Authority of Anger: *Three Guineas* as Case Study," *Signs* 16 (winter 1991), 362. Also, on the question of the politics of rhetoric in Woolf's writing, see Pamela L. Caughie, *Virginia Woolf and Postmodernism: Literature in Quest and Question of Itself* (University of Chicago Press, 1991), pp. 113–42, and Krista Ratcliffe, "The Troubled Materialism of Virginia Woolf's Feminist Theory of Rhetoric," in Neverow-Turk and Hussey, *Virginia Woolf*, pp. 258–67.

41 Woolf, "Women and Fiction," in *Collected Essays*, vol. II, p. 145. In this essay Woolf also comments on Charlotte Brontë and other writers in a way relevant to her discussion in *A Room of One's Own.*

42 On this point, see Mary M. Childers, "Virginia Woolf on the Outside Looking Down: Reflections on the Class of Women," *Modern Fiction Studies* 36 (spring 1992), 61–79.

43 James Baldwin, "Stranger in the Village," in *Notes of a Native Son* (Boston: Beacon Press, 1990), p. 165.

44 Audre Lorde, "The Uses of Anger," *Women Studies Quarterly* 9 (fall 1981), 8.

45 Kant, *Critique of Judgment*, p. 159 (1.1.34).

46 Quoted in Jonathon Green, *The Encyclopedia of Censorship* (New York: Facts on File, 1990), p. 201.

47 The quotation from Shakespeare is taken from *The Riverside Shakespeare*, ed. G. Blakemore Evans (Boston: Houghton Mifflin, 1974).

48 Lorde, "Uses of Anger," 7.

49 Jordan, "Clear and Present Danger at Yale," p. 94.

50 Peggy Kamuf, "Penelope at Work; Interruptions in *A Room of One's Own*," in Neverow-Turk and Hussey, *Virginia Woolf*, p. 194.

51 Wojnarowicz, "In the Shadow of the American Dream: Soon All This Will Be Picturesque Ruins," in *Close to the Knives*, p. 33.

52 Nancy Armstrong and Leonard Tennenhouse, "Introduction, Representing Violence, Or 'How the West Was Won,'" in *The Violence of Representation: Literature and the History of Violence* (London: Routledge, 1989), p. 9.

53 See Karl Marx, *The Eighteenth Brumaire of Louis Bonaparte* (New York: International Publishers, [1935]), p. 26.

54 John Milton, *Eikonoklastes*, in *John Milton: Complete Poems and Major Prose*, ed. Merritt Y. Hughes (New York: Odyssey Press, 1957), pp. 790, 806.

55 William Blake, "Marginalia," in *William Blake's Writings*, ed. G. E. Bentley, 2 vols. (Oxford: Clarendon, 1978), vol. II, p. 1405. (I omit the editor's interpolated punctuation.)

56 William Blake, "Notebook," in *William Blake's Writings*, vol. II, p. 938. In terms of my argument here, it is notable that in spite of all his rage against war, Blake once engraved a prospectus for a war monument designed by John Flaxman. See David V. Erdman, *Blake: Prophet Against Empire* (Princeton University Press, 1954), p. 320.

57 Adrienne Rich, "When We Dead Awaken: Writing as Re-Vision," in *On Lies, Secrets, and Silence*, pp. 37, 48–9.

58 Adrienne Rich, "Disloyal to Civilization: Feminism, Racism, Gynephobia," in *On Lies, Secrets, and Silence*, pp. 303–4.

59 Virginia Woolf, "Professions for Women," in *Collected Essays*, vol. II, pp. 286, 288.

60 Lesage, "Women's Rage," pp. 420, 428.

61 Lorde, "Uses of Anger," 10.

62 Friedrich Nietzsche, *Human, All Too Human: A Book for Free Spirits*, trans. Marion Faber with Stephen Lehmann (Lincoln: University of Nebraska Press, 1984), p. 93. See also Nietzsche's argument about the radical differences between Jewish and Christian conceptions of anger in *Daybreak: Thoughts on the Prejudices of Morality*, trans. R. J. Hollingdale (Cambridge University Press, 1982), p. 27.

63 David Hume, *An Enquiry Concerning Human Understanding*, ed. Eric Steinberg (Indianapolis: Hackett , 1977), p. 10.

64 Woolf, "Thoughts on Peace in an Air Raid," p. 175.

65 John Dryden, "The Author's Apology for Heroic Poetry and Poetic Licence," in *Essays of John Dryden*, ed. W. P. Ker, 2 vols. (Oxford University Press, 1926), vol. I, pp. 181–3.

66 John Dryden, Dedication to *Examen Poeticum*, in *Essays*, vol. II, pp. 2–3.

67 John Ashbery, "Houseboat Days," in *Houseboat Days* (New York: Viking, 1977), p. 39.

68 Thomas De Quincey, "The Spanish Military Nun," in *De Quincey's Works*, 14 vols. (Edinburgh: A. & C. Black, 1862–3), vol. III, p. 48.

69 Wojnarowicz, "Post Cards from America," p. 109.

70 James Joyce, *Ulysses* (New York: Random House, 1934), p. 35. The speaker is Stephen Daedalus.

71 Wojnarowicz, "The Suicide of a Guy Who Once Built an Elaborate Shrine over a Mouse Hole," in *Close to the Knives*, p. 169.

72 Borges, "Babylon Lottery," p. 72.

73 Kant, *Critique of Judgment*, p. 222 (1.1.541).

74 Arthur Schopenhauer, *The World as Will and Idea*, trans. R. B. Haldane and J. Kemp, 3 vols. (London: Routledge and Kegan Paul, 1964), vol. I, p. 406.

75 Plato, *The Republic*, in *Dialogues*, vol. I, p. 819 (8: 561).

76 Borges, "Babylon Lottery," p. 65.

8

The discomfort of strangeness and beauty: art, politics, and aesthetics

PETER DE BOLLA

The artwork is a knowing.

One-time candidate for the republican nomination for the presidency of the United States, Patrick Buchanan, in an attempt to initiate what he announced as "a cultural revolution in the nineties as sweeping as the political revolution of the eighties," published the following comments in a national newspaper:

Culture – music, literature, art – is the visible expression of what is within a nation's soul, its deepest values, its cherished beliefs. America's soul simply cannot be so far gone in corruption as the trash and junk filling so many museums and defacing so many buildings would suggest. As with our rivers and lakes, we need to clean up our culture; for it is a well from which we all must drink. Just as poisoned land will yield up poisonous fruit, so a polluted culture, left to fester and stink can destroy a nation's soul . . . We should not subsidize decadence.[1]

Buchanan was moved to make these comments in the context of an exhibition of the work of the artist Andres Serrano. More specifically one of these works, a photograph of a crucifix submerged in his own urine and entitled *Piss Christ*, seems to have prompted Buchanan in his zeal to initiate a counter conservative program of "culture." Buchanan argues that while the right has been busy running world affairs – in his approving words "busy winning primaries and elections, cutting taxes and funding anticommunist guerrillas abroad" – the left has been surreptitiously colonizing culture. Buchanan, with the clarity of an ideologue, claims to discover how this miserable state of affairs has come to pass: "The reason for all this is simple. Those who believe in absolute values such as God and beauty do nothing, and those who believe in existential humanism have captured the culture. Businessmen, political leaders and bankers have failed to recognize the importance of culture as a force for good and force for evil" (*Washington Times*, May 22, 1989).

Buchanan went on to fan the flames of a conservative backlash against the arts and art funding in the United States which was prompted by a further outcry against an exhibition of photographs made by the artist Robert Mapplethorpe.[2] Again the question of the purposiveness of the artwork was raised, and again charges of obscenity were deemed to be decisive in relation to the "worth" of the artwork.

More recently in Britain a public debate surrounded a work made by the artist Rachel Whiteread, entitled *House*, a cast of the last remaining house of a demolished terrace in Bow, east London. On this occasion the decisive issue did not hinge on questions of obscenity but on whether or not the cast could be entitled to be considered as an artwork. Of course a number of very topical political issues flowed through the work, most obviously those concerned with housing but also including the politics of memory and of the public commemorative function of art. In this sense Whiteread's *House*, given the terms upon which it was funded and constructed, was always doomed to destruction since the artwork itself articulated the timeliness of aesthetic forms. In all these examples, however, whether or not charges of obscenity were brought to bear, the central question concerns the epistemological status of the artwork, on whether it may be understood to ground itself as art irrespective of its subject matter, material form, or political meanings. While the debate around Mapplethorpe's photo- graphs often circled the related but not identical question of who may decide this issue, that is to say who may make judgments about whether or nor something is an artwork (this issue was also invoked, though less directly, in the discussion of Whiteread's *House* through the familiar tactic of taking soundings from the "man in the street"), it nevertheless remains the case that the core of the problem concerns the grounding of the object in something we call, perhaps with a good measure of philosophical illiteracy, "the aesthetic realm."

Over the last few years this kind of argument has surfaced in a great variety of distinct locations. In literature, for example, the question over who decides what shall count as literature, and – more politically fraught – which works so designated will be included in the canon, has become a topic of intense debate. In relation to

205

abstract visual art this kind of question has been close to the surface of public consciousness since the early part of this century – coincident with artistic experiments in nonrepresentational forms. And since then flashpoints have occurred for a variety of reasons which have brought these issues into the open. Carl Andre's bricks at the Tate Gallery in London is just one such example. However, even though these debates are not new, have histories, our public awareness of the philosophical issues underpinning them is extremely rudimentary. Patrick Buchanan, for example, seems to think that the production of artworks is precisely identical to the production of ideology, and in a capitalist ideological environment this leads him to suppose that if subversive liberals can support, promote, and commission "trash" and "junk" which disseminates "nihilist values," then "Conservatives and the religious community that comprise the vast middle-American population should actively support those artists that advocate the same values and ideas as they do" (*Washington Times*, May 22, 1989).

A great part of the problem, as I see it, lies in the fact that we have neglected to discuss, openly and publicly, the philosophical arguments which attempt to ground what we call the aesthetic as a distinct domain. That there is a politics in holding to this view is more than clear, but to focus upon that political motivation is to resist asking in enough detail and to a great enough depth the artwork to account for its aesthetic materiality. My point here is that we have not taken great enough care of the aesthetic, of that distinct area of experience that is called in the post-Kantian tradition affective response. And we have neglected to take care of this even while we have often, unthinkingly or in the service of a reactionary ideology, taken great pains to preserve, catalog, and market the artwork. We have, then, been silent when we should have spoken, distracted from the central issue when we should have made great efforts to ensure that precisely the central issue was understood.

This neglect is nowhere more apparent than in arguments concerning the political aspects of the artwork. Buchanan is not the only person confused here, though he may well be more dangerous than many, since his notion that because an artwork may have effects within culture at large, and that of course encompasses the political, it is therefore conditional upon and constructed by politics is deeply ignorant of what grounds the object we call an artwork. In other words, Buchanan believes that the reason why there are so many artworks he finds disturbing, subversive, amoral is because subversive, amoral, and disturbed people have been given encouragement and grants to make such works. This implies that an artwork is merely a representation and nothing more, that it simply represents the world and in so doing states a set of political or ideological beliefs held by the person who made it. Furthermore, and yet more confused, Buchanan, along with his conservative critic allies, also believes that it is within the preserve of individuals, or collections of individuals – say art critics or museum curators – to decide whether or not something should be understood as "art." And, holding to this belief, it is only "natural," as it were, that he should also hold to the view that such individuals or collections of individuals are politically and ideologically motivated in their decisions.

Now it is clearly the case that art critics and museum curators (not to mention candidates for presidential nominations) are politically motivated. Indeed they are so in the practice of their professions. But this is merely to signal that all actions undertaken by human agents are in some sense *motivated*: that is they are undertaken on behalf of certain interests (and it does not matter in the least to this argument if those interests are coincident solely with an individual). Although it may be the case that such individuals do in the course of their professional activities confer upon the works they discuss or purchase or choose to display the status of the artwork, it is not this which makes of an object art, and it is a poor reflection upon the health of our culture that such arguments are too often intoned. This is the kind of argument that has it that anything I deem art, as long as I have sufficient cultural capital to make such pronouncements and for them to be upheld, is art. It should be said that this argument is not only made by conservatives, it is also mobilized, in very profitable ways, by an art market willing to commodify anything, whether or not it be art. The opposite side of this populist coin states that I do not know whether or not something is art but I do know what I like (and I am prepared to pay for it). In all these cases what is lacking is a properly philosophical account of the epistemological status of the artwork; that is a grounded description of what makes an object an artwork, i.e. what is within it that makes it so and not what surrounds it or the uses to which it might be put. If, and only if, we take care to ensure that we continue to investigate the aesthetic in regard to this question will it be possible to understand the complex relations between aesthetics and politics in such a way that those relations are not taken to merely reproduce current political objectives. Thus, the question of the political, as it arises in

Peter de Bolla

the artwork, should properly be seen as logically posterior to the question of the epistemological grounding of the aesthetic. Politics here is something that is affected by or represented in the artwork, and not something which determines the status of the object designated as an artwork. It is for this reason that we should first be clear about the aesthetic motivation of the form before we make that motivation over to the interested gaze of the political. Consequently, politically motivated embraces of the artwork remain at one remove from that which grounds aesthetic form. An artwork is not made in politics though it might have effects in that register, and indeed its political resonances may cause us to diminish the value we attach to it. But in noting this we are here insisting on the relations between aesthetics and politics in order to keep them distinct. There are, it seems to me, a good number of political readings of artworks which do not do this, which take the political register to have effects at the level of the status of the object as art. Such readings are not sufficiently aware of the epistemological grounding of the artwork, and it is for this reason that what follows concentrates upon this to the exclusion of explorations of the relations between the political and the aesthetic. I hope that this is not taken to imply that a logically prior set of issues, the epistemological status of the artwork, are also prior in terms of value or interest. While part of the presentation is speculative and philosophical it ends with an attempt to be with an artwork in order to investigate the discomfort of affective response, and therefore to open out the terrain upon which relations between an aesthetic form and the political might be built.

A KANTIAN DETOUR

There is a curious moment in Kant's *Critique of Judgment* which has attracted very little commentary. It comes in the section entitled "Of the divisions of an investigation into the feeling of the sublime" (section 24), and concerns what Kant calls "the movement of the mind bound up with the judging of the object."[3] I want to take this moment and press it a little in order to make some speculative statements about the epistemological status of the artwork.

The first thing to note in this curious Kantian formulation is the phrase "movement of the mind," which is, in some manner, bound up with or connected to an affective response. What is this mind moving over, or through; what is the destination of this movement? I

208

think that the most effective way to answer this is to present an account of an aesthetic experience which I shall do in conclusion. For the moment let us stay with this unremarked Kantian description. The text continues: "Now this movement ought to be judged as subjectively purposive (because the sublime pleases us), and thus it is referred through the imagination either to the faculty of cognition or of desire" (85).

It is very clear that this movement is aroused by the feeling of the sublime: "for the feeling of the sublime brings with it as its characteristic feature a movement of the mind" (85). Thus, according to Kant the sublime is that name we give to the affect which arises in us when we contemplate the artwork; it is, in the formulation above, generated by a movement of the mind which is referred not to the faculty of reason but through imagination to the faculty of cognition or desire. Kant is clear that this feeling is not located in natural forms ("sublimity . . . does not reside in anything of nature" [104, §28]) and the knowledge we have about the object which arouses this feeling is not cognitive in the usual sense: "if we are to call the sight of the ocean sublime, we must not think of it as we [ordinarily] do, as implying all kinds of knowledge (that are not contained in immediate intuition)" (110).

However, this does not mean that the sublime affect has no reference to the cognitive faculty, since, as we have seen, the affective response which Kant labels the mathematical sublime is the result of the imagination referring the movement of the mind to the faculty of cognition (while reference to the faculty of desire determines the response as the dynamical sublime). So the prospect comes into view that something is known in affective experience, and that knowledge can only be a property of the object which arouses the response, since if it were a property of the perceiving subject it would be known through the usual channels of cognitive certainty, that is through the exercise of the understanding. Consequently one of the properties of the artwork is its knowingness.

In order to open this out a little further, we can retrace some of the steps of Kant's aesthetic theory since it is here, in the Western philosophical tradition, that the most extensive discussion of the nature of the artwork and our response to it takes place. Kant's more general philosophical project is to justify the claim that objective knowledge is possible. It is, therefore, somewhat strange that he should turn in his third critique to the question of the aesthetic realm, since aesthetic judgments are notoriously difficult to ground in objective criteria. Kant's way around this is to demonstrate how judgments of taste have universal validity, and therefore do approximate a form of "objectivity," but they attain this via the insistence on the subjective nature of all such judgments. The famous Kantian solution to this seemingly insoluble problem is to make a set of arguments about the "disinterestedness" of aesthetic judgments, which renders such subjective evaluations both universal and necessary. In fact Kant's entire corpus is concerned to distinguish the distinct domains of the ethical, aesthetic and philosophical and to demonstrate how something we might call knowledge is contained within the domain of the philosophical, and this is held to be separated out from ethical judgment or aesthetic experience. At first glance, then, Kant's philosophical project would seem to preclude the possibility of art containing a cognitive component. It is often held that in the light of this, aesthetic judgments, given that they are "disinterested," cannot have ethical or more generally political values. It is worth following the steps in the Kantian argument in order to circumvent this particular reading.

It could be said, perhaps quite fairly, that this common reading is partly encouraged by the *Critique of Judgment* itself, since it begins by attempting to divorce aesthetics from all other forms of judgment and knowledge. It is useful, here, to rehearse the reasons for the turn to aesthetics in the first place, which in the German Enlightenment tradition, at least, is the culmination of an inquiry into the grounds of knowledge and of the self's relation, through what we call knowledge, to the world. The problematic of the aesthetic, then, is this: is it possible to have a knowledge of the world and our relation to it through experiences of aesthetic forms, since these experiences are singular and individual? On the basis of these singular experiences, is it possible therefore to reach universal conclusions, that is valid for all persons, when they are grounded in individual or subjective sense experience? The judgments we make in respect of these experiences, aesthetic judgments, are, in the Kantian terminology, subjective, but this does not preclude the possibility, according to Kant, that they might also be understood as necessary and unmotivated. In other words, Kant sets out to show how my judgment is not simply something to do with me but is also necessitated by the objects I encounter in the aesthetic realm. For this reason, the *Critique of Judgment* begins by investigating what it means to say that an aesthetic judgment is subjective and Kant does this by pressing hard on the category he calls the "aesthetical." He writes:

In order to distinguish whether anything is beautiful or not, we refer the representation, not by the understanding to the object for cognition, but by the imagination (perhaps in conjunction with the understanding) to the subject and its feeling of pleasure or pain. The judgment of taste is therefore not a judgment of cognition, and is consequently not logical but aesthetical, by which we understand that whose determining ground can be no other than subjective. (§1)

Kant then goes on to enumerate what he understands as the eight characteristics of a purely aesthetic judgment. Firstly, as we have seen, it is grounded in feelings of pleasure or pain. Secondly, it is immediate; that is, such judgments are not based on a process of reasoning. Thirdly, these judgments are particular; they are the result of an individual experiencing subject responding to a specific object. Fourthly, the judgment is nonconceptual, not based upon our cognitive judgments which would make aesthetic judgments equivalent to ethical judgments. For this reason aesthetic judgment is said to be imaginative. Fifthly, aesthetic judgments are subjective, in spite of the fact that they must also have universal validity by which they not only apply to the person making the judgment but to all other persons.

In the Kantian argument this is possible because of the sixth characteristic of aesthetic judgment. This holds that an aesthetic judgment is universal because the purely aesthetic response abstracts from the merely contingent features of the experience. The aesthetic response transcends emotion or the "attraction" exerted by the object on the observer. Indeed, in its purest form even the existence of the object is taken to be irrelevant. This is the famous thesis of disinterest which holds that the object's use-value or material value is irrelevant to the aesthetic judgment. The seventh point is that the "formal" features of the object provide the focus for the aesthetic judgment, and lastly, the eighth point, the purest kind of response is based on the disinterested appreciation of the harmony that is implicit in the form of an object. It is this, the so-called disinterested thesis, which has been developed most fully in the literature following Kant, since it has been taken to imply that aesthetic judgments are absolutely distinct from ethical, social, or political considerations. It is precisely this line of argument which leads to the notion that the artwork is beyond or outside the realm of politics or ethics.

Now there are a number of complicated steps in the Kantian argument itself which bear upon this matter, most obviously in regard to the imperative that accompanies an aesthetic judgment. Kant writes: "The judgment of taste requires the agreement of everyone, and he who describes anything as beautiful claims that everyone ought to give his approval to the object in question and also describe it as beautiful" (§19).

In this manner, aesthetic judgments are overlaid upon ethical imperatives, even if the distinctness of the two realms is preserved. In a similar vein, Kant's contention that aesthetic judgments are distinct from cognitive judgments does not necessarily imply that aesthetic experience is without a cognitive component. While such judgments are indeed nonconceptual, ungrounded in cognitive appeals to what is known, nevertheless what results from the experience which generates the noncognitive judgment, that is an aesthetic judgment, may itself have a component that could be called a knowledge quotient. Here there is a distinction to be made between what it feels to be in the presence of the sublime and those judgments we make as a result of that affective experience. In other words, the "movement of the mind" with which I began is to be taken as precisely opening up the cognitive aspect of an affective response. Thus the possibility arises that something is known to us in aesthetic experience which is not available to us as knowledge in other forms of experience.

THREE PROPOSITIONS

The artwork is a knowing.

Our attempt to know that knowing is called our affective response to or experience of the artwork.

This experience or response raises in us the feeling of sublimity; hence what we know of that knowing is called the sublime. Sublimity, then, is the name we give to what we recognize, or know, as that which we have yet to know: the artwork is a knowing.

THEIR ELABORATION

What one knows is usually taken to be directly the property of an individual, although this property may be exchanged or transferred between others, and insofar as what is known is known to myself, to a subject, it is unknowable to others. Thus, within the concept of knowledge there is a corner which remains out of reach of the notion that knowledge is a quantity available for circulation. So, just as what I know and how I know what I know is ineradicably bound up with me, the subject-who-knows, or knowing subject, it does not matter for these purposes, since another cannot know this, whether the subject who knows is taken to be a thinking consciousness or not. In other words, it makes no difference whether or not the thing that knows is an object or a human agent since in either case I know that I cannot know how the knowledge that is known to the other is known, nor can I know that knowledge *as knowledge*, although I can know that I do not know it, insofar as knowing it is to think it. This is like saying that I cannot wear another's glove or think another's thought. We do not, therefore, need a special theory of knowledge (except insofar as this is such a theory) in order to make the statement that the artwork is a knowing. However, knowing something, like knowing I shall die, is most often like knowing a fact, even though we often claim to know things, like knowing a city or how to read, that are not known to us as facts. But the artwork is not a fact, nor is it knowable in the sense of knowing a person, as if we might make the acquaintance of the artwork. Our knowing the artwork, or knowledge of it is precisely contained in and by our response to it. Thus the limits of what can be known to us of the artwork are identical to our affective response. It therefore follows that the knowing that is the artwork must, to some extent, remain hidden to us since the affective response is uniquely that which cloaks or veils our knowing anything outside the experience. This is because affective experiences tell us about ourselves, tell us that we are subjects, engross our minds so that we become engrossed with our selves. Sublimity is the name we give to this enlargement of the sense of self. Yet this is also the name we give to the cloaking of knowledge in our experience of the artwork, the designator of what remains unknown knowledge, and the sign of something we call insight. The revelation that is the affective experience of the artwork is an insight into the supersensible subject of the experience, and the feeling of awe which accompanies it erases the object which first gave rise to our affective response, erases the knowing that is the artwork. In a sense, then, the artwork is destroyed in the moment of rapturous appreciation, and so the knowing of the artwork can only be reconstructed in our attempts to capture the harmony that exists between the form of the artwork and our perception of or affective response to it. This is why those artworks which move us the most are those which allow our affective responses and the formal aspect of the work to be knotted together more harmoniously than others.

This interweaving of our response with the form of the work allows us to enter the time-world of the work and in doing so we come to recognize that an experience of the artwork, while in time, is not of it. On account of this, the artwork does not tell the time and in this sense is distinguished from all other objects we place ourselves in an experiential relation to. Insofar as our affective response correlates to the time-world of the artwork, we glimpse an example or exemplum of being in time but are not subject to it. For this reason our experience of the artwork is timely, in the strictest sense, since it serves to demonstrate how difficult it is to be with time. The time that we glimpse in the artwork, then, is a shadow thrown across the face of being without time, or being in time.

APPROACHING THE ARTWORK

I would like to turn to another text in order to explore further the distinct quality of the experience of the artwork. This time it is a painter who struggles with the conceptual grounding of the sublime, the American abstract expressionist Barnett Newman. The essay I shall be concentrating on is quite well known and is entitled "The Sublime is Now"; it was originally published in the *Tiger's Eye* on December 15, 1948.

The first pages of the essay are substantially a reading of the discussion of the sublime from Longinus, through Burke and into Kant and Hegel (this in fact takes up only a paragraph). Newman then turns to pictorial tradition, and explains the Renaissance in terms of a struggle between the sublime and the beautiful. According to Newman modern art found it so difficult to follow the standard set by Michelangelo that it developed the desire to destroy beauty. However, without a correlative sense of the sublime, modern art merely became entangled in and obsessed with the materiality of the artwork. In effect, this meant that considerations of beauty always superseded the attempt to redefine the sublime. Michelangelo "set the standard for sublimity" and thereafter the pictorial tradition failed to meet this standard. As Newman writes:

modern art, caught without a sublime content, was incapable of creating a new sublime image, and unable to move away from the Renaissance imagery of figures and objects except by distortion or by denying it completely for an empty world of geometric formalisms – a *pure* rhetoric of abstract mathematical relationships became enmeshed in a struggle over the nature of beauty, whether beauty was in nature or could be found without nature.[4]

214

Consequently, the heroic stance taken by the American artist, or at least some American artists, in the face of this lack of the sublime. Newman proposes that it is only because America has no history, so to speak, it is "free from the weight of European culture," that it became possible to contemplate creating a sublime art in a context which lacks the sublime. As Newman says: "The question that now arises is how, if we are living in a time without a legend or mythos that can be called sublime, if we refuse to admit any exaltation in pure relations, if we refuse to live in the abstract, how can we be creating a sublime art?" (328).

The answer comes in the form of a temporal wager: we must face up to our being in the now of history, must cut ourselves loose from the burden that is time as it is manifested in history. In so doing it becomes necessary to be in the here of the now in a way that is self-propelling, and this because we are unable to recreate the now of the past, the sublime of Michelangelo. This is, of course, because the structure of the sublime prevents it from being iterable. Newman writes:

We do not need the obsolete props of an outmoded and antiquated legend. We are creating images whose reality is self-evident and which are devoid of the props and crutches that evoke associations with outmoded images, both sublime and beautiful. We are freeing ourselves of the impediments of memory, association, nostalgia, legend, myth, or what have you, that have been the devices of Western European painting.   (328)

In other words, Newman makes a call for an exit from history in order to experience the past as the present to hand, to remake the sublime as the now of history. He concludes the essay: "Instead of making cathedrals out of Christ, man, or 'life,' we are making it out of ourselves, out of our own feelings. The image we produce is the self-evident one of revelation, real and concrete, that can be understood by anyone who will look at it without the nostalgic glasses of history" (328).

In this new proclamation that the sublime is now, we are led towards an explicit interrogation of time in the artwork. But, more importantly, we are required to respond to our being made present to the artwork in ways which are emphatically not determined by us, the viewer, but by the artwork itself. Newman's art in fact became obsessed with what he called "the idea of making the viewer present."[5] It is this being made present to hand which causes a certain discomfort, one of the hallmarks of being in the presence of art, and which will be the topic of my concluding section.

Peter de Bolla

VIR HEROICUS SUBLIMIS

Newman: "My paintings are concerned neither with the manipulation of space nor with the image, but with the sensation of time."

I suppose it might be said by some people that this is not art. Arguments might be made on behalf of this view, such as those which are based on a curious imperative that the artwork be, in some sense, the product of a more than ordinary person, more than humdrum talent. This kind of argument is based on something like the notion of genius, since it holds that if anyone can make the artwork, say fill a canvas with red paint, if even I could do this, then the object cannot be art. Other arguments, say about the lack of representational forms, or the negation of a certain painterly tradition, might equally be marshaled against this canvas. But these arguments and others like them are all poorly grounded; indeed they are illiterate in relation to the philosophical content of what we call the aesthetic realm. In order to know whether or not this is an artwork we have to experience it, and that experience, whether we like it or not, cannot remain indifferent to the knowing that is presented by this canvas. That our response is not an articulation of this knowing is one of the lessons we should draw from Kant. So, first of all we need to understand how we might begin to experience this artwork and that, by necessity, means that we must first attempt to look at the canvas.

This, as with a great deal of abstract art, is not as easy as it might at first appear. How might one prepare the eye for its work, how begin to look so that we might be able to see? Let us begin in a very rudimentary way, by taking the measure of the image. Let us attempt to size or scale the canvas, grasp its almost 8-foot by 16-foot presentation. Grasp the size of its autistic eloquence. This, for a start, puts it in the orbit of the Kantian sublime. Its scale prepares the eye for an extension of the time of looking since scale usually determines a temporal measure to the look, but on this occasion the physical size of the canvas is placed in tension with the subject presented: color. The eye, then, can both take the image in at a glance and is required to travel over the scale of its expanse, extending the glance into a gaze.

Let us blink. Is there a texture to the surface, a narrative of form, of material, a line of movement which might echo "the movement of the mind that is bound up with the judging of the object" (Kant, *Critique of Judgment*, §24)? Is this line of movement itself figured in the vertical lines, the stripes of color which punctuate the monotone

216

of red pigmentation? There is, for sure, a synaptic break, a syntactic articulation on the left-hand side which seems to disjoint the canvas, separating the left segment from the rest, while simultaneously balancing the muted incision of the black-blue stripe. This certainly introduces a temporal aspect to the look, since it causes the eye to track back and forth across the surface of the image in a series of comparing and contrasting shots. And, as it does so, the bare, naked expanse of undifferentiated color which must be traversed each time another contrastive shot is taken comes to seem more and more threatening, as if the eye, frightened of confronting its agoraphobia, feels compelled to jump over the chasm which begins to open up in the center of this image. And is this the feeling of terror, of fear we most commonly associate with the sublime? It is for this reason that the eye hugs the peripheries, seeks out the edge of vision, finds comfort in the quiet interruptions of the stripes. Draw back, zoom the image into the middle distance. That is more comfortable, a better perspective. Now the segments merely frame the central panel, give it contour, definition.

From this distance a calmness comes over the eye in direct response to its shrill monotonous silence. How long does this calm last; how long is the eye held in the comfort of taking this distance? Repose only magnifies the imperative to look harder, but that imperative immediately gives way to the seductions of gawping in anxious wonder. Already a structure to the view is beginning to emerge, a structure in which the eye shuttles back and forth from stillness to agitation, a pulsation of the look which is, of course, the pulsation of the sublime. As soon as the eye recognizes its inactivity, notices itself staring, it starts off again, skimming and scanning the surface for indications of depth, for moments of incident that will give a point of purchase on the shiny surface of the picture plane. But the flatness of the surface will not, as yet, reveal its contour, still less will it open to reveal its representational interior: its knowing remains veiled by its presentation. So the eye becomes anxious, its movements between stasis and agitation become more frequent, marking time by the irritation caused on the retinal surface. Back again. Blink again.

Close the eyes. Concentrate on the after-image. Something stands out, something winks at us from the picture plane. Note it. We can begin to ask some questions, now that the eye is blind, begin to disturb signification. What does it mean to paint color, to reduce the world to a single, punctuated color. We are not quite at the furthest remove of this project, in the single presentations of Reinhardt, but the same questions are nevertheless raised. Is the ambition of this canvas to know the world, know it in the full simplicity of knowing as the object knows? Or, rather, is its ambition to master the world, hold it at bay, erase it through the incredibly hubristic depiction of a single sentence: this is color. Is this what the image knows, and tells; shows in its mute speaking forth: here is? This attempt to present the unpresentable is, of course, another defining characteristic of the sublime.

Open the eyes. Look again. How many lines punctuate the in-different wash of red? Five, or four, six or seven since the border at each edge of the canvas could be further repetitions of the white line to the left? Is this white an incision into the flatness of the red, or merely the absence of pigmentation? Is it an opening or a layering? Let us look at it segment by segment. It feels natural to move from left to right, as if we might respect the syntax of the image by so doing. But beginning at the far left-hand side seems somehow wrong since the eye is constantly drawn to the center. Nevertheless let us attempt to remain within the tramlines, let us force the movement of the eye towards verticality and resist the continuous pressure towards horizontality. It is difficult to do this because the eye keeps wanting to zone the image, order it sequentially, feel time. There is, then, a kind of power play going on, as if the image disciplines the look, requires it to traverse. But struggle a little harder to look up and down, uncomfortable though it is, and feel the axis of space. It is flat, flattened out, pummeled into a gossamer-thin line of chromatic punctuation. It is nothing but a syntactic mark. Space has been etiolated into the nothingness that lies behind the canvas.

Now the white line begins to assert its seductive power, drawing the eye into its ambivalent depth; for here there is an opening in the canvas, an incision into the representational surface which gives it the appearance of depth. It is almost as if we might begin to see behind the image, behind its back and witness the void from which this heroic presentation of color has sprung. And now of course the movement of the mind has succumbed to the desire of the eye in its return to the comfort of horizontality, to the retinal pan. Stand back. Zoom in and out of different perspectival distances. Now the canvas begins to take on another dimension. Are those four stripes, those excluding the white line, are they overpainted? Or has the red wash been applied up to, abutting the stripes of a different color? And if these are overpainted, does it differentiate them from the white stripe which seems to show no evidence of background color? What

Art, politics, and aesthetics

is the temporal narrative of execution of the image; which color was laid first?

The movement of the eye gives us some clues here, clues to the questions we might phrase to the image even if those questions will not yield the certainty of a knowledge we might know. As the horizontal pan tracks across from side to side, the central panel begins to feel like another, different, painterly narrative structure. It begins to feel remarkably like a polyptych, an excavated narrative of a life, say, of the idea of color. And now I begin to read into this central panel a nativity, say the birth of representation, and into its side panels moments in the life of this idea, the life of redness. It is a narrative of color coming into its being. A narrative of the artwork coming into its knowing.

And now another register enters the affective sphere, the register of waiting, for the response to end, for the narrative of knowing to conclude. This is like waiting for presence to be at hand and the discomfort it produces is like the embarrassment that another might know what we are thinking, the paranoid fantasy of telepathy. Perhaps it is because of this, in the light of such discomfort, that we feel a certain kind of relief. It is this feeling of relief which slowly stains the retinal surface; a sense that the effort to see will, in the end, yield no more than this. Relief that the waiting, waiting for the image to give up its knowingness, is over; that the discomfort of this strange beauty has a point of termination.

What this feels like, then, is an internal blushing in the face of the gaze of the artwork; as if the eye registers its own surveillance. The movement of the mind here constantly swings out towards the desire of the canvas, its wish to impart what it knows of knowing. Our discomfort, then, which is the feeling of contemplative wonder irritated by the eye's longing for relief, must face up to the fact that the artwork keeps its own counsel. What happens now, what we do with that and how we deal with it, is where the politics of seeing begins, and that place is ineluctably outside the time-world of the artwork itself. So it is that the worldliness of the political must always remain adjacent to the timeliness of the aesthetic.

Notes

1 Patrick Buchanan, "Losing the War for America's Culture?," *Washington Times*, May 22, 1989, §D.

2 The full scale of this public debate is represented in a collection of newspaper articles, transcripts of broadcasts and senate hearings edited by Richard Bolton, *Culture Wars* (New York: New Press, 1992).
3 Immanuel Kant, *Critique of Judgment*, trans J. H. Bernard (London: Macmillan, 1931), p. 85. Subsequent references will be given within the main text.
4 Barnett Newman, "The Sublime is Now," in *Abstract Expressionism*, ed. David Shapiro and Cecile Shapiro (Cambridge University Press, 1990), pp. 325–8. Subsequent references will be given within the main text.
5 Quoted in Jean-François Lyotard, "Newman: The Instant," in *The Lyotard Reader*, ed. Andrew Benjamin (Oxford: Blackwell, 1989), p. 247.

9

The political autonomy of contemporary art: the case of the 1993 Whitney Biennial

MICHAEL KELLY

The 1993 Whitney Museum Biennial was one of the most controversial art shows in recent memory in New York City and in the art world in general.[1] Critics from across the political spectrum objected either because the art was political at all, or because it was political in the wrong way.[2] Believing that the meaning of art must be intrinsic to the works themselves, the first group argued that the Biennial failed this test because the art was subservient to political messages. The second group acknowledged that art can be political, but insisted that it can be so only through the formal conventions of art, not its content. Comparatively little was written by either group about the aesthetics of the Biennial, except to declare that political art is bad art. In fact, very little of the art was reviewed or discussed in any detail.[3] According to one critic from the first group, it was impossible to review the show because it was so "heedless of the needs of the eye," so indifferent to "visual pleasure," that it defied description and, lacking description, *could not* be reviewed.[4] Critics of the second group also tended to ignore the aesthetics of the show, claiming that the art "privileged the signified" by being political through its content and thus neglected the signifier, the natural focal point of aesthetic interpretation.[5]

Most of these critics did not even acknowledge the first of three criteria according to which the chief curator of the exhibition, Elizabeth Sussman, had hoped the art would be evaluated: "despite a widespread belief to the contrary, art committed to ideas is not lacking in what are thought of as the traditional aesthetic qualities, for instance, sensuality, contradiction, visual pleasure, humor, ambiguity, desire, or metaphor."[6] She asked viewers to evaluate the 1993 Biennial in terms of how well the art synthesized aesthetic and

221

political concerns rather than to dismiss it as if such a synthesis was either undesirable in principle, or necessarily unsuccessful given the particular strategies employed by the artists.[7] Sussman's aesthetics–politics criterion was supported by testimony from the director of the Whitney at the time, David Ross, as well as by two participating artists, Glenn Ligon and Janine Antoni.[8] At a symposium at the Whitney in the spring of 1993,[9] these two artists showed slides of their work, which had been read by the critics largely in political terms. They insisted, however, that their art be evaluated in aesthetic terms as well, for they had produced it according to their under-standing of these terms, though in ways that also accommodated political issues of feminist and gay black identity.

Were Sussman, Ross, Antoni, Ligon, and the rest of the 1993 Biennial organizers and participants merely employing rhetorical devices in anticipation of, and later in reaction to, the criticisms that the art in the Biennial was too political? While it might be proble-matic to privilege their intentions in evaluating the show, there is something behind their comments which bears philosophical scru-tiny and which is borne out by some of the art. The Biennial represented a challenge to a false choice between art and politics – art is either aesthetic/autonomous or political[10] – which is pervasive in discussions about art in general and which underlies most cri-tiques of the show. The first group of critics of the Biennial believed that since art is autonomous it cannot be political, as politics is one of the things of which art is allegedly independent.[11] And the second group believed that to preserve its autonomy, art can be political only on a formal level, as if it would lose its autonomy if its content were also political. But the Biennial contained numerous examples of art that was clearly aesthetic and political at the same time.

Were the artists unaware of the virtual prohibition on political art imposed by the art–politics choice, or were they combining art and politics in order to challenge (whether intentionally or in effect) that false choice? I think they offered a challenge which compels us to rethink the genealogy and present constellation of the art–politics relationship. In fact, with respect to the understanding of this relationship, I think art is ahead of theory here. This suggestion will likely surprise some people, for it is often said that today's art, and particularly the art represented in the 1993 Biennial, blindly follows theory. But art is placing a serious demand on theory to come up with a better account of the art–politics relationship than theory now offers. While the Biennial did not create this demand on its own, as contemporary art has been moving toward it for some time, and while the Biennial cannot satisfy the demand on its own, the exhibition is important for encouraging us to take it more seriously.

ART–POLITICS CHOICE

The first thing to be said about the art–politics choice is that it is false for two reasons. First, the choice is historically too simplistic. Autonomist art – such as Robert Motherwell's *Elegies to the Spanish Republic* – can also be political; and political art – even Bertolt Brecht's theatre – presupposes the autonomy of art.[12] Second, neither side of the choice can be sustained without the other, as Theodor Adorno argues: "Each of the two alternatives negates itself along with the other: committed art, which as art is necessarily detached from reality, because it negates its difference from reality; *l'art pour l'art* because through its absolutization it denies even the indissoluble connection to reality that is contained in art's autonomy as its polemical a priori."[13] Each side needs the other to define itself, so art and politics are mutually dependent. This is something most artists in the 1993 Biennial seem to have understood, so far as one can tell from the art they created.

If this choice is indeed false, how is it that critics of the 1993 Biennial – and even some of the artists[14] – became entangled in it? The source of the entanglement is, I believe, a common but mistaken belief about modern and postmodern aesthetics.[15] The mistaken belief is that modern aesthetics separated art and politics and that postmodern aesthetics reunited them.[16] On this belief, modern art is generally understood as the pursuit of purely aesthetic ideals made possible by art's autonomy from politics: as distinct from premodern art and its commitment to mimesis, a modern (or at least modernist) picture is to be seen, so Clement Greenberg claims, "as a picture first."[17] By contrast, postmodern art is thought to begin, in part, as a critique of the separation between art and politics; it is self-con-sciously political and willingly minimizes, if not forfeits, the autonomy of art for the sake of what its proponents regard as a richer notion of art.

The problem with this belief is that modern *aesthetic theory* did not typically separate art and politics any more than modern *art* typically did (though certainly some modern*ists* aspired to separate them).[18] What makes this belief even more problematic is that it has often served as a normative principle in accounts of modern and postmodern aesthetics; that is, it does not merely reflect an historical claim about these forms of aesthetics, but a normative claim about how they ought to be understood. And it is precisely this norm which informs the critics' judgments of the 1993 Biennial; they objected to (postmodern) art that synthesized aesthetics and politics because they thought (all) art should keep them at a proper distance. I think it is this distance which the Biennial artists transgressed, and it is their transgression which occasions the present rethinking of the belief about modern and postmodern aesthetics with respect to the art–politics relationship. How have they been related? Not far behind that question is again: How ought they to be related? While many contemporary theorists seem to be mistaken in their answers to these questions, at least the first one, the artists in the Biennial seem to have a good sense of how to answer them, especially the second one.

It is not difficult to show, however, that art and politics are not as independent within *modern* (let alone postmodern) aesthetics as the modernists among the critics of the 1993 Biennial tend to believe.[19] Instead of holding on to a false choice between autonomous and political art, it would be more accurate – historically and philosophically – to acknowledge both (a) that art is autonomous only under certain political conditions, and (b) that art is political only after it is autonomous. That is, it would be more accurate to speak about the *political autonomy of art.* I will clarify this notion by tracing the genealogy of the art–politics relationship within the history of modern and postmodern aesthetic theory from Immanuel Kant to Jean-François Lyotard. This genealogy shows, I think, that art and politics have always been intimately related in modernity, though with significantly diverse and competing (and not always clearly defined) notions of politics and art.[20]

In the light of the genealogy of the political autonomy of art, the 1993 Biennial art would be best appreciated, I think, as embodying different and even competing ways of understanding the art–politics relationship. The artists' efforts to embody these ways is what makes the Biennial important, despite its reception and at times despite itself, and their success at doing so is how they would best be evaluated (see below). I will not end this discussion, however, merely by affirming a pluralism of strategies for handling art and politics. For if it is presented as a single doctrine, pluralism runs the risk of lumping all the Biennial art together, just as the two groups of critics did, which has the effect of closing off instead of revealing the multiple approaches to art and politics that this art embodies. The question at the end will rather be: While contemporary theory may not offer us an adequate understanding of the relationship between art and politics, what has the Biennial art revealed to us about this same relationship? Even to be in a position to ask this question, we must first discuss how the theories that informed the critiques of the Biennial prevented it from being asked. Critics were blinded by their normative theoretical commitments about the art–politics relationship and thus were unable to see the Biennial art (as art) at all, let alone to see it in a way that just might illuminate this relationship. Some of the critics' questions may emerge again at the end, but not in their original form. The issue will no longer be: "Is it art?" or "Is it necessarily bad art?" But rather: "As art, are its voices, strategies, and ideas convincing aesthetically as well as politically?" Much needs to be clarified, I believe, before this question can be addressed.[21]

KANT, HUME

When the topic of aesthetics and politics arises in contemporary art theoretical debates, Kant is often credited, for good or for bad, as the philosopher who irrevocably separated these two realms, because he insisted on the autonomy of aesthetics from all other human interests, practices, and material conditions, including politics. But he does not deserve the credit or scorn he has received on this issue. His goal in *Critique of Judgment* was to give more coherent theoretical expression to the philosophical aesthetics inaugurated by Alexander Baumgarten, Joseph Addison, Francis Hutcheson, David Hume, and others earlier in the eighteenth century. As is well known, he did this by trying to clarify the uniqueness of aesthetic judgment as being both universal and subjective. While Kant's solution may be unique, and though it may or may not be successful or relevant today, my interest here is in the philosophical significance of the problem of autonomy he inherited from his predecessors.

The very problem of the uniqueness of aesthetic judgment was part of the on-going effort at the time to establish aesthetics as an autonomous discipline. As even a cursory study of the historical context of eighteenth-century aesthetics will reveal, there were political conditions enabling this effort. The autonomy of aesthetics was possible only in a social world in which autonomy or freedom was a prominent, if as yet largely unrealized, political (and moral) concept. The point is not that aesthetic autonomy itself was always expressed in political terms, for it was not. Baumgarten, for example, was defending the autonomy of sensible knowledge relative to logical (conceptual) knowledge, a claim that people today who criticize autonomy may still want to defend. Rather, the point is that the general Enlightenment notion of autonomy was an indispensable condition for the historical possibility of autonomous aesthetics and art. In Hume's words: "it is impossible for the arts . . . to arise . . . among any people unless that people enjoy the blessing of a free government."[22]

The general history within and about which Hume was writing is familiar enough, though its implications for aesthetic theory have often been overlooked, especially with respect to the aesthetics/politics issue. Prior to the eighteenth century, art was generally subject to the authority of religion and politics, while politics itself was under the hand of monarchical rule. With the help of capitalism, the American and French Revolutions violently changed these relationships by introducing the ideal of democratic politics. This ideal was accompanied by a newly embraced belief in the autonomy of the arts, which had been developing since the Renaissance along with the rise of the bourgeoisie. The arts aspired to be free from politics (and religion) as politics (and religion) struggled to become independent of the king. The point here, however, is not only that politics liberated the arts along with the citizenry, for politics is indebted to the arts. In Hume's words again: "If we consider the matter in a proper light, we shall find that progress in the arts is rather favorable to liberty, and has a natural tendency to preserve, if not *produce* a free government."[23] The goal of establishing an autonomous practice of art required numerous other practices and institutions, namely, cafés, theatres, newspapers, art criticism, and museums. These practices and institutions established an art and literary public sphere. It was partially the ideal of the extension and democratization of this sphere that contributed to the larger public sphere, which in turn provided the site of autonomy for politics. That is, the public sphere in which bourgeois democratic politics developed began, in part, as an ideal extension of an art and literary sphere that was distant enough from politics to attain its own autonomy and, at the same time, to provide a model for politics to move toward autonomy.[24]

The relationship between aesthetics and politics is perhaps best understood in terms of the connections between the autonomous domains of art and politics: modern art and politics emerged within a shared bourgeois public sphere regulatively based on the principle of autonomy. The relationship between aesthetics and politics was established within a newly emerged public sphere where art and politics related to one another from positions of relative autonomy. The autonomy of the modern public sphere both assured and assumed the autonomy of these subspheres. Thus, (Kantian) autonomy does not separate art/aesthetics and politics, it actually unites them via a common philosophical presupposition and historical condition.

Kant would of course insist that, if aesthetics is going to be autonomous, it cannot be conditioned by politics in any way that bears on the philosophical foundation of aesthetic judgment, for judgment can be universal (unconditional) only if it is unconditioned. This was an important issue for Kant because being universal is not only possible only for autonomous aesthetics, it is also constitutive of what it means for aesthetics to be autonomous. Yet aesthetic judgment is immanently, if indirectly, conditioned by politics not only because autonomy is a political as well as an aesthetic (and moral) concept, but principally because autonomy is an historical condition of aesthetic judgment. There would be no object – art – and no judge – aesthetic subject – were it not for the condition of autonomy Hume describes. According to Salim Kemal, "Kant's insistence on individual autonomy in aesthetic practice and judgment affirms the social and political value of subjectivity, imagination, and creativity . . . Nor is the autonomy of fine art permitted to obscure its basis in cultural practice."[25] Since aesthetics shares its autonomy with politics (and morality), aesthetic judgment shares its autonomy with its political (and moral) counterparts. So, again, Kantian autonomy does not separate art/aesthetics and politics, it unites them in a uniquely modern and reciprocal way that is still unfolding today, albeit often under the guise of postmodernism.

ROMANTICISM

Historically, almost as soon as art had been honored with a philosophical defense of its autonomy, J. C. F. Schiller converted his interpretation of Kant's notion of aesthetic autonomy into a defense of art's political function: "If man is even to solve the problem of politics in practice he will have to approach it through the problem of the aesthetic, because it is only through beauty that man makes his way to freedom."[26] Schiller pursued the twin projects of aesthetics and politics by offering a political rationale for art while

defending art's inherent value.[27] The coherence of this twin project –
called "aesthetic education" – rests on the notion of autonomy. For
it is only insofar as politics is autonomous that we have freedom at
all; while art is the domain of beauty, it is only in autonomous art
that we can understand beauty as freedom in appearance; and it is
only because beauty is free that art can help us to develop further the
autonomy that we need to conduct politics.

Inspired by Schiller, though not always sharing his political views,
the Romantics espoused similar ideas about the art–politics relationship; they, too, defended art's political function while presupposing
and safeguarding its autonomy.[28] In making art a necessary constituent of political autonomy, they also recognized the political conditions necessary for autonomous art. Friedrich Schlegel, for example,
believed that the proper sphere of art is pure enjoyment, that is,
enjoyment separate from morality and politics. Yet he also believed
that aesthetic enjoyment, the highest form of which is love, can be
realized only among free and equal persons.[29] Art was able to
(re)unite with politics after it attained its autonomy only because
politics itself was autonomous. That is, art became political without
risking its autonomy only because politics was based on autonomy,
too. So from a position of aesthetic autonomy, the Romantics asserted
art's political authority, transforming art from a symbol of morality,
as it was for Kant, into a tool of political enlightenment.

In short, Schiller and the Romantics established the political
authority of modern art from a position of aesthetic autonomy from
politics. What makes this position coherent is that there are two
different notions of politics: art is free from nonautonomous (non-
democratic) politics; once it is autonomous in this sense, art is
linked with politics and even serves as a model for the further
development of political autonomy. Once again, autonomy unites art
and politics.

L'ART POUR L'ART, MARX

The aesthetics–politics pendulum seemed to swing away from the
political during certain periods of the nineteenth century. For
example, art received one of the strongest defenses of its autonomy
from politics (and morality) from the *"l'art pour l'art"* movement in
the first half of the nineteenth century (Benjamin Constant, Théophile Gautier, Charles Baudelaire, Paul Valéry, Mallarmé, *et alia*). As
Gautier expressed the key belief of this movement in the well-known

228

preface to his *Madamoiselle de Maupin* (1835), "nothing is truly beautiful except that which can serve for nothing; whatever is useful is ugly." This "cult of beauty" began as a critique of the instrumentalization of art in bourgeois culture, including the Romantics' political uses of art. The aesthetic focus was now to be primarily, if not exclusively, on the intrinsic qualities of the work of art, as it was for most critics of the 1993 Biennial.

Yet even *l'art pour l'art* was more political than it is often represented as being (taking "political" here in the general sense of the cultural). Baudelaire, for example, combined his dedication to beauty with an equally strong devotion to modern life, much the way Schiller and others pursued aesthetic and political tasks at the same time. This dual focus is immanently reflected in Baudelaire's notion of beauty: "Beauty is made up of an eternal, invariable element, whose quantity it is excessively difficult to determine, and of a relative, circumstantial element, which will be, if you like, whether severally or all at once, the age, its fashions, its morals, its emotions."[30] Every "scrap of beauty" has this double composition, for without the circumstantial element, eternity is beyond our power of comprehension; while without the moment of eternity, the circumstantial would offer only meaningless fragments. Baudelaire's famous *flâneur* is identified as "the painter of the passing moment and of all the suggestions of eternity that it contains."[31] So even for the aesthete or dandy, beauty is both aesthetic and political; for as capricious, indulgent, and flighty as the dandy seems to be, his aim is to understand the present and in a sense become part of it (at least its eternity). Far from being committed to the idea of an absolute separation between art and politics, *l'art pour l'art* confirms that modern autonomist aesthetics has retained a link with politics by being unified with life in the present, albeit one that has been aestheticized by beauty.

Almost contemporaneous with the deinstrumentalization of art by *l'art pour l'art* was the Marxist repoliticization of art. Karl Marx challenged art's presumption of autonomy and argued that it was determined by political economy, though in such a way to think that it was autonomous; he thereby explicitly (re)invested art with politics. At the same time, Marx was equally inspired by the political authority of autonomous art, even that of the romantic legacy; that is, he adopted the political challenge autonomous art represented to society and demanded that autonomy be given a more concrete embodiment in society.[32] Where he differed dramatically from that

229

same legacy, however, is that he seemed to believe art had to forfeit its aesthetic autonomy because it was symptomatic of reality's state of class conflict, which was itself a barrier to political autonomy's full realization. If only art and society could be unified, then reality could realize its immanent goal of a classless society whose only members would be autonomous individuals.

A problem with Marx's view, however, is that by denying art was autonomous once it became political, even if only ideally, he contributed to the antagonism between aesthetics and politics instead of overcoming it, as he had aspired to do. He failed to realize that art is political in the very way he demanded only insofar as it is autonomous in the way he did not seem to allow. Hoping to expand the political authority of art, Marx challenged its autonomy with the hope of realizing the political vision that earlier art represented under the protection of autonomy. His motivation in denying art's autonomy was thus political. The underlying problem was that political society at the time was incapable of realizing the political vision art embodied. If art's autonomy is forfeited so that its political vision can be realized in political reality, yet that reality is not ready to do so, then the very source of the vision to be realized has been lost without any concrete possibility of realizing it.[33] Thus, while the Marxist critical imperative about political reality may be well justified, the price art must pay because of reality's deficits is self-defeating for politics as well as for art.

AESTHETICISM, AVANT-GARDE

The seesaw between politics and aesthetics has continued unabated into the twentieth century, which witnessed the rise of the historical avant-garde art – Marcel Duchamp, dadaism, futurism, cubism, surrealism, etc. On the one hand, the avant-garde seems to be an extension of the political camp within modern art, for the artists identified with these movements often made political claims and gestures; on the other, the avant-garde echoes the modern aesthetes' claim that art be integrated with life, though on noninstrumental terms. This composite identity stems in large part from the impasse that aestheticism (Walter Pater, Oscar Wilde, *et alia*) had reached at the end of the nineteenth century. While aesthetes perhaps came the closest of any other group in modernity to reaching the goal of fully autonomous art, they also aspired to be reunited with life; they first demanded, however, that the life with which they wanted to be reunited be transformed, and that it be transformed by art. How could they transform the life from which they were autonomous in order then to reunite with it? That they could not do so reveals what Peter Bürger characterizes as "the nexus between autonomy and the absence of any consequences."[34] The aesthetes' position is thus untenable, according to their own demands. One way to explain why it is untenable is to reemphasize the political autonomy of art: the full autonomy of art at which aestheticists aimed first required the full autonomy of political society, yet they were impotent to change society because of their autonomy from it.

The avant-garde reaction to the impasse of aestheticism was to reestablish art's relations with what Bürger calls the "praxis of life." They did not attempt this through the content of art, nor through its formal structure; they chose instead to change the very institution of art by making it more integrated with life. Duchamp, for example, was not looking to have more things (e.g., a urinal or a shovel) included within the pantheon of artworks, he was in effect questioning the grounds of judgment by which works of art are distinguished from the everyday objects around them. At the same time, the avant-garde also recognized the need to change praxis, for political reasons, before reuniting with it. They resisted the instrumentalized bourgeois life just as much as the Romantics and aesthetes had done before them. Since life is not so easily changed, however, at least not by art, the avant-garde attempted "to organize a new life praxis from a basis in art."[35] They thus seemed to retreat behind the protective walls of autonomous art, which means, however, that the distinction between aestheticism and the avant-garde was blurred since the latter had distinguished itself by tearing down aestheticism's walls. The result of the avant-garde's pragmatic experimentalism was therefore to highlight rather than overcome the art–life dichotomy. At the same time, this failure of the avant-garde serves as further evidence of the political autonomy of art; for it is because the avant-garde did not fully recognize the political autonomy of art that it failed.

ADORNO

While Kant represents early modern philosophical aesthetics, Adorno is his late modern counterpart. He is particularly relevant here because of his direct and indirect influence on the critics (and even some artists) of the 1993 Biennial.

Michael Kelly

Adorno argues that there are two dialectics constitutive of modern art: it *both* shows reality for what it is – divided and unreconciled with itself because of the dialectic of subjectivation and reification, which means, in short, that every advance in political freedom is accompanied by repression – *and* represents, through the dialectic of semblance, a possible reconciliation of reality with itself in a utopian future.[36] Art must maintain a distance from political reality, not because of a failure on art's part or because of an aesthete's impulse, but because of reality's own failure to realize its immanent goals; as a result, art is autonomous from the very political society to which it belongs. Adorno thus defends the autonomy of art from politics but does so on political grounds. Moreover, modern art is political for Adorno only because it is first autonomous and only insofar as it remains so: "As eminently constructed and produced objects, works or art . . . point to a practice from which they abstain: the creation of a just life."[37] His position is perhaps best understood in relation to its implicit Kantianism: there is a political basis for the autonomy of (Kantian) aesthetics which now allows (Adorno's) aesthetics to become political.

The dual relationship that art has to political reality creates a dilemma that, according to Adorno, is endemic to the genealogy of modern art: "If art cedes its autonomy it delivers itself over to the machinations of the status quo; if art remains strictly for-itself, it nonetheless submits to integration as one harmless domain among others."[38] If art is too autonomous, its separation from society appears to be indirectly responsible for reality's immanent failure; so, as was the case with Marx, art is thought to be complicitous with the failure of politics. But if art is not autonomous, then it loses the critical distance from which it can make us aware of the failure of politics. In trying to resolve this dilemma, Adorno does not think that art has the power to resolve reality's nonreconciliation with itself, for that is not art's task. Contrary to the idealist aesthetics that emerged out of romanticism's response to Kant, art is not the site of such reconciliation: there is no "aesthetic state." Rather, as long as the dialectic of subjectivation and reification continues to block true reconciliation in political society, art's task (even its truth) is to sustain the dialectic of semblance: "Through the irreconcilable renunciation of the semblance of reconciliation, art holds fast to the promise of reconciliation in the midst of the runreconciled."[39] which in turn accounts for art's mimetic function; it "imitates" reality's nonreconciliation while holding up a mirror to the possibility of reconciliation. Thus, the tension between art and politics stems from a strain within political reality itself rather than from a failure of art.

Despite Adorno's recognition and subtle articulation of the political autonomy of art, however, the aesthetics–politics relationship he envisaged is problematic for three reasons. First, instead of dealing with the question how two relatively autonomous subspheres of the bourgeois public sphere can relate to one another, Adorno argues that art must remain separate from external, concrete politics. He is rather final on this point, as was clear in his early debates with Georg Lukács and Brecht.[40] At the same time, he argues that art can be political while separate in this sense, but only in terms of its form. As a result, Adorno internalizes the art–politics relationship in much the same way the avant-garde did, following aestheticism.[41] He, too, perpetuates the false choice between art and politics for he separates more than relates them. Second, the progressive development of the formal techniques of the production of modern art, if it exists at all, can no longer be trusted as the primary locus of the politics of art, because, as Bürger, Fredric Jameson, and others have argued, it is not as independent of bourgeois capitalism as Adorno believed. Formal art is no more autonomous than content-oriented art, since artistic forms can be put to fascistic uses just as easily as they can to critical uses. Third, despite Adorno's materialism, he insisted on seeing the aesthetics–politics relationship in only one way. But it is inconsistent with the genealogy of the modern art–politics relationship not to see it as dynamic, always adopting new shapes as the definitions and demands of art and politics change. For these reasons, we need to look for a different theory to capture the political autonomy of art.

LYOTARD

If the basis for Adorno's late modern aesthetic theory is established by Kant's early modern theory, then the transition from Kant to Adorno – via romanticism, *l'art pour l'art*, Marxism, aestheticism, avant-gardism – is from one mode of *modern* aesthetic theory to another rather than a radical step beyond modernity. It is a transition that becomes apparent *in* or, perhaps better, *as* postmodernism, of which Lyotard remains one of the best theoretical representatives, at least during this transitional period. Lyotard offers a provocative account of the interrelationship between modern and postmodern aesthetics, which in turn suggests yet another model for understanding the political autonomy of art. Like Adorno, Lyotard is particularly relevant to the 1993 Biennial because of his direct and indirect influence on contemporary art and art theory.

In *The Postmodern Condition*, after explaining that "postmodern" designates "incredulity toward metanarratives,"[42] Lyotard argues that "the aesthetic of the sublime is where modern art . . . finds its impetus, and where the logic of the avant-garde finds its axioms."[43] The sublime occurs, he continues, following Kant, "when the imagination in fact fails to present any object that could accord with a concept, even if only in principle."[44] For example, we have the idea of political reality's reconciliation with itself but no sensible representation of it. "One could call [these ideas] unpresentable."[45] The genealogy of modern art accordingly devotes its techniques "to presenting the existence of something unpresentable. Showing that there is something we can conceive of which we can neither see nor show – this is the stake of modern painting."[46]

The sublime, according to Lyotard, both divides and unites modern and postmodern art. For the postmodern sublime serves as a symbol *that* something is always unpresentable in modern art and *as* a stand-in for what is unpresentable. So postmodern art is not after modern art, as the "post" would suggest; on the contrary, "A work can be modern only if it is first postmodern. Thus understood, postmodernism is not modernism at its end, but in a nascent state, and this state is recurrent."[47] In other words, according to Lyotard, postmodernism is immanent in modern art; it renders explicit what is implicit in modern art from the start; it is only in postmodernism that we finally begin to achieve the aesthetic of the sublime that defines modern art.[48]

Lyotard's analysis of the postmodern sublime is relevant to the political autonomy of art, for art's relationship to politics is part of what is unpresentable in art. Whereas modernists infer from the unpresentability of art's politics the conclusion that art is apolitical, postmodernists infer that art is political and that its thinking that it is not is, as Marx argued, politically determined. In postmodernism, art now knows it is political, but that is not to say it understands the particular political conditions by which it is governed. They always remain unpresented, at least until after the fact; conditions that are operative are not presentable, and ones that are presentable are no longer operative. This fact bedevils attempts within postmodernism to reveal art's political conditions.

What is unfortunate about Lyotard's views about the postmodern aesthetic of the sublime, however, at least with respect to the art–politics problematic of the 1993 Biennial, is that after rejecting Adorno's confidence in the politics of art's form, he also eliminates much of art's content through his critique of representation. Without form or content, it is hard for art to exist, let alone to be political. According to Daniel Herwitz, Lyotard's notion of the sublime is "too abstract to capture much of the actual art of resistance it is meant to capture."[49] That is, while Adorno argued that art holds a mirror up to a reality that is not reconciled with itself, *and* holds up a mirror to the possibility of an eventual reconciliation, Lyotard retains the first mirror but abandons the second. The hope of reconciliation is replaced by the sublime, which thus becomes merely a sign of hope's absence. There is apparently little room for politics in Lyotard's postmodern aesthetic theory.

Taking Lyotard as representative of postmodern philosophy, perhaps it is now actually the postmodernists who inscribe the false aesthetics–politics choice into the ontology of art. For if, following the genealogy of the political autonomy of art, the modern understanding of this relationship was much subtler than is typically imagined, postmodernists who perpetuate the misconception of modern aesthetics through their critiques of modernism are actually responsible for sustaining the false choice.[50]

HAACKE

What is the political autonomy of contemporary art? To answer this question, I now want to explore how the genealogy of the political autonomy of art opens up critical reflection on the 1993 Biennial in aesthetic as well as political terms. But I first want to analyze briefly an example of contemporary art not included in the Biennial which sets the stage for discussion of it. This example also makes it clear that the issues here are not confined to the Biennial.

A well-known contemporary artist struggling with the relationship between art and politics is Hans Haacke.[51] An example of his subtle handling of this relationship is *Photo Opportunity (After the Storm/ Walker Evans)*, a work in his spring 1992 show, The Vision Thing, at the John Weber Gallery in New York City (fig. 9.1). He placed two photographs side by side that have strikingly similar formal compositions: one was the famous Walker Evans photograph, *Alabama*, of a poor woman standing with her hungry child in the doorway of their rickety home; the other was a newspaper photo-

Michael Kelly

Fig. 9.1 Hans Haacke, *Photo Opportunity (After the Storm/Walker Evans)*, 1992

graph of then President and Mrs. Bush standing in the doorway of a home destroyed by a Florida hurricane. While the first photograph was from the 1930s Work Projects Administration (WPA) art program and was explicitly political at that time as part of the documentation of the depression, it has since assumed a place in the history of photography as an exemplar of art *qua* social commentary. As a result, the Evans photograph has lost much (though not all) of its original (and any other political) content; in a word, it has been aestheticized (especially but not only for those without any memories of the depression). When Haacke placed it next to the Bush photograph, however, the Evans photograph was repoliticized. Rather, the fact *that* it had political content and could, in the proper context, acquire it again was reactivated by the politics of the Bush photograph. While the politics of this second photograph seemed explicit and immediately accessible, if only because of the then impending 1992 presidential election, it was actually deferred in this context because of its placement next to the aesthetic photograph; its politics worked through the aesthetic level of the Evans photograph and was displayed on that level. At the same time, the overall effect of Haacke's juxtaposition of these two photographs was that the political became aesthetic, for the Bush photograph was

236

rendered aesthetic (on the level of formal composition) as it (re)politicized the Evans photograph.

So a political photograph, presumed not to be aesthetic (because it was merely journalistic), works through an aesthetic photograph, once but no longer political, to make the aesthetic political. None of this transference of politics to aesthetics and aesthetics to politics could be recognized and understood, I believe, were it not for the political autonomy of art.[52]

Although Haacke both offers a subtle strategy for integrating politics into the form and content of the work of art, and recognizes that the line between art and politics can never be eliminated without abandoning art in the process, I am not suggesting that his work be employed here as a standard for judging the 1993 Biennial. There is no such standard for the art–politics relationship because, in light of the genealogy of the political autonomy of art, there is no one way to understand or practice it. But the subtlety with which Haacke handles this relationship does suggest a guide for seeing how the Biennial embodied different ways of relating art and politics (some of which have historical precedents, some of which do not). The pluralism of the Biennial on this score challenges both the idea that art and politics ought not to mix *and* the idea that there is only one single way to define their relationship. So both the apolitical and singularly political views are questioned by the Biennial, which both confirms the genealogy of the political autonomy of art and allows us now to reassess the Biennial. The artists I will discuss have not been selected because they offer highly articulate senses of what a new theoretical account of the aesthetics–politics relationship may be, but because they make art which such an account must be able to cover. I do not evaluate the efficacy of the political "messages" of the Biennial art, but rather analyze the aesthetic–political presuppositions, techniques, and contexts that make it possible for this art to have such "messages" and which thereby open up the need for such evaluation.[53] Finally, because of the understanding of this relationship that their art embodies, these artists provide guidelines for this account. Art guides theory.

GOBER, JAMESON

Robert Gober is a good example to begin with here since Elizabeth Sussman introduces him as being paradigmatic of the general temperament of the 1993 Biennial, and because he subtly combines a poetic sensibility with gay, environmental, feminist, and other political issues.[54] This combination is manifest in his handling of sculptural material and his choice of metaphors to voice his aesthetic and political concerns. One of Gober's works in the Biennial was *Newspaper*, (fig. 9.2), a work comprising several stacks of newspapers tied up in preparation for recycling and "discarded" throughout the museum in gallery spaces, the lobby, and in the hall outside the bathrooms. On top of each stack was a silkscreened page from the *New York Times* with the stories and advertisements edited by Gober to reflect his personal and political priorities; for example, he mentioned the death of an artist on the front page, and inserted his own image in an advertisement for a wedding dress with the copy "Having it All" – both under an article with the headline: "Vatican Condones Discrimination Against Homosexuals."[55] On a political level, an everyday throw-away object – a newspaper – that conveys real contemporary issues becomes evidence of how these same issues are treated by the major media, at times as if they are mere "fillers." At the same time, the aesthetics of the piece is a function of both the role of newspapers in the history of modern art

Fig. 9.2 Robert Gober, *Newspaper*

(collages and debates about high and/or low art), and the interactions among the stacks and other art in the show established by their relative placements in the Whitney Museum. The stacks were at times as invisible as art as the stories and images in the newspapers Gober selected. In the end, *Newspaper* also seems like an apt metaphorical strategy, reflected in the choice of aesthetic materials, for responding to the critique of political art as being reducible to journalism. In effect, it has the appearance of a "journalistic" response to this critique which, like the photograph of Bush, operates through aesthetic means. What is asserted here, in short, is the power of art to raise political issues on its own terms while incorporating the terms of those who would deny artists the possibility of making such assertions.

Jameson offers an at times insightful but, I think, unnecessarily restrictive interpretation of Gober's work (produced before the 1993 Biennial): "[it] is meant to stress, over against [Haacke's] deconstructive operation, the production of a new kind of mental entity, but at the same time to exclude the assimilation of that entity to any kind of positive representation."[56] Why is Jameson so reluctant to have the artist identify this "mental entity," a utopian space that defies specification? Gober certainly need not offer blueprints for this space; for that is not the way art should be political any more than it is the way we could do politics today – one person's utopia is another person's hell. But this does not mean an artist cannot set deliberate parameters for the new space, as well as poetically communicate specific senses of why it is desirable.[57] The virtue of Gober's work, as I understand it, is that it provides viewers with something to which they can react aesthetically and politically, though without making them feel that some singular aesthetic or political reaction is being expected of them. In the 1993 Biennial, for example, he deliberately addresses contemporary political issues on personal and social levels which are very timely and clear yet sublime, that is, which are open to interpretation on aesthetic as well as political grounds. So, in contrast to Jameson's analysis, which I think risks making Gober's work so vague that the reasons why people respond to it today are unfathomable, I think that people are engaged by it precisely and principally because of its deliberateness in relation to the present in a way which does have "positive representation," though one that can bear multiple interpretations.

Michael Kelly

SIMPSON, KRAUSS, BUCHLOH

The issue of how "positive" or deliberate the politics in/of art should be was the topic of a 1993 roundtable discussion in the journal *October* about the Whitney 1993 Biennial. The exchange between Rosalind Krauss and Benjamin Buchloh regarding Laura Simpson's installation *Hypothetical?* (fig. 9.3) was very provocative and revealing on this issue. In her description of Simpson's work, Krauss focused on the grid structure of the wall of mouthpieces from various musical instruments which were interacting with the photograph of a person's lips on the opposing wall roughly fifteen feet away; together they constituted "two different taxonomic spaces" of an object and the body. Her description stopped with these first two walls, even though there was a third wall – a small-scale newspaper clipping of the then Mayor Bradley of Los Angeles being asked whether he was afraid after the Rodney King verdict, to which he answered that he was not afraid but angry. On Krauss's account, this third wall was not part of the "texture of the work," that is, its form, what was being shown visually. It was, at best, "irrelevant to the piece" and, at worst, disruptive of its "material level" which "constitutes the signifier." Moreover, since the play of the signifier and

Fig 9.3 Laura Simpson, *Hypothetical?*, 1992

240

acts of interpretation of this play are part of public political space, when this play and interpretation are restricted, the work that does so, in this case the newspaper clipping, is "profoundly unpolitical."[58] By "simply looking at the work," Krauss thus argued that what seems to be the most political part of *Hypothetical?* actually makes the work as a whole *un*political.

Buchloh challenged Krauss's assumption that the public would or should universally accept her idea of political art, namely, art that is political only through its form or, as she also calls it, its material level. Several alternative notions of political art were embodied in the Biennial: "Why can't one say, I define my project to be opening up new venues, addressing new audiences, providing models of enactment, empowerment, articulation?"[59] The suggestion here is that in order to understand Simpson's *Hypothetical?* we cannot allow our theoretical commitment to one idea about the politics of art to blind us to art that may be political in a different sense. Buchloh also challenged Krauss's assumption that viewers of *Hypothetical?* would so readily see what and, more importantly, see *only* what she described. For many viewers, the Bradley clipping was indispensable to the piece both as art and as politics. To make this point we need not rely on Simpson's intentions, nor the analysis of her work by Golden to which Krauss objected; rather, we can simply begin with a description of the work which is more complete than Krauss's. That is, instead of arbitrarily excluding this wall and then either interpreting the work on purely aesthetic grounds or else arguing that it is unpolitical simply because it includes that wall, the interpreter has to include the third wall as part of the description of *Hypothetical?* and from there begin to interpret the piece on political as well as aesthetic grounds.

The issue of the interpretation of Simpson's *Hypothetical?* – and especially of the interpretation of its political dimension – therefore goes back to the description of it. Is the newspaper clipping part of the description or not? What is important in addressing this question is, as I have claimed, the set of assumptions about the art–politics relationship informing any answer. It seems clear that the newspaper clipping is an integral part of *Hypothetical?* because, to return to Krauss's incomplete but otherwise insightful description, this third wall activates the other two walls by provoking the conversation between them. They need not talk in univocal terms about the Rodney King affair, nor need they talk always and only about politics. But this clipping starts them talking, and we interpreters must then follow the three walls (and their many voices) where they lead us.

Krauss rightly argued that art can be political only if the artists and interpreters do not completely jettison the work of the signifier, which is why she placed the emphasis on the formal/material dimension of art, for that is where the signifier dwells. But her perhaps even more basic philosophical point, on which she and Buchloh seem to agree, was that artworks must be capable of multiple interpretations. But are there no limits to interpretive multiplicity? What prevents it from collapsing into radical indeterminacy?

What can separate multiplicity from radical indeterminacy is, I think, the degree of deliberateness which is included in the work, intentionally or otherwise, and which is thus part of the work's description and/or interpretation. The goal here, in the case of political art, is a mixture of diverse and subtle politics compatible in turn with multiple aesthetic interpretations. This is what much of the 1993 Biennial art was proposing, albeit with artistic means rather than in theoretical terms. Instead of expecting artists to aim for (1) *deliberate indeterminacy*, why not hope they aspire rather to (2) *indeterminate deliberateness*? The difference here is between (1) aiming to be differently interpreted with little or no attention to politics or while assuming that the achievement of multiple interpretations is itself a political act, and (2) being deliberately political but in a way that can be differently interpreted on both political and aesthetic grounds – that is, being historically (culturally, personally) of one's time but without imposing any single reading of that time at the expense of art. As was the case with Gober, deliberateness (timeliness and historicity) is not a restriction on interpretation but is actually a condition that makes multiple interpretations possible; it generates rather than precludes multiple interpretations, while allowing multiplicity to stop short of radical indeterminacy. Simpson provided a perfect example of this, as the roundtable discussion of *Hypothetical?* demonstrates, and I believe she succeeded in doing so precisely because she included the third wall. As in the case of Gober's contribution to the Biennial, a newspaper again unifies aesthetics and politics.

WILLIAMS, ANTONI, SHERMAN

Sue Williams may represent the deliberate end of the deliberateness–indeterminacy spectrum. She offers, by most accounts, an explicit in-your-face brand of feminist political art, reflecting what some have called the "bad girls' attitude." The titles of her paintings alone are quite revealing on this score: *It's a New Era* (fig. 9.4), *Are You Pro-Porn or Anti-Porn?*, and *The Sweet and Pungent Smell of Success.* Her aesthetic style, which would be called anti-aesthetic by some, is shaped by cartoon- or graffiti-like images of violence to women with hand-drawn writing offering statistics and commentary about abuse to women (including, at least her in earlier work, abuse

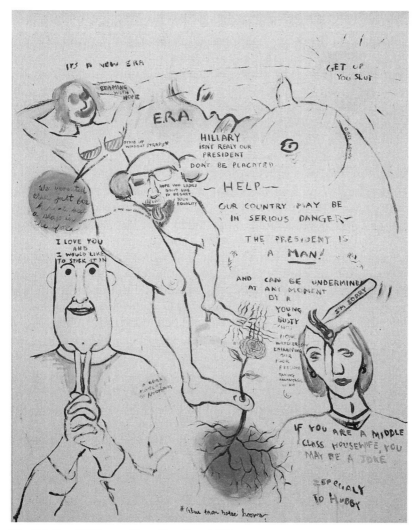

Fig. 9.4 Sue Williams, *It's a New Era*, 1992

and neglect of them by male artists and the male-dominated art world).[60] She thus embodies one mode of political art and one that is as legitimate as it is necessary, at least so long as the issues she addresses demand urgent attention, as is regrettably the case regarding feminism in the art world and more generally.

Critics of the Biennial claimed, however, that Williams crossed the line between aesthetics and politics. Perhaps she crossed the line, but the line remains even when it is crossed; in fact, the crossing reconfirms that there is a line, even if it is moved as a result of the crossing, and the presence and persistence of the line is evidence, in this case, of an integral relationship between aesthetics and politics. Perhaps, as many critics also claimed, she crossed *over* the line – in the sense that her crossing is unforgivable from the aesthetic point of view – when she placed a plastic cast of what appears to be vomit on the floor in front of her paintings. Or was she, in effect, conveniently providing a metaphor for the reaction to her paintings she might well have expected to receive from the critics? Might the vomit also be a metaphor for the reaction of the people caught in the abuse situations depicted in the paintings? If so, which is more revolting? The abuse that is depicted in the paintings or the depictions of abuse as paintings? Most people reacted as if they thought the latter, and it is for them that the vomit was likely provided in anticipation of their reaction.

Some critics would say, however, that if the focus of such political art is on the art itself rather than on the political content of what is depicted in the art, then the work is a failure.[61] But that is, I think, to judge the art on political terms alone, as if successful political art were invisible as art relative to the political content it embodies; if it were invisible, however, it would no longer be art. Moreover, since when is art that draws attention to itself deemed a failure for that reason alone, given that one of the criteria of modernist art is precisely its self-reflective quality, and given that postmodernist art only seems to have heightened this feature even as it takes an ironic stance toward it? Is the problem then that self-reflective art is supposed to be pleasurable as well, and, if so, is this why Williams's work is a failure? But, surely, there is no necessary connection between self-reflection and pleasure, though the two have long been features of modern and modernist art. All in all, I think Williams's work is important as art for raising all these aesthetic and political issues combined.[62]

Janine Antoni was another artist in the 1993 Biennial whose work raises questions about aesthetics and politics. Her piece *Chocolate Gnaw* (fig. 9.5) comprises one large (36" × 27" × 27") cube of chocolate next to an equally large cube of lard; they are both part of a larger installation that includes lipstick made out of the lard. On her account, she chewed on the chocolate after making the cube, spat it out, made cosmetic boxes out of it, and then made lipstick from the lard; finally, she displayed the boxes on glass shelves in a mirrored alcove similar to those found in up-scale department stores. Critics and supporters of Antoni pointed to her work as a metaphor for women's eating disorders, since the lard, chocolate, and lipstick form a vicious circle linking the beautiful with the fat, and there had been much discussion at the time about these feminist, cultural–political problems. At a Whitney symposium in the spring of 1993, however, the artist distanced herself from this type of interpretation, denying that she had an eating disorder and that she was concerned

Fig. 9.5 Janine Antoni, *Chocolate Gnaw*, 1992

with such problems, at least in her Biennial contribution. Why did she make the cubes? Because she likes them – for aesthetic reasons. Once she made the chocolate cube, she had to decide what to do next, so she ate some of it, altering the cube's geometry in the process. She then extended the material life of the cubes – transforming the chocolate into beautiful boxes, and the lard into lipstick. The rest of the chocolate and lard cubes slowly melted in the gallery of the Whitney until they were practically reduced to liquid state, perhaps ready to be consumed or transformed again. So, while many critics saw cultural–political issues in Antoni's work, she also pursued aesthetic concerns: the appropriation of minimalist monochrome cubes (or the appropriation of Fluxus material in earlier work).

Some other critics have argued, however, that while there is indeed a relationship between art and politics in Antoni's work, it is not captured by the interpretation that focuses on the most apparent feminist reading. Rather, they argue, Antoni makes an institutional spectacle out of feminist and political art of the 1970s which consciously resisted institutionalization; she has created a depoliticized version of that earlier political art.[63] Perhaps. But perhaps she is offering a new way of addressing feminist issues, perhaps the spectacle is now an appropriate political strategy, or one of few available – especially now that the Karen Finley style of performance art has been publicly restrained. The state of politics in contemporary art is too pluralistic for anybody to decide a priori what is or is not political. The more relevant question is which political art is more or less effective, but that assumes we first understand the political strategy and aims at issue. It is not clear that these critics of Antoni had such understanding or even that she has settled yet on her own strategy and aims. In any case, these different types of aesthetic and political interpretation of Antoni's work do not stem from her disingenuousness, or from a privileging of her intentions, or from the critics' arbitrary projections on to her work, but from the work's complexity and depth, or lack thereof, relative to the aesthetic and political matters that inform it.

Although Cindy Sherman was perhaps already so well known before the 1993 Biennial that she cannot be considered an integral part of it, I think she is an important example here nonetheless because she successfully (if unwittingly) synthesizes art and politics on a variety of levels. She contributed seven untitled photographs (each an average of 45" × 60") (fig. 9.6) of mannequin-looking figures

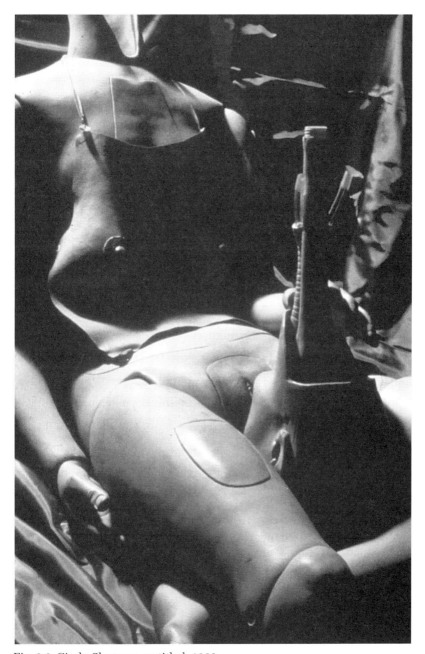

Fig. 9.6 Cindy Sherman, untitled, 1992

composed of medical-supply prosthetic body parts arranged in provocative, often grotesque, if sexual, poses. One prominent type of interpretation of Sherman's work has been that it concerns the construction/deconstruction of the identity/difference of female subjectivity by the male gaze (mostly in art, as in the film stills used in her earlier work).[64] She has also been interpreted as the visual equivalent of Judith Butler's notion of performative identity; on this type of interpretation, her photographs personify the fact that subjectivity and identity are social constructs, effects of factors that seem as mechanical as the mannequins and camera yet as playful (performative) as the acts of subjects who constantly assume different identities.[65] Although the photographs in the Biennial are clear on gender terms, they also represent – a third type of interpretation – startlingly uncanny products of psychoanalytic imagination. Yet two more types of interpretation are offered by Krauss and Arthur C. Danto, each of whom deemphasizes in very different ways the feminist readings in favor of more emphasis on either the signifiers in the work or on the significance of her work for the human condition, respectively.[66]

The reason for mentioning the variety of types of interpretation of Sherman's work is to provide evidence that she makes art which is open to diverse and even competing interpretations. This multiplicity is made possible, I think, by the work's deliberate dimension, at least part of which is political. That is, the feminist politics of Sherman's work, in which she need not have any personal interest, brings the work to the attention of people who then interpret it in aesthetic as well as political terms. While I would agree with those who insist that political art be understood on aesthetic terms, too, I would disagree with some of the same people who would insist that aesthetics necessarily comes first. In Sherman's case, the politics seems to come first (for us, if not for her) because, without it, it is questionable whether her work would ever have received as much or the same (if any) attention that it has. While this is, of course, something that would be impossible to prove, it seems clear that the politics of feminist identity provided the first major context of the work's reception. This context did not exclude aesthetic interpretations; for, clearly, if Sherman did not understand the medium of photography (the production of the signifier), as she obviously does, few people would have been interested in her work, despite its political reception, and certainly nobody would have remained as interested in the work as people have. Drawing on the notion of the political autonomy of art, it would perhaps be more accurate to say that politics and aesthetics are equiprimordial in Sherman's art, which is why it has been susceptible to being interpreted in such a variety of ways.

KIM, LIGON

Byron Kim was discussed at great length by the curator and artists at the 1993 Whitney symposium because his work embodied the aesthetic and political mixture to which all the art in the 1993 Biennial was thought to aspire and according to which they hoped it would be evaluated. The individual monochrome paintings in his *Synecdoche* (fig. 9.7) were each small (8" × 10") but there were many of them which, combined, covered a large wall area. On first impression, they were reminiscent of abstract paintings, perhaps from the 1950s, and they may have passed for only that in a less political art world. But while each painting has only one color, the color varies from one painting to the next. As it turns out, the color of each painting is the skin color of the racially diverse people who have visited the artist's studio. The notion of flesh tone is expanded

Fig. 9.7 Byron Kim, *Synechdoche*, 1991–2

to include many varieties of it in the (art) world, and thereby color (aesthetics) becomes racially encoded (political).

The political dimension (racial issues) of Kim's work was invisible, at least to the innocent eye. Yet it was clearly visible once it was pointed out (as it was in the catalog) how the paintings were produced. So the viewers seemed to have to look elsewhere than in the paintings to see them for what they were. But if, as critics of modernism have been reminding us for years, there is no innocent (racially insensitive?) eye, and if Danto is right that interpretation is constitutive of works of art, we should expect to "look" elsewhere to see the art in front of us. Or if, as Norman Bryson argues, interpretation or "reading" is "as fundamental an element [of painting] as the paint," painting is encoded with interpretation from its inception, waiting to be read as well as seen.[67]

In his *Notes on the Margin of the "Black Book"* (fig. 9.8), Glenn Ligon appropriated photographs from Robert Mapplethorpe's *Black Book*, which contains sexually provocative images of nude black gay men. Interspersed among the photographs on the wall were brief statements about them and about Ligon's appropriation of them. Part of the political dimension of this piece is the fact that the photographs are sexual and particularly that they are homosexual, which is political in the current social climate where there have been numerous National Endowment of the Arts controversies about such art.[68] Another part is their racial dimension, given that a white man photographed black men, many of whom have since died of AIDS, as Mapplethorpe himself has. While a white man's desire for black men is not racist, it is typically only the white artist who has the privilege to show such photographs in an art gallery or museum. Would it matter if Ligon had taken the photographs? The result would have been very different, of course, but would that difference be more than an aesthetic difference between the Mapplethorpe "style" and that of Ligon? What would that "more" be? A different racial perspective? A third political dimension, though one that is more confined to the art world, is that Ligon appropriated the images and that he received advance permission from the Mapplethorpe Foundation to do so. Although appropriation has become commonplace in contemporary art, it is still controversial, if only on legal grounds. Ligon's advance permission, which eliminates the legal angle, adds a new twist to appropriation since it seems an anathema to the practice of appropriation to ask first. How is appropriation different when it is "legal"? Ligon's contribution to the 1993 Biennial is to

Fig. 9.8 Glenn Ligon, *Notes on the Margin of the "Black Book"*, 1991–3

have stimulated debate about these important political and aesthetic issues.

The aesthetic of the *Black Book* is initially Mapplethorpe's, of course, but it is transformed once it is appropriated by Ligon. The Mapplethorpe photographs were originally very politically as well as sexually charged, because they were not simply documentary pictures of sexuality from which the artist remained distant. The artist lived the sado-masochistic homosexuality depicted in his art, so the photos embody his sexuality as well as that of the subjects of the pictures. Such embodiment is political in a world where homosexuality is controversial. More recently, however, beginning with Mapplethorpe's retrospective show at the Whitney in 1989, and especially as a result of the later Cincinnati censorship trial, Mapplethorpe's art has been aestheticized, that is, depoliticized by being somewhat removed from the world out of which its political force and aesthetic identity originally emanated. Critics increasingly discuss his art in largely formalistic terms, mentioning its sexual and political dimensions but no longer letting them be constitutive of the art's aesthetic as well as political value.[69]

By appropriating Mapplethorpe's images of black males, Ligon may seem to be contributing to this aestheticization process because he exhibits them in an art institution. But, in fact, he halts that process, at least temporarily, because his identity as a black gay male reactivates the content of the photographs, not unlike the way the Bush photograph repoliticized the Evans photograph in Haacke's work. As a potential subject or object of homoerotic desire himself, Ligon reanimates the subjects of the photographs, and thereby their political as well as sexual identity. And, as Thelma Golden expresses it, Ligon identifies with Mapplethorpe's portrayal of gayness but critiques his portrayal of blackness.[70] Thus, when Ligon's appropriation is seen in the context of the aestheticization of Mapplethorpe's art, it becomes political on yet one more level, though one that retains a clear aesthetic, albeit one that is now Ligon's.

CONCLUSION

There are other examples of political art in the 1993 Biennial and even some nonpolitical work. But the examples I have cited should be ample evidence of the subtlety of the artists' handling of the political autonomy of art and the diversity of strategies for relating art and politics. Their work is indeed aesthetic as well as political, as is clear from the fact that in each case it is open to multiple aesthetic as well as political interpretations because of, not despite, its deliberate dimensions. I have focused on multiplicity in the discussions of the artists to show that the fear expressed by critics of the Biennial – that political art is incapable of multiple interpretations since it is, in effect, reduced to its political message – is unfounded.

Now, what is the relationship between the earlier genealogy of aesthetic theory and the discussion of the 1993 Biennial? Ultimately, what would be optimal here would be for there to be a reciprocity between theory and art which we would then expect theory to articulate and art to embody. But it appears that we have not yet attained this reciprocity in the present case of contemporary art and theory, at least as they are represented in the 1993 Whitney Biennial. While *modern* aesthetic theory and *contemporary* art have worked from similar assumptions about the political autonomy of art, it is impossible, for obvious historical and philosophical reasons, to return to an earlier form of theory to judge and appreciate today's art. Yet *contemporary* criticism and *postmodern* art theory have worked from assumptions that seem at odds with the political autonomy of art and are thus inapplicable to contemporary art.

The outstanding philosophical problem is that among the presently dominant art theories I have discussed, no single theory is adequate to articulate the art–politics relationship in contemporary art, because each theory tends to make false assumptions about aesthetics. The postmodern sublime, whether Lyotard's or some other, is quite alluring, but it is merely a symptom of theory's inability to say anything constructive about the political autonomy of art. If we cannot turn to theory, where else can we turn?

Following the lead of the 1993 Biennial art, the relationship between art and politics must be understood in strategic and dynamic terms and in the context of a pluralistic culture. We can no longer say that the two practices must be kept separate, nor that one always has priority over the other. Just as those today concerned about identity are careful not to essentialize it, concerned art theorists should not essentialize the art–politics relationship either. The notion of the political autonomy of art is expressive of this nonessentialism. Sometimes (political and other) forms of identity need to be critiqued, and sometimes they have to be constructed. Likewise, the balance between art and politics may have to lean toward politics in some cases or contexts, because of the urgency of the political matter(s) in question (for example, AIDS, racism, feminism). And sometimes aesthetic matters will dominate when the political urgency subsides (though likely only to surface somewhere else in the public sphere). But in all cases, aesthetics and politics are allies rather than adversaries, whether they are used for critical or constructive purposes.

Yet pluralism, even of the strategic variety, cannot be the basis on which the political autonomy of art is articulated and defended; for to adopt a pluralistic doctrine – on the level of art theory or aesthetics – is to propose one more singular way of understanding it on the level of art. Even if pluralism is right, and perhaps because it is, it cannot and need not take the form of a doctrine; for as such it is not better – no less singular and exclusive – than any of the doctrines that have shaped the genealogy of modern and postmodern aesthetics. As a doctrine, pluralism would have the effect of lumping all art (of the Biennial) together (as both groups of critics did) and would thereby only undermine the multiple approaches to the art–politics relationship embodied in this same art. Since it is these approaches which make the 1993 Biennial important, pluralism as a doctrine must be avoided. The notion of the political autonomy of art is an alternative to pluralism as well as to essentialism, since it opens up multiple and subtle ways of relating art and politics. It is one of the main conditions which makes such ways possible, and which in turn opens up multiple interpretations of artworks produced under this same condition.

While I have argued that the theoretical accounts from Kant through Lyotard of the aesthetics–politics relationship are not adequate to contemporary art (particularly but not only as it is reflected in the 1993 Biennial), and though I have not yet provided a nuanced alternative account of this relationship, I hope I have made a convincing case that such an account is needed because contemporary art demands it of theory. And I offer the notion of the political autonomy of art as a way to begin moving beyond both the (modernist) art–politics and modern–postmodern divides. In suggesting that we move beyond those two divides, however, I am not proposing another "post." Rather, I propose that, using the notion of the political autonomy of art as our conceptual tool, we continually redraw the art–politics line(s) and that in doing so we look to contemporary art for guidance.

Notes

I would like to thank Alex Alberro, Lydia Goehr, Daniel Herwitz, Gregg Horowitz, and audiences at Cooper Union and Columbia University for their helpful comments and criticism.

1 This chapter was first written in 1994, while the controversy about the 1993 Biennial was still quite passionate. Since then, the negativity toward the show has become legendary and has even been institutionalized at the host museum. For example, in a recent (spring 1998) interview on the television show *Charlie Rose*, David Ross, recently departed Director of the Whitney Museum (and now at the San Francisco Museum of Modern Art), was asked whether he had any regrets about his tenure, to which he responded: only one, the 1993 Biennial (see note 8 below). There was little discussion about his point, as if it were self-evident why he would regret it. Such lingering critical reaction to that show has undoubtedly put a damper on the politics of contemporary art over the last five years. If this fact is combined with the United States Supreme Court's June 1998 decision to uphold the National Endowment for the Art's "Decency Clause," then we can only expect the politics of art to end this decade and century in a rather vulnerable position. All this makes my attempt to open up another round and level of debate about the 1993 Biennial all the more imperative, if not more difficult.

2 My reason for not giving full weight to the differences between the two groups of critics of the 1993 Biennial is that I want to analyze certain assumptions which they share about art and which perpetuate the false art–politics choice. At the same time, I am overlooking other kinds of objections to the Biennial since they are not directly related to this choice. One other objection, which has been raised in response to this chapter on the several occasions I have delivered it publicly, is that while art can and in fact should be political, the art in the Biennial was bad on aesthetic grounds. I will not discuss this objection here, since the majority of critics denied that there were any aesthetic grounds at all because the art was political. I am resisting such resistance to the Biennial art in order to get to the position where this other type of objection can be addressed. Finally, I should mention that there were a few critics who defended the Biennial. For example, Thomas McEvilley said that most of the art was "serious and focused work that deserves to be leveraged into mainstream cultural awareness" (*ArtForum* [May 1993]). Ironically, many of the artists in the show have indeed become mainstream, despite all the critical overreaction to them in 1993.

3 According to Laura Cottingham, there was "a kind of hyperbolic condemnation indicating that the critic has chosen not to view the art, but to condemn all the selected works in one angry swoop" ("The Pleasure Principled," *Frieze* [spring 1993]). At the same time, most critics who

defended the Biennial did so by criticizing its critics, not by analyzing the art in the show.

4 Jed Perl, "From Tung Ch'i-ch'ang's China to David Ross's Manhattan," *New Criterion* (April 1993), 50–2. Another critic from the first group said there was no need to review the Biennial at all because it had nothing to do with art (Hilton Kramer, "The Biennialized Whitney: Closed for Deconstruction," *New York Observer* [March 29, 1993], 1). Yet another objection was made by Peter Schjeldahl: "Beyond active offense, the biennial suffers from what is turning into a chronic weakness of an art culture that has too long stripmined the formal resources of past art without replacing them" ("Missing: The Pleasure Principle," *Village Voice* [March 16, 1993], 34, 38).

5 See "The Politics of the Signifier: A Conversation on the Whitney Biennial," *October*, 66 (fall 1993), 3–27, which is discussed below.

6 Elizabeth Sussman, "Coming Together in Parts: Positive Power in the Nineties," in *1993 Biennial Exhibition* (New York: Whitney Museum of American Art–H. H. Abrams, 1993), pp. 12–25, esp. p. 14. Michael Kimmelman acknowledged this aesthetic criterion but said that the show did not live up to it because it offered "zero visual pleasure" and exhibited "virtually no sensitivity to art that demands a certain silence and space around it" ("At the Whitney, Sound, Fury, and Not Much Else," *New York Times* [April 15, 1993]).

7 Sussman's request was reiterated by another Whitney curator, Thelma Golden: "I think the way in which the critical response to the show has delineated a political art certainly wasn't an aesthetic that we were looking at . . . We were looking at people who certainly were making statements, but not necessarily calling it political art, as such" (transcript from the *Charlie Rose* Public Broadcasting Service television show of April 6, 1993).

8 Ross stated on *Charlie Rose* that "Art's independence, art's autonomy, art's dependence, art's engagement, are both parts of what art is" (transcript from PBS show March 5, 1993). See note 1 above.

9 The symposium was organized by Norton Batkin, Director of the Center for Curatorial Studies at Bard College, New York.

10 The "autonomy of aesthetics" means that aesthetics is an independent discipline among the human sciences. Such independence has been asserted in the history of aesthetics through various types of arguments claiming that there are, for example: (1) aesthetic judgments (independent of cognitive, moral, and other forms of judgment); (2) uniquely aesthetic experiences; (3) objects called works of art that are ontologically separate from mere things; (4) aesthetic qualities or properties of objects, whether works of art or mere things; or (5) aesthetic terms, concepts, or even an aesthetic point of view. Central to each of these autonomy theses is the belief that aesthetics is independent of politics.

The "politics of art" can mean several things: (1) art's relations to social/cultural institutions (including museums and art schools) and practices; (2) questions of the identity of artists (in terms of race, gender, ethnicity, sexual preference, and the like); (3) viewpoints that artists adopt in response to current affairs; (4) factors that influence which artists get monetary and critical recognition from the art world; (5) the material conditions affecting the production of art; and (6) the dynamics of art criticism, that is, critics staking out territory for their preferred artists or art form, often in connection with a prominent exhibition, such as the Whitney Biennial.

The "autonomy of art" means that art is independent of all the levels of politics just outlined and that it can therefore be discussed in terms of one of the modes of the autonomy of aesthetics.

In what follows, I invoke most of these versions of the autonomy of aesthetics/art and the politics of art, sometimes more than one at a time, depending on the theorist, critic, or artist under consideration.

11 As one anonymous critic announced, "[t]he debate about this Biennial rests on the question of whether the politicization of art is good or bad" (*New Yorker*, March 22, 1993).

12 Discussing Brecht, Adorno argues that the primacy of pure lesson over form became a formal device, that is, the didactic play became an *autonomous* artistic principle (*Aesthetics and Politics: Debates Between Ernst Bloch, Georg Lukács, Bertolt Brecht, Walter Benjamin, and Theodor Adorno*, trans. R. Taylor [London: New Left Books, 1977], pp. 182–8).

13 Adorno, "Commitment," in *Notes to Literature*, vol. II, trans. Shierry Weber Nicholson (New York: Columbia University Press, 1992), p. 70.

14 Some artists adopted an anti-aesthetic stance in combination with their political art as if they, too, believed that art and politics do not mix. Some artists who wanted to be political thought that to be so required that they challenge modern aesthetics; and other artists who wanted to resist modern aesthetics, whether for political or nonpolitical reasons, thought a ready-made form of resistance was political art. These artists were thus unknowingly complicitous with the critics, thereby diffusing the challenge to the false choice between art and politics.

15 I use the terms *modern* and *modernity* to refer to the history of art since the end of the eighteenth century, which also marks the beginning of aesthetics. The term *modernism* refers to the movement within modernity which began at the end of the nineteenth century and culminated in abstract expressionism in the 1950s. The terms *postmodern* and *post-modernism* refer to art that emerged at the point that modernism (though not necessarily modernity) waned; this point in history is different in the various art forms.

16 Other problematic beliefs held by the modernist critics of the 1993 Biennial are that *modernist* and *modern* aesthetics are the same and, in turn, that *modernist aesthetics* is synonymous with *aesthetics*. Such beliefs seem natural enough if one looks at history, since the discipline of aesthetics began with modernity. But it conflates an historical form of

aesthetics – called modernist – with modern aesthetics or even with aesthetics *tout court*, which means that the critics were using a non-contemporary (modernist) form of aesthetics to judge the contemporary (postmodernist) art of the Biennial. This conflation led critics to think that political art was antimodern as well as anti-aesthetic, and that to defend modernist aesthetics against postmodern political art was to defend modern aesthetics. The critics' judgment and the conflation on which it is based in turn perpetuated the false art–politics choice, further obscuring the possibility, if not the fact, that the Biennial was challenging it.

17 Greenberg, "Modernist Painting," in *Clement Greenberg: The Collected Essays and Criticism*, vol. IV, *Modernism with a Vengeance, 1957–1969*, ed. John O'Brian (University of Chicago Press, 1993), pp. 85–93, esp. p. 87; the word *first* is significant here, because it allows for art to be seen in political terms so long as it is seen as art first.

18 If this is true, as I will argue it is, it raises serious questions about the rationale for postmodernism, at least on this score.

19 At the same time, it is possible to show (though with more difficulty) that aesthetics and modernist aesthetics are not the same. The reason they are so easily conflated, besides the fact that aesthetics and modernity have common historical origins, is that late twentieth-century aesthetics is at an historical juncture: the modernist paradigm (as well as the modern paradigm in general) has been challenged, if not undermined, for a host of artistic, theoretical, and political reasons, yet no alternative paradigm has been clearly articulated. On its own terms, postmodern(ist) aesthetics has so far been mainly a stage of modern(ist) aesthetics where the "post" represents a negation – particularly (but not only) of the modernist art–politics relationship – and has as yet little content of its own – in this case, a new way of understanding this same relationship. One of the aims of the following genealogy of modern and postmodern aesthetic theory is to move toward such an understanding.

20 While this genealogy may appear to reflect a linear, unified narrative, there is no claim to unity here. Genealogy is generally different from narrative, though in (other) ways I cannot enumerate here.

21 In Kay Larsen's generally positive review of the Biennial (*New York*, March 22, 1993, 71–2), she warned that there is a fine line between giving artists a chance to speak and sanctioning their politics. Perhaps this fear of sanctioning is what worried critics more than the art in the show. If so, they were the ones who politicized the Biennial by assuming that they – or anybody – needed, or had the right, to sanction what the artists had to say. In any case, is this line really so fine?

22 David Hume, "Of the Rise and Progress of the Arts and Sciences," in David Hume, *Political Writings*, ed. Knud Haakonssen (Cambridge University Press, 1975), p. 61. Or in Adorno's words, autonomy was "a function of the bourgeois consciousness of freedom that was itself bound

up with the social structure" (*Aesthetic Theory*, trans. Robert Hullot-Kentor (Minneapolis: Minnesota University Press, 1997), p. 225.

23 David Hume "Of Refinement in the Arts," in Hume, *Political Writings*, p. 111 (emphasis added). Hume makes it clear in this essay that he considers the refinement of the arts a philosophical and not a political question (p. 114).

24 See Jürgen Habermas, *The Structural Transformation of the Public Sphere: An Inquiry into a Category of Bourgeois Society*, trans. Thomas Burger (Cambridge, Mass.: MIT Press, 1989); Raymond Williams, *Culture and Society: 1780–1950* (New York: Columbia University Press, 1958, 1983); Reinhardt Koselleck, *Critique and Crisis: Enlightenment and Pathogenesis of Modern Society* (Cambridge, Mass.: MIT Press, 1988); Thomas Crow, *Art and Public Life in Eighteenth-Century Paris* (New Haven: Yale University Press, 1985); and David H. Solkin, *Painting for Money: The Visual Arts and the Public Sphere in Eighteenth-Century England* (New Haven: Yale University Press, 1993).

25 Salim Kemal, *Kant and Fine Art: An Essay on Kant and the Philosophy of Fine Art and Culture* (Oxford University Press, 1986), p. 275. See also p. 101: "Kant ascribes necessity to beauty and finds an analogy between beauty and morality on the basis of their autonomy."

26 Schiller, *On the Aesthetic Education of Man in a Series of Letters*, ed. and trans. E. M. Wilkinson and L. A. Willoughby (Oxford University Press, 1967), p. 9.

27 See Martha Woodmansee, *The Author, Art, and the Market: Rereading the History of Aesthetics* (New York: Columbia University Press, 1994), ch. 3.

28 The major German romantic theorists were Friedrich and August Schlegel, Novalis, F. W. J. Schelling, Hölderlin, and Ludwig Tieck, some of whom were also artists. For an excellent discussion of Romanticism with special attention to the art–politics problem, see Frederick C. Beiser, *Enlightenment, Revolution, and Romanticism: The Genesis of Modern German Political Thought, 1790–1800* (Cambridge, Mass.: Harvard University Press, 1992), esp. chs. 4 and 9–11.

29 Cf. ibid., ch. 10.

30 Charles Baudelaire, *The Painter of Modern Life and Other Essays*, ed. and trans. Jonathan Moyne (New York: Phaidon–De Capo, 1964), p. 3.

31 Ibid., pp. 4–5.

32 Cf. Ernst Fischer, *The Necessity of Art: A Marxist Approach*, trans. A. Bostock (Harmondsworth: Penguin, 1963), pp. 52–62.

33 Cf. Fredric Jameson's introduction to Henri Avron's *Marxist Aesthetics*, trans. H. Lane (Ithaca, NY: Cornell University Press, 1973), p. x.

34 Peter Bürger, *Theory of the Avant-Garde*, trans. M. Shaw (Minneapolis: Minnesota University Press, 1984), p. 22.

35 Ibid., p. 49.

36 The dialectic of semblance is discussed in Adorno's *Aesthetic Theory*

Michael Kelly

while the dialectic of subjectivation and reification is introduced in Adorno and Max Horkheimer's *Dialectic of Enlightenment*, trans. J. Cumming (New York: Continuum, 1972). For a clear and critical discussion of Adorno's views on autonomy, see Lambert Zuidervaart, *Adorno's Aesthetic Theory: The Redemption of Illusion* (Cambridge, Mass.: MIT Press, 1991), pp. 29–32, 82–92, 217–23, 225–34.

37 Adorno, *Aesthetics and Politics*, p. 194.
38 Adorno, *Aesthetic Theory*, p. 237; cf. p. 252.
39 Ibid., p. 33. Cf. also p. 134: "Reconciliation is the comportment of artworks by which they become conscious of the nonidentical."
40 See Adorno, *Aesthetics and Politics*.
41 While it is true that form is content for Adorno, this only compounds the problem here by further internalizing the false art–politics choice.
42 Jean-François Lyotard *The Postmodern Condition* (Minneapolis: Minnesota University Press, 1984), pp. xiii, xiv.
43 Ibid., p. 10.
44 Ibid. For more on Lyotard's notion of the sublime and its Kantian roots, see his *Lessons on the Analytic of the Sublime*, trans. E. Rottenberg (Stanford University Press, 1994).
45 Lyotard, *Postmodern Condition*, p. 11.
46 Ibid.
47 Ibid., p. 13. Lyotard may very well be conflating modern art with modernism as I understand them.
48 As Albrecht Wellmer interprets Lyotard, *aesthetic* postmodernism is a radical form of aesthetic *modernism*, "a modernism that has become conscious of itself" (*The Persistence of Modernity*, trans. David Midgley, [Cambridge, Mass.: MIT Press, 1991], p. 42). In Daniel Herwitz's words, "Lyotard's theory of the postmodern condition is a modernist theory of postmodernism closely tied to the idea of the avant-garde" (*Making Theory, Constructing Art: On the Authority of the Avant-Garde* [Chicago University Press, 1993], p. 274).
49 Herwitz, *Making Theory, Constructing Art*, p. 280.
50 There is an important difference here between the modernists and postmodernists, however: while modernists seem to separate art and politics for the sake of the autonomy of aesthetics, postmodernists who separate them do so largely because of their desire to remain distant from the political world since it does not live up to their expectations.
51 In analyzing one of Haacke's most infamous political works, *Shapolsky et al. Manhattan Real Estate Holdings, a Real Time Social System, as of May 1, 1971* (1971), Leo Steinberg argues that its status as *art* "is contingent on the continuing validity of the modernist enterprise" ("Some of Hans Haacke's Works Considered as Fine Art," in Brian Wallis, ed., *Hans Haacke: Unfinished Business* [New York and Cambridge, Mass.: New Museum of Contemporary Art and MIT Press, 1986], p. 12). Talking about Haacke's *Isolation Box*, Steinberg adds that

"Haacke may be more threatening to the continuance of modernism than any postmodern of the new figuration"; by being *art*, this work "asserts itself in the cracks of modern aesthetics" (p. 15). In the terms I introduced earlier, Haacke is a modern artist, not a modernist or postmodernist.

52 In some of his major work, Haacke shows *that* the art museum/gallery that traditionally thinks of itself, under modernist assumptions, as being apolitical is in fact political. Fred Wilson, one of the artists in the 1993 Biennial, shows *how* the art museum/gallery that now seems to concede that it is political reveals its politics in the aesthetics of its exhibitions (everything from the architecture to the content and labeling of the art).

53 My own image of the 1993 Biennial is of a group of artists distinguished by race, gender, sexual preference, and ethnicity – as well as by artistic mediums, temperaments, and the like – clamoring at the glass doors of the Whitney Museum for many years demanding, on political grounds, that they be recognized as the artists they are. Suddenly, or so it seemed, these artists found themselves on the inside of the museum, with the help of several politically sympathetic and creative curators. Yet much of the art actually exhibited in the 1993 Biennial by these same artists was produced while they were still outsiders, or at least while they operated with an outsider's mentality, both aesthetically and politically. So while the art was inside, some of it was demanding attention as if it were outside. These artists simply need time to adjust to their new position relative to the museum, knowing that it cannot be taken for granted. My sense is that many of the critics of the 1993 Biennial wanted these artists to remain outsiders and were angry at what they saw as political capitulation on the part of the Whitney. I have no sympathy for such a political stance. But what I am focusing on here are the aesthetic arguments used to back it up, which I think generally appeal to conceptions of the autonomy of art that are fictions, or so the genealogy of modern and postmodern aesthetics I have offered would suggest.

54 Sussman, *Biennial Exhibition*, p. 13.

55 In an earlier work with newspapers, *Untitled* (1991), Gober printed a facsimile of a *New York Times* obituary page combined with other news. Among the obituaries was an account of the death in his own home town (Wallingford, Connecticut) of a six-year-old "Robert Gober," who would have been the same age as the artist at the time of his death in 1960. While imagining one's own death is perhaps evidence of an anxiety about dying, it is at the same time an indubitable Cartesian declaration that one is alive after all.

56 Fredric Jameson, *Postmodernism; or, the Cultural Logic of Late Capitalism* (Durham, NC: Duke University Press, 1991), pp. 161–72, here p. 165. He is discussing Gober's *Untitled Installation*, which was not in the 1993 Biennial.

Michael Kelly

57 I use the word *deliberate* to mean that artists respond in their work to social–political–cultural issues definitive of their time. The use of "deliberate" is also intended to evoke "deliberation," specifically in the sense of "critical reflection," through art, on these issues.

58 Krauss, "Politics of the Signifier," 6.

59 Buchloh, "Politics of the Signifier," 12.

60 There are, of course, numerous art-historical and aesthetic precedents for "writing" with paint. The 1994 Cy Twombly show at the Museum of Modern Art, for example, provides a recent and popular precedent. Twombly, too, scratches and writes as he paints and, while his content is literary rather than political, it still violates the strict modernist mandate to eliminate all referents. And he, too, creates an overall effect on the canvas in handling these different compositional devices, while also allowing the devices themselves to be manifest on the surface of the paintings.

61 Arthur C. Danto makes this type of criticism of some art in the 1991 Whitney Biennial (*Nation*, June 3, 1991).

62 Williams's most recent work, some of which was included in the 1995 Whitney Biennial, is less "in your face," but no less political for that reason. She seems to be working the aesthetics–politics line from the other side, as it were. In the 1993 work, politics dominated aesthetics, albeit for aesthetic purposes, in the form of a resistance to people's expectations that aesthetics exclude politics. And in the latest work, aesthetics dominates politics, albeit for political purposes, as she draws in the viewer who earlier would not look at her work by making it appear more pleasant, only to expose the attentive viewer to many of the same pleasures and abuses depicted more vividly in the earlier work. Once the viewer is drawn in, she or he becomes implicated in what is depicted, whether it is pleasurable or abusive; whereas in the earlier work she or he was repulsed by the vomit on the floor in front of Williams's painting, turned away, and thus could not be implicated. Ironically, it turns out that the vomit was a safeguard. So viewer beware, now more than ever.

63 See "Round Table: The Reception of the Sixties," *October* (summer 1994), esp. 3–21, 14–15.

64 Cf., e.g., Laura Mulvey, "A Phantasmagoria of the Female Body: The Work of Cindy Sherman," *New Left Review* 188 (July/August 1991).

65 Judith Butler, *Gender Trouble* (New York: Routledge, 1992).

66 Arthur C. Danto's *Cindy Sherman: Untitled Film Stills* (New York: Rizzoli, 1990), and *Cindy Sherman: History Portraits* (New York: Rizzoli, 1991); Rosalind Krauss, *Cindy Sherman: 1975–1993* (New York: Rizzoli, 1993).

67 Norman Bryson, *Looking at the Overlooked: Essays on Still Life Painting* (Cambridge, Mass.: Harvard University Press, 1990), p. 10, and cf. his *Calligram: Essays in New Art History* (Cambridge University Press, 1988), pp. xxii, xiv.

262

68 See *Culture Wars: Documents from the Recent Controversies in the Arts*, ed. Richard Bolton (New York: New Press, 1992).
69 Cf. Douglas Crimp's analysis of this issue in his *On the Museum's Ruins* (Cambridge, Mass.: MIT Press, 1993), pp. 6–13.
70 Thelma Golden, in *1993 Biennial Exhibition*, p. 30.

Index

Index

Borges, Jorge Luis 174, 175, 185, 197–8
Boucher, François 92
Bougainville, Hyacinthe Yves Philippe
    Potentien, baron de 85, 93–4, 98,
    100
Bradstreet, Anne 182
Brecht, Bertolt 223, 233
British Museum 183
Brontë, Charlotte 179, 186, 194
Bryson, Norman 248
Buchanan, Patrick 204–5, 206–7
Buchez, Philippe 146
Buchloh, Benjamin 240–1
Bürger, Peter 231, 233
Buffon, Georges Louis Leclerc, comte de
    87
Burden, Chris 176
Burke, Edmund 214
Bush, George Herbert 179, 236, 238
Butler, Judith 246

Calero, Adolfo 176, 179
Cambodia 126
Canada 92, 175
Capus, Pierre 162
carnival 166, 197
Carroll, David 3, 5–6, 112–39
Central Intelligence Agency 176, 179
Cellini, Benvenuto 164
censorship 11, 13, 18, 29, 175ff.
Charles I, king of England 190
Charles II, king of England 190
chef(s) d'œuvre 161ff.
Cicero 179, 180.
class 6, 125, 140ff., 230
cognition 54–6, 58, 209, 210, 212
colonialism 122
colonization 3, 85ff.
color 216–19
commerce 5, 29, 85, 101–2, 146, 148, 149
communitarianism 54
compagnonnage 152, 158, 159ff.
Condillac, Etienne Bonnot de 95
Congress, US 1
Constant, Benjamin 228
Corbon, Antime 156
Corneille, Pierre 90
Corot, Jean Baptiste Camille 156
Corpus Christi 13, 19, 20, 33
Crashaw, William 19
creolization 5, 133ff.
cubism 230
culture, high 117, 133, 148
culture, folk, low, popular 117, 136, 143

dadaism 230
dandy 229

Danto, Arthur C. 246, 248
Daubigny, Charles François 156
David, Jules 149–50
Delessert, Benjamin 149
democracy 79ff.
Department of Defense (US) 176–7
Deruineau, Pierre 140, 142
Descartes, René 54
Diderot, Denis 5, 85–102
drawing(s) 160–1
Dryden, John 195
Duchamp, Marcel 230, 231

Earl of Leicester's Men 16
Ecole gratuite de dessin 155
Ecole polytechnique 157
Egypt 86, 97
Elizabeth I, queen of England 11, 12, 13,
    16, 23, 28, 35, 37
empire(s) 85ff.
esprit national 96ff.
Essex, Earl of 3
    rebellion of 24ff., 31, 37
Etex, Antoine 144, **145**, 146, **147**, 153–4
ethics 51–2, 76, 77, 81, 89, 92, 96, 98,
    112, 148, 211, 228
Evans, Walker 235–7, 251

Fascism 1, 113, 119, 120, 233
feminism 7, 182ff., 222, 238, 242ff., 254
Fluxus 244
Finley, Karen 245
First Amendment (US Constitution) 176
Fischer Gallery, Lucerne 1
Foley, Barbara 176
free speech 18–2, 176, 177, 190
Frégier, Antoine-Honoré 149
French Revolution 113, 226
Fuller, Thomas 9
futurism 230

Gadamer, Hans Georg 4, 56ff., 76, 77, 80
Gauny, Gabriel 155
Gautier, Théophile 228–9
Gellner, Ernest 114–16, 117, 118, 119, 127
Ghiberti, Lorenzo 164
Gilbert, Sandra M. 182, 183
Glissant, Edouard 5, 112, 133ff.
Globe theatre 12, 13, 14, 25
Gober, Robert 237–9, **239**
God 14, 15, 22, 181, 188, 189, 190, 193,
    195, 204
Golden, Thelma 251
good(s) 55–6, 66, 69, 75, 77, 78–9
Gosson, Stephen 15, 22
Goujon, Jean 164
goût 89, 91, 93

265

Index

Index